The Philosophy of Arson

Ken Baxter

For Jenny: who walked on broken glass

And Alex: who went one step too far

Contents

Act Three - The Literal Warrior 199

Foreword

Shortly after meeting Ken Baxter in the Winter of 2018, he asked if I would be willing to read the book he had written. He described it as the story about his time in prison and then added that it was over 800 pages. He said the number in a proud way, like he had accomplished something just with its length alone. Normally, I would have paused at such a request by a new, unproven writer. But Ken is anything but usual, so without hesitating, I said I would.

His question and my answer launched our working partnership which has evolved into one of the most challenging and compelling professional and personal relationships I've ever had. I wish I knew exactly why I said yes to him on that day. Believe you me, I have questioned it many times during the past two years. All I know is this – when I looked into the depth of his eyes, when I heard the rich tones of his singing voice, and when I heard his story leap off the page – I believed in him and his ability to do what so many others desire to, but never can. Do the work of writing the truth of their own story.

The book you hold in your hands does exactly that. But this book is not the 800 pages I read.

How did this happen? That in and of itself could be its own book. In May, 2018, I asked Ken to be a part of a pilot program I was running called Write It Together, LLC. The concept was to work with one other writer in a mutual way. For both of us to share drafts and provide feedback to each other. The philosophy behind this is that we learn as much from reading and providing observations to others about their writing as much as we do from receiving it on our own. He answered yes to me even quicker than I had answered him a few months earlier. We spent a week together at an ocean-front house at Sandbridge Beach, Virginia mutually working on his memoir manuscript and also working on the early pages of my own.

It was an immersive time and I quickly learned how enervating and exhausting Ken can be. His sharp intellect, creative instincts, and his fascination with his own life are a wonder and also require a lot of wrangling to keep him on task and on the page. By day three, we were shouting at each other across the kitchen counter. By day four we were high-fiving and crying when the opening paragraphs got crafted so perfectly. By day six, Ken had a plan of attack for his manuscript.

And attack he did. For the next year, we spent nearly every Friday together. We filled large flip chart paper with the full journey of his story, with the overarching themes, with character maps detailing the large and small details of the people who populated his story. Ken wrote, wrote, and re-wrote. He has said that I've been tough on him, but don't believe him. He's much tougher on himself. Every single thing I asked him to do, he did. Every single thing he could do to make this book the best it can be, he's done it.

He's done it by uncovering the truth of his own life. In that early 800-page draft, Ken wrote down everything - I mean everything - that happened to him in prison. This attention to the details laid the basis for the plot, structure, and the flow of this book. But what I believe that Ken has learned along the way is that a true memoir is about the "in". What happens inside a person as situations and events and the consequences of choices are occurring. This book masterly tells what happened to Ken and in Ken. Both are vital for a well-written memoir.

It's one thing to be willing to delve deeply into your life and honestly try to come to terms with it, especially those moments of pain, loss, and responsibility. It's quite another to then figure out how to best write it as a cohesive and compelling narrative.

I've witnessed Ken coming to terms with the emotional truth of his life and his story. His struggle to put himself honestly on the page has taken its own kind of courage, courage that is very different than the kind he needed to run into a burning building as a professional firefighter. To face the burnt ruins of your own life and acknowledge that you were the one who lit the matches takes guts and stamina. Ken has both in abundance as you are about to find out.

Few things in life have their own perfect arcs. As I write these words, I'm looking out at the Atlantic Ocean just about a mile from that beach house where Ken and I first began our work together two years ago. It's an honor for me to write this Foreword for *The Philosophy of Arson* because I have had the privilege to witness its evolution in such a personal way. I could not be more grateful because I have been challenged to read more closely, listen more deeply, and broaden my own abilities as a writer.

I have called Ken many different names over the years, but I am proud to call him friend.

I'm even prouder to call him author.

Beth McLaughlin, MFA
Sandbridge Beach, VA

Introduction

How is it that the knowledge to make proper choices in life were never fully taught to me? How stupid I feel sometimes, and what a shame. How many decisions made in the moment will forever alter the rest of your life? The answer, I've come to learn, is all of them.
One August afternoon, I dropped a MEPPS Burner into the attic of a house filled with gas fumes. It was the perfect vapor expansion.

The explosion blew out the windows and doors of the rest of my life.

Act one

Reason

SEVEN MINUTES

When that steel door slammed shut, a part of me said, "Cool." I grabbed the bars. I was impressed by how thick and sturdy they were, surprised by the level of security required for me. I pressed my face against the damp, unsympathetic wall, straining to catch a glimpse of the TV monitor mounted at the far end of the block. It was the only thing that resembled any form of familiarity in my quickly fading world. I wondered how many before me had done the same thing and recoiled. Walpole State Prison was old. It had once been the third most dangerous prison in America. I tried to force this thought from my mind, but like my surroundings they held me captive.

This mammoth structure seemed more like a condemned building coaxed out of retirement. Already a fresh coat of paint peeled off in scaly chunks. Having painted myself, I noted the shoddy job. Attention to detail was not a priority here. After all, the décor consisted of one-color scheme. Gray.

I released my grip on the bars and turned to survey my new home. I did the math. My 6 x 8 feet of space combined with the 9-foot ceiling provided me a total surface area of 348 square feet. The volume of oxygen made it seem larger at 5184 cubic inches. Oxygen was a generous description given the single, filthy air vent high on one wall. There was no window. The only light came from a single fluorescent bulb mounted tenuously to the ceiling. There were also other objects short- circuiting my equations: the bunks, the desk, the small shelf with five hooks, the sink, and the toilet. These last two huddled so closely together I renamed them my "soilet." I was the final impediment. My thesis on air in a prison cell would take longer than I thought. Fortunately, I had the time.

My attention turned to the two bunks bolted to the floor. They consisted of two pieces of sheet metal welded together, fastened through the wall with additional bolts. I stared at the second bunk and considered the fearful ramifications of a roommate. The mattress was extremely thin, which was in fact, it's best feature. The stains appeared to be a combination of sweat, urine, spots of blood, and other excretions I could not bear to look at.

The desk, also bolted to the wall, would have been vastly more useful had the seat not been ripped from its moorings. The feat of strength required to do this worried me more than anything else.

Lastly, I looked at the soilet. The sink was oddly small and equipped with a tiny button. I pressed it and the smallest amount of water trickled out. The attached toilet had a similar button which brought into question their proximity. There was no toilet seat to remember to put down. I anticipated the icy wake-up call this metal surface would elicit on a future winter morning.

I was told that toilet paper would be doled out at a ration of one roll per week. When it was gone, it was gone. I suspected many a fight broke out over its scarcity. The last of my pride would be gone as I squatted in plain view. I would eventually learn, by observing my neighbor, how to rig a privacy screen by securing a sheet from the corner of the bunk and sink.

I began to pace from one end of the wall to the other. I made adjustments to my gait until they equaled four evenly spaced steps. I quickly learned to perform this routine with eyes closed. All the prison movies I had ever seen began to flash through my mind. I envisioned the exercise routines. Where was the best place for me to do push-ups so I didn't touch the soilet? Would the rails of the bunk hold my weight for pull-ups? Could I straddle the bed in order to fully stretch my hamstrings?

I focused on all of these distractions to avoid the one thing I was not ready to face... Me! Would I be forgotten in here?

If you were to look up the word "forget" in the Oxford English dictionary it would begin simply: *fail to remember, to put out of one's mind. If you delve deeper it becomes more personal, as if the Author himself had experienced what it meant to be forgotten, Overlooked, disregarded, devolved into, left behind, and eventually, ignored, and shut out completely. It woefully concludes with to say goodbye forever, to deep six, to consign to oblivion.* This left me groping for its antonym, "to be remembered." What would I do to be remembered? Was how I was remembered out of my control now? As sad as it was to be forgotten, the desire to be remembered often led one down unintended paths with questionable moral choices. It certainly was the case for me.

Suddenly, with rushing clarity, I saw myself for the first time. I saw the fraud I had been, the games I had played, the life I was wasting. This place at least could be a place to start.
I must admit, in that moment, my knee touched the floor. When it did, I laughed at the hypocrisy of making deals with a God I didn't want to believe in. I slumped back on my bunk and the echo of that slamming door reverberated in my cellular memory like the snap of my father's belt and the explosion of that gas burner.

I wondered if anyone was thinking about me at that moment. A rather conflicting thought from a man whom had done everything to push those closest to him away. Why had I done that? I had an ex-wife whom I still loved and an untrustworthy girlfriend I didn't. I had two sons: one of this world and one not. I wondered which one would visit me more? My sister would cry and come see me for all the wrong reasons. My brother, my hero growing up, would feel whatever his wife told him to feel. He would never come visit, claiming, in his defense, that I kept the truth from him. My mother, brilliant artist and classical pianist, her mind laid barren by Alzheimer's, would discover each morning that her youngest child resided in state prison, this knowledge forgotten before her breakfast was finished. My father was dead, and I would not miss him.

Out of my quiet, a cacophony of half-conversations floated around me from the darkness outside my cell.

"Yo, H, what's for chow?"

"That all you think about, K?"

People had letters for names?

"G, what time is it?"

"Time for you to get a watch, dawgg."

"Come on, G. What's the time?"

"Nine thirty-seven."

Seven minutes. I had been here for seven minutes.

It seemed like hours ago I was processed in New Man's Land, handcuffed and shackled after the bumpy, crowded van ride from the county jail in Worcester to Walpole. As I was escorted down the central corridor to the maximum-security side known as the East Wing, I saw a clock outside the chow hall. It read 9:30. I'd only been here for seven minutes.

"I can't do this." I said out loud. I was suddenly consumed with a crippling thought as I came face-to-face with the unrelenting reality of this place. I wanted to die. Seven minutes... and I already wanted to die. How did I choose this?

But I did. I did choose this. To go forward, I needed a new beginning. I knew my mind all too well. My propensity to fool myself into change would no longer be an option. I needed to burn the proverbial bridge, like Cortez, who, upon arrival in the new world, burned his ships in the harbor to motivate his men. There was no turning back now. There was no retreat. There was only what lay ahead. Although the story of Cortez was a myth, in that moment I would choose the myth.

My head began to burn. I needed oxygen. I realized I had been holding my breath. With difficulty, I regulated my breathing. In. Out. In and Out. This, I knew how to do. Years of martial arts training, and endless hours of controlled breathing in the inferno of a house fire, listening to the sound of my Scott 4.5 SCBA, conserving oxygen; conserving the difference between life and death.

I focused on a spot on the wall and relaxed. As though through a fog, dozens of images began to reveal themselves. I had not noticed them earlier. Like ghosts, these faded symbols materialized: crucifixes, satanic pentagrams, Chinese characters, and Koranic letters. The desperate etchings of previous occupants seeking solace, salvation, or simply the desire to be remembered. With every gouge and scratch, I felt their individual yearnings.
I would not allow myself to be one of them. I refused to leave my mark here. I would not lament my punishment, banning the tendrils of self-pity. I was locked in, but the world was locked out. I would learn to find my way somehow. I would learn to make time my companion. I was alone now. Soon the gate would open and I would be thrust into the pit. I was no longer young at fifty, and I most certainly did not know the rules here. The horrifying uncertainty of prison life would become the catalyst for a new philosophy. I could feel it. And, I wouldn't have it any other way.

I would burn my ship in the harbor.

TRAUMA

Prison was like the trauma of a car accident. I should know. I spent 25 years as a first-responder.

My mind drifts to an early morning tragedy of black ice and a tree. The engine block of the small sports car has severed the torso of a young man and pinned him to his seat. It is the only thing keeping him alive. He asks me to help find his cell phone so he can call his wife, to tell her he will be late, unaware that I will hear the last words he will ever speak.

Now, I was the one bleeding out. I was the one in shock, numb and clueless to the extent of my injuries, and no one was coming to rescue me.

I paced the floor of my cell, eyes closed, four steps and then four more. I stood in lines when one formed. I ate what appeared to be food, although most of it looked unrecognizable. I looked up at the TV and watched Jerry Springer referee a fight between two long-haired women. Strange choice of television shows in prison I thought. I saw people talking on phones. They looked like pay phones. Could I talk on these phones? Who would I call?

My confused state of mind quickly turned to paranoia when a State police woman took my DNA and claimed it was standard procedure. I stared at the vial of my blood and wondered where it was being sent. Another piece of me lost forever to this vast system.

I wandered for hours back and forth between yellow lines painted on the floor, careful not to step on or over them. They must be there for a reason. No one would tell me. No one told me anything. I was certainly not going to ask. Everything here seemed random and irrational.

"Alright! I can't take this any longer," came a voice.

It was a different voice. I was talking in a different voice now?

"You're the firefighter, right? What's your name?"

I should answer.

"Ken. My name is Ken. Ken Baxter." Wow, I got that right. My name was Ken Baxter.

"I'm Ed," came the reply. "Listen, I can't stand here and watch you anymore. You've got to get a grip. First of all, hold your head up and stop staring at the floor. You look like an idiot."

Ed looked about my age and if he wasn't wearing prison garb, he'd look like a professor or an accountant.

"Second, get your towel and get in line. You stink! I had the misfortune of standing behind you at chow this morning. After that, come see me. I'm in nine."

The shower was a single stall. I had been standing in line wondering if Ed was sending me off to some prison indoctrination. Before I had time to dwell on that, it was my turn. I held in one hand the infinitesimally small bar of soap that came in my gift bag when I arrived. The Prison starter kit also included three new pairs of white, overly starched underwear and three tee shirts. The underwear was already chafing my inner thighs. There was an elfin-sized toothbrush, I assumed to discourage one from sharpening it into a weapon. The generic toothpaste came in an equally minute amount measured in micro grams. Then there were the Bo-Bo's. Once I put the Bo-Bo's on, I never wanted to take them off. Not only were they comfortable, they doubled as my shower shoes.

I felt better standing in the doorway of Ed's cell. He was intent on telling me everything I needed to know. I heard his words, but had difficulty processing and storing all of the information. I tried to focus.

"Get shower shoes." He said, "You don't want to even think about what grows in there."

I perked up and took a step forward. My shoes left a wet mark on the floor.

"How do I dry these?"

He shook his head and continued, "The first thing is to learn patience. No one cares if you're inconvenienced. No one. Second, get used to lines. Third, if you don't have money, you're screwed. If you do, don't tell anyone, or you're screwed."

I nodded and tried to look like I remembered everything he just told me. All I seemed able to focus on was how the damp canvas Bo-Bo's were beginning to itch the top of my foot.

Ed looked up at me, "Your brain will straighten itself out

soon enough." He flipped me a book, "This'll help you calm down. Don't lose it."

Back in my cell, I stood looking at the cover of *"All The President's Men"* thinking I saw the movie once. Dustin Hoffman and who else was that. I can see his face. Why can't I remember his name? It's, it's, Robert Redford. Yes, so there is hope for me.

This book was my first gift inside. I devoured it. Like many inmates, I would read everything I could get my hands on. For me, it wasn't just about passing time. It was about a quest to know, to hear my thoughts echoed in someone else's words or to learn something I could have never imagined myself.

I soon discovered that Ed was a lawyer from Fall River. He liked to talk, not only about the minutiae of prison, but also about the mundane characteristics of a regular life: marriage, children, where you lived, and where you went to school. The distraction of dialogue more akin to those between two strangers strapped beside each other on a long airplane flight. While he seemed prison-savvy, Ed's true experience could still be measured in days.

"I thought you'd been here for years," I said as I lingered in Ed's doorway, still unsure of the protocol for entering.

"This is the process side, the Green side," Ed began. "Every man is evaluated here. If a guy's a real problem, or he got a "smoker," he's sent to the Super Max up in Shirley."

"If you smoke, you're sent to the Super Max?"

Ed laughed. "You should talk as little as possible in here. A 'smoker' is a long sentence, like twenty or thirty years. See that Asian kid over there with the long hair. He's eighteen. He just got a "natural." That's life without parole, or for as long as you survive."

I winced at the thought of "as long as you survive."

"Most people here are like you. Just trying to fit in and understand the rules," Ed paused as he placed stamps onto several envelopes. "You'd be surprised though how many are in here for the second, third, even fourth time. Not me," he exclaimed, "I'm never coming back."

I wondered at this. How could anyone want to return here?

"Trying to sleep on one of these pieces of metal is the hardest thing to get used to," Ed thumped the mattress with his fist.

I nodded in solidarity, but didn't tell him the truth. Sleeping in prison, or anywhere, was not a problem for me. After my divorce, I couldn't sleep in a bed for over a year. Instead, I slept on top of things: Hose beds, reclining chairs, leaning against the engine compartment of the fire truck on a long night of fire watch. At the station I slept on the couch, denim fire jacket draped over me and the TV on all night as a companion. The winter coat I was issued in prison was almost identical, though a slightly lower quality. In place of the honorable fire emblem on the front, there were oversized white letters on the back, D.O.C, branding me as property of the Department of Corrections.

My other advantage came from my close encounters with lightning. I have been struck twice in my life, leaving me nearly deaf in my left ear. My wife and I were building a beautiful post and beam house in the deep woods of Barre, Massachusetts. It was our last-ditch effort to escape our hometown of Worcester and salvage the remains of our marriage. While I was unloading furniture, a tremendous, fast-moving storm tore through the area. It was so powerful I took refuge in the cellar and waited for it to pass. As I re-appeared the sun was breaking through the clouds. I continued to unload when time suddenly took a detour. One minute I was picking up a bike, the next I was kneeling in the driveway, soaking wet, spitting out pieces of my teeth. The fillings in my molars were blown out. Both eardrums collapsed. I tasted metal for days. A doctor later told me after examining me that it was the equivalent of standing next to a stick of dynamite going off. It was a full year before performing music didn't sound like I was singing inside a shoe box.

The second time was in Smithfield, Rhode Island at a crane company while loading generators onto a flat-bed during a thunderstorm. I remembered the strange metallic taste, the sound of a steam engine in my one good ear, and the salty tinge of blood in my mouth where I bit my tongue. I managed not to lose complete consciousness this time. Progress at least.

All I had to do now to sleep in prison was to simply press my right ear against the wafer-thin pillow and the blessed silver lining of silence followed.

With sleep came improved brain function. As Ed predicted,

what first felt like information-overload now seemed more like kindergarten instructions. Daily I studied the requisition forms available in a wall-mounted unit near the East Wing's front desk. It resembled one of those small, unmanned welcome center kiosks located off an interstate highway. There were forms for everything from ordering food and clothing to an application for a sex change operation. As the initial shock began to wear off, the real weight of where I was began to sink in. For the first time, I met with my caseworker who informed me in less than twelve words of the nothingness that lay ahead for my next five to seven and a half years. There were no educational opportunities. There were no musical instruments. This was nothing more than a Human Warehouse.

Prison would become a dichotomy of opposites for me. As crowded as my surroundings appeared, I would spend as much time as possible alone. As much as the imminent threat of danger demanded my attention, my train of thought would remain for the most part, internal. I would spend as much time as possible reading. I would read myself to sleep. The alternative was sitting motionless on the corner of my bunk for hours staring into nothing, reliving every moment of my life. Every success, every failure. Every second guessed regret. Over and over and over again.

MOVING ON

"Five minutes to count. Five minutes to the major count."

Counts were held first thing in the morning, before lunch, after lunch, before and after dinner chow, and in the evenings after lock in.

"Count time. Count time. Stand for count. Stand for the major standing count. Face front. Shirts on. Lights on."

In all my years in prison I never experienced a minor standing count.

Some guards were more enthusiastic than others. It hadn't occurred to me that the guards would be people too.

Sleeping through or not standing for count could be over-looked if it appeared to be an honest mistake. Tickets, or written reprimands, were a kind of demerit system. Some inmates, even though they specialized in pushing the boundaries, would constantly complain that they were being singled out for punishment. I would avoid these.

Inmates called me "citizen" because I had a job in the outside world that required training and a degree of intellect, so I was not to be trusted. Certain guards would accuse me of throwing away a civil service job, a job that they couldn't get. Resentment aimed at me from both sides of the bars. Even in prison I didn't fit in.

My first few weeks already felt like years. I was struggling to adapt. There was a huge relief knowing that this was not where I would be spending the next several years of my life. The close proximity of three- and four-time repeat offenders housed alongside first-time white-collar criminals seemed a volatile mix destined to end badly.

As it turned out, there were several "green blocks" in Walpole, "green" denoting the poorly fitting, itchy D.O.C. garments you wore until you were classed. Unlike the movies, where the brother of a murder victim (usually his wife or sister) has himself put in the same prison as the murderer so he can take his revenge in a very dramatic nighttime encounter, all underscored by suspenseful music, didn't happen here. The D.O.C conducted thorough background research to ensure known enemies such as rival gang members, co-defendants, and family members were separated to stave off these possible deadly encounters. This was the first of many prison myths to be exposed. Not everything in prison was what it appeared.

There was the Orientation Unit known as the PC block or protective custody unit. This block was for high profile cases. It also housed individuals who requested placement here out of fear for their lives, as well as those at high risk of suicide and those with a high media profile that made them too vulnerable for the general population.

Guards were at times in more danger than inmates. It wasn't hard to imagine that compassion withered under the stress. An inmate with nothing to lose can cause considerable damage at a moment's notice. In every profession, there were those who did a good job and those who didn't live up to expectations. Prison guards were no different. There were guards that were respected and guards that were not. You got what you gave for the most part.

By a strange twist of fate, the guy in the adjoining cell turned out to be someone I had met in a holding cell right after my trial. Although I thought I was calm that day as I waited for my sentencing, my constant pacing freaked this guy out. He described to me what sentencing would be like and about the van I would travel to prison in. He also said I would get more time than I was probably aware of because I was a "good story." On this assertion, he turned out to be prophetic.

Now, here he was, my neighbor. When he remembered I had absolutely zero prison experience, his previous efforts to inform me morphed into figuring out ways to exploit me. I was an easy mark and he began his attempts to extort items from me which he claimed was part of the process.

After one week, there were no bulletins I hadn't read, no questions I hadn't asked, no corner of the block I hadn't examined. I waited as patiently as possible for my turn to go to the library where I devoured any book, I could get my hands on, anything that transported my mind somewhere else. I procured an order form from the wall box which was a feat in itself. You had to be quick. Most inmates would grab twenty or thirty of the same forms at once, emptying the box seconds after it was filled. I had no idea what the point of this was. You could only submit one form a week. I guessed it was some form of he who dies with the most toys wins.

I had my last paycheck in my pocket upon arrival which I was told would be placed in an account for me though I wouldn't be allowed to access it for a while. Even so, just the thought of being able to purchase a T.V. someday or sneakers to run in once I graduated out of the green block was some far-off dream that seemed somehow unobtainable. Your expectations drop dramatically once incarcerated.

In the meantime, I ordered the few items I was allowed to own: a plastic mirror, some very much needed deodorant, an actual bar of soap, and my one extravagance, a cherry Chapstick.

The air was unbearably dry in here and I'd wake up with my lips cracked and stinging. Complaining about chapped lips did not enhance your street-cred as far as toughness goes. Heeding Ed's warning, I avoided anything else that might indicate I had money in an account. Ed, as it turned out, was already being targeted as a "person of means" by two unsavory characters in on their fourth bids and headed for the Super Max in Shirley. What bothered me was the fact that it didn't take a trained psychiatrist to tell you at least one of them was suffering from some form of mental illness. When I mentioned this to Ed, he shook his head and rolled his eyes. Being a lawyer, Ed was quite aware of the problem. He explained that in Massachusetts most mental health facilities had closed down years ago which meant that the prison system was left to warehouse the mentally ill alongside your run-of-the-mill common criminal. These two unstable veterans knew how to manipulate or intimidate for their own selfish ends.

The week's end promised a break in the monotony. We were finally going to eat in the chow hall. Initially, we were being fed in our block. I guessed the D.O.C. had reservations about unleashing the new arrivals in the chow hall which made me think about what they knew. I had caught a glimpse of the rows of aluminum tables bolted to the floor when I was first brought in that night that seemed a life time ago instead of the short time it had actually been. Ed explained that the customary seating was done by the city you were from. There was no way I was sitting at the Worcester table. I came to prison to escape the place of my birth. I agreed to sit with Ed at the Fall River table which was unfortunately run by the two guys that were shaking him down, which meant that I would be next.

My first visit to the chow hall was christened by an actual prison fight. The fight itself was amateuristic. Two guys from different blocks wrestled each other to the floor. To my surprise, once the fight began, all the guards stationed along the walls ran for the exits out of the chow hall. They promptly slammed the gates shut locking us in and them out. I realized that this was much the same as a Fire Department protocol. Never create secondary victims. It made perfect sense. Once the combatants got tired, the doors opened and the guards rushed in with pepper spray and various beating instruments. The inmates usually suffered more damage on the way out then during the fight. Everyone else in the chow hall was individually patted down one at a time, slowing the exiting process immeasurably. The combatants would be dressed in red and shipped off to Ten Block, the solitary confinement ward where they would nary see the light of day. Doesn't seem worth the roll on the floor in my book.

This day would also bring another first. My first contact with the outside world. No one knew where I was. No one was at my sentencing. I had cut myself off from everyone long before that day.

The phone felt sticky in my hand. I could smell the breath of its last user and tried to wipe it clean with my shirt. I had filled out the proper forms, set up an account, and stood in line. All I had to do now was dial and speak, yet I hesitated. My son Nicholai was the only person I wanted to talk to. Emotion roiled upward from deep within me, a nervousness followed by the sinking humiliation of hearing the computerized voice announce a phone call from Cedar Springs Correctional facility with an option to accept or decline. I imagined that Cedar Springs sounded less threatening than Walpole. Nicholai's voice was distant and distorted, but his worry came through loud and clear.

"I'm just glad you're okay," he said.

The sound of his voice left me filled with guilt and shame. Two new emotional cell mates to wrestle with. I yelled into the phone so he could understand me. I was surprised how quickly my composure betrayed me as I tried to explain that everything was going to be fine all while the computerized voice announced the count down to the end of our two- minute exchange. Everything in prison was controlled and counted.

"What have I done?" I said out loud as the line went dead. There was so much to say. Had I lost my other son? I stood paralyzed; the phone still clenched in my hand. The next person waiting in line put his hand on my shoulder.

"It gets better, dude," he said.

I retreated to the solitude of my cell as my eyes filled with tears. I went over every word that Nicholai managed to get in before we were cut off.

"No one knew where you were." He said, "How long will you be in there?"

I had not thought about his reaction. All I could manage to say was that I was sorry.

"Sorry for what?" he questioned

"Everything." I replied.

The list of oversights resulting from my choices were growing longer. My first foray with the outside world just made my incarceration painfully tangible. Yet, I did not want to run from these thoughts, I wanted to wrap myself in them. I formulated a plan. I would write everything down. In my past life, the thought of leaving anything in print was horrifying, as I believed it would eventually be used against me. That would have to change. Every moment of my life, good or bad should be exposed. I would hide from nothing. There would be journals explaining everything, and I would grow from this. Every fear, every fantasy. I would write about it all. I would also educate myself somehow. I would share this progress with Nicholai the old fashion way, in letters. These would become my legacy of learning, my legacy of punishment, my legacy of shame, forgiveness, and perhaps redemption.

MOVING UP

As cold as the late December air had become, as soon as I was offered Yard time, I took it. Most days only a handful of people braved the yard. Once you went out, you couldn't come in. I used to be a runner and I believed that my body, given time, could be a runner again.

I did not have the proper outdoor wear and, at age fifty, I no longer enjoyed the cold as much as I used to. I also didn't have sneakers. Man was born without shoes, so running mile after mile around a dirt track in my paper-thin Bo-Bo's was an opportunity I was going to pretend was really cool. The motivation to run was met with side-cramping protest, but survival was best achieved by constant motion. Stopping was not an option. If you did, the cold quickly crept into your bones. No one cared if hypothermia set in. You were stuck out there until Yard Time was officially over.

One extremely cold day there were just three of us that braved the weather. These guys were big. Just the way they walked screamed "Don't mess with me!" One of them wasn't even wearing a coat. I could see spiderwebs tattooed on his elbows. The other one was about six foot four with bright red hair. His hands were stuffed into the front of his green pants in an effort to protect them from the cold, a sign of some mortal weakness at least. On my fourth time around, the red-haired guy swung his arm out and stopped me.

"You've been running non-stop for a week. Where you going?"

"Running off a little frustration," I said.

"I can see that," said the spider-tattoo guy whose name turned out to be Spider. "You don't look like you belong here. Where you from?"

"Worcester," I said, "unfortunately."

"I know Worcester," said the red-haired guy whose name turned out to be Red. Go figure.

I liked these guys. They kept things simple. We talked of people we knew and places we had frequented.

Upon discovering I was a firefighter, Red said, "I thought I recognized you. You used to play in a band at The Blarney Stone."

"Nauset," I said.

"Like the beach on Cape Cod?" asked Spider.

"Exactly."

"How the hell did you end up here?"

"That's kind of a long story."

"You got someplace to be?" asked Red, putting his arm around my shoulder.

We walked for a while as I gave them the Reader's Digest version of my life. After every lap, we stopped at a set of pull-up bars and did as many as we could just to keep warm. I joined in like I knew the ritual when in reality, I was grinning ear to ear because this 'was' exactly like the movies. Something about it felt refreshing and familiar like I was exactly where I was meant to be.

I liked Red and Spider. But I wasn't supposed to like criminals. It seemed, I needed to change my attitude on a whole lot of things.

Red was sympathetic to my story.

"Man, you got smoked."

Spider broke in, "You got to leave everything about you on the other side of that wall. That world doesn't exist for you no more. You having any trouble on your block?"

"I'm adapting," I replied.

"You stand out like a sore thumb. I repeat. You having any trouble on your block?"

"I could use some advice." I explained about Ed and the two guys who were trying to shake us down.

"The lawyer." said Spider. "How's he doing?"

"His learning curve is a couple of weeks ahead of mine."

"Don't worry. We'll take care of everything."

I couldn't help but wonder how they would do this considering they were housed across the way in another classification block. By the time the guards called yard, I had forgotten all about being cold.

That evening at chow, Red yelled out from across the huge hall in a booming voice. "Fire Fighter! You sit here from now on."

As I approached, I could feel the eyes of everyone in the chow hall upon me.

"If you come to chow first, you come here," Red ordered.

Even the food tasted better that night.

By the next week, I had recovered from the trauma of my metaphorical car accident. My cerebral abilities were on the rise. I could play chess again. I looked forward to reading. When I did venture out of my cell, no one bothered me. The two career criminals that were harassing myself and Ed barely made eye contact. Don't know what Red and Spider did to make this happen, and I didn't care. Chow, although disgusting, was something I looked forward to. I even got Red and Spider to jog a little in the yard. Our conversations were now centered around what prison placement to request. They informed me that I could ask for a medium (the level of security), but that I would never be allowed to go to a minimum due to the length of my sentence and the severity classification of my crime. Spider suggested Gardner.

"So, blowing stuff up," Red said, his eyes glittering. "You were on the fire department for years. You can blow stuff up, right?"

I paused at his question. I owed them, and well, I was a criminal just like them. We discussed the combination of bleach-soaked rags and linseed oil, ammonia and drain cleaners, all garden variety bomb stuff, nothing too specific. Red loved the idea of two Styrofoam cups, one filled with ammonia and the other bleach, placed on the floor behind the driver's seat of his good-for-nothing girlfriend's car, the imminent chemical reaction waiting for the first bump or turn to be unleashed.

Spider interrupted. "If you know so much about all these things, why did you blow up a house with gasoline and get caught? Why were you even in the house?"

I smiled.

"You're the first person to make that observation. That's a story for another day."

The rule of thumb in prison was nothing ever happens until it does. Our block was to attend a "meet and greet" in the auditorium. We were to be introduced to all the department heads who would each say a few unenthusiastic words of welcome. The superintendent spoke about the journey we would be taking together. The head of security warned of the consequences of stepping out of line. The Property sergeant growled about the necessity of correct paper work and the requirement to fully complete all forms before wasting her time. I spent most of the seminar staring at the stage wondering if I could put on a music show up there like the Blues Brothers.

Then came the PREA (Prison Rape Elimination Act) video on prison rape. It showed an inmate walking into his room and discovering a candy bar on his bed (it was a Pay Day). The next badly-edited cut had him running out to the flats and declaring to the entire block that he would not be a part of any such bribery. The audience began to giggle like a group of seventh graders at their first sex education class. Staff stressed the importance of reporting transgressions.

"Is that a Payday in your pocket or are you just happy to see me?" erupted a voice from several rows in front of me. The guards-controlled grins underscored the absurdity of the film.

Our exit from the auditorium was slowed by the laborious pat-down search that was a carbon-copy of the one we got on the way in. As I stood with my row waiting our turn to exit, I heard someone yell.

"Firefighter!" The voice came from the front of the auditorium which was strange because that was where the administrative staff was standing.

"Come here!" barked a sergeant, pointing directly at me.

There was a collective head turn as all the inmates trained their gazes on me.

"What's your name?" he demanded.

"Baxter." I replied.

He grabbed the identification tag off my shirt, the one you're never supposed to be without. "You lose this, you're screwed!" was the warning passed out with the Prison I.D. that first day in New Man's Land.

"Nice picture," he handed back my ID.

"Not my best day," I replied.

"Tell me your story," he ordered, and I noticed that several of the upper staff members took a step closer.

I quickly recounted what had now become the standard version, one I could recite in my sleep. Sweat dripped down my neck as I rushed through the chain of events that delivered me here. I could feel the glares of inmates burning a hole in my back.

"Jesus Christ, Baxter," he said. "Where you thinking of requesting?"

I told him how "my people" had suggested I go to Gardner medium.

"No. You should stay here."

"Isn't this Max security?"

"I'll bring you down with the Grown-ups." He said, "You'll work on the permanent work force. You're not going anywhere for a long time. This will break up your bid. Trust me, it's your best option."

Things moved quickly after that. Within a few days, someone stuck their head in my cell.

"They're calling you at the front desk."

I was finishing up *The Hound of the Baskervilles*, lost in my own world with Sherlock Holmes. I had already made a dent in reading every book ever written. I made my way to the front desk and stood there waiting to be acknowledged. Without looking up, the guard snapped, "Pack it up, Baxter. You're moving up. You got five minutes."

You sit and you wait for weeks and nothing happens, then you're told you have five minutes to jam all your possessions into a garbage bag. I was gone before anyone knew it.

My journey took me all the way across the hall. It was only a few feet, but it was progress. It meant part one of this expedition was behind me. I also got to change the color of my uniform to gray.

"Progress is good," I thought.

My new cell was the exact reverse mirrored version from the lay out of my first cell. Other than that, everything was identical. I never got a chance to unpack my garbage bag of meager possessions. Within a day I was on my way to the far end of the building. The West Wing. A-1. The permanent work force. I never saw Red or Spider again.

A-1

Permanent work force. What a foreboding sound. It's seventy-two occupants surpassed the population of the Green units. The tiers encircled the entire block like the indoor running track of an old YMCA, except the walk ways were barely wide enough to accommodate a large man, let alone two people walking in opposite directions. This oversight was just begging for confrontation. Otherwise it was the same gray palette that I had just come from in the East wing. Although there were subtle differences that suggested hope: a day room with a pool table, a ping pong table, and microwaves. Hints of civilization. The sergeant did say the grown-ups lived here.

The massive bars of my former cell were now replaced by a modern sliding metal door outfitted with a small opening. For me, this solid door created a feeling of privacy, not claustrophobia. As a firefighter, confined spaces were familiar. The best part of my new cell, I had a window to the outside world. It only opened two inches and the rusty metal screen made seeing clearly a challenge. Still, I had a window. Mine looked out at the west wall. I could see Tower Eight which faced east. The wall extended past that, disappearing around the corner. I would come to spend hours tracing the setting sun and its slowly changing angles along with the stages of the moon's orbit visible in my patch of sky. In time, I realized why the Ancients had such a grasp of the stars and their movements. It wasn't that they were equipped with some lost knowledge or forgotten insight, they simply had nothing else to do.

My first day there, I wondered why the place was nearly empty. I assumed everyone was at work. The thought of what constituted a job in here made me nervous. It wasn't that I doubted that I could do a prison job, but I was beginning to realize that new things made me uneasy and probably had for the majority of my life. This must become a priority. Overcome the uncomfortable.

There were chin up bars at one end of the third tier. I wandered up to try them out. There were showers located on each tier, one giant shower with three heads. As it turned out, only one shower head was ever functional at any one time. I wondered if this was by design or neglect.

I heard the clamor and shuffle of inmates coming down the hall. I retreated to my cell. No one had spoken to me yet. I could hear the grumbling voices as the group impatiently waited for the guards to let them back into the cell block. I noticed two guards tending the gate when I arrived and then suddenly, they were standing in my doorway. The difference between these guards and those of the East Wing were noticeable right away. They were at ease.

"Settled in?" one asked.

"It doesn't take long to unpack five items," I said.

"You're the firefighter?"

I nodded.

"You'll have to tell me about that sometime," the first guard said and walked away. Someone was yelling "on the gate," a phrase I had witnessed guards using when they want to be let in, but this sounded like an inmate yelling.

"You get to yell 'on the gate' when you come back from work?" I asked.

"If you want to come in," replied the C.O.

"Lock in's at 9:30. Doors crack at 7:30 AM after count. Don't sleep through it," he warned. "Everything else, a dog could figure out."

I spent the next few hours listening to other people's phone calls. They were mounted right outside my door. There were two phones to a tier and there were always people on them. The phones were horrible. Both speaking and listening were close to impossible. The prison phone system was a private interest gold mine. Inmates with no money were encouraged to have family members on the outside pay into "Prison Phone" accounts which would be drained on occasion without any explanation. Nicholai tried once and then gave up. The account was charged an upfront fee of several dollars just for the act of dialing, even if no one answered. Then, there was a minute-by-minute charge. An out-of-state call was billed at twenty or so dollars. Setting up an account on the inside was more cost effective (less institutional graft), but I wasn't about to ask anyone to send me money so I could communicate with the outside world. Nicholai lived in Los Angeles now, but he still had a Boston cell number from his time at The Berklee School of Music, otherwise our phone calls would have been un-affordable. I told him I would write instead. I was pretty certain that old-fashioned written correspondence seemed archaic to my 23-year-old son who was steeped in the world of Hollywood music and sound engineering. I hoped he would be game so we could maintain a bond despite being so distant.

My welcome wagon came in the form of Spearzie. He was large and had the look of someone who liked to fight after a beer. Spearzie was on me the second I stepped out my cell door. He talked non-stop: Where was I from? Was this my first bid? Talk to this guy. Don't talk to that guy. The same routine I had been through with Spider and Red in Green. Then a strange question:

"What do you need?"

No one but Ed the Lawyer had ever been concerned with anything I might require.

"Do you play cribbage?" He didn't wait for a response. "You want a cup of coffee?" He turned and climbed the stairs beckoning me to follow.

At that moment, the inmate in the cell directly across from mine caught my attention. He was leaning against the door of his room studying a book on chess entitled *Checkmate in Two*. He glanced up at me.

"He's cool," he said softly, sensing my trepidation.

I trusted him immediately, an unusual thing for me. Maybe it was the book.

I followed Spearzie upstairs. His cell was on the third tier and had the distinct look of a well lived-in shoe box. The standard amenities were present, but Spearzie had a T.V.

"You get cable?" I kidded.

"They screw us out of anything good, but we get the regular stuff," he clicked thru the stations at warp speed. "I'll wire yours for sound when you get it. When I'm at work, you can watch mine. It'll be a couple of weeks till you get a job, even longer till you get your own tv. Anything you need, just ask. Here." He pushed several order forms into my hands. "You'll need these. I have this great collection of magazines." He reached under his bunk.

There must have been thirty magazines, everyone was of the motor vehicle variety.

"Most of my porn is on loan, but you can get on the list," he dropped his wooden cribbage board on the bed. "Cut for deal?"

"You deal," I said; I ignored his porn offer.

"I'll make you one of these too." He held up what appeared to be a hotpot with auxiliary wires running through the bottom. In seconds, I was drinking a cup of coffee. "Keep the cup until yours comes in."

He pulled a bag out from underneath his bunk and dumped its contents on the bed. He had several extra blankets, none of which seemed like the ones they passed out in New Man's Land. Everything in his room was either handmade or altered in some fashion.

"Where did you learn to do all this?" I marveled. Spearzie was busy digging through an assortment of wires and what appeared to be parts of dismantled headphones and radios. Without looking up, he said, "You pick up all sorts of things. I have consecutive fifteen to twenty's, here they are!" he said triumphantly. "I can wire your T.V!"

The RCA brand televisions were see-through, clear plastic shells whose purpose was obvious: to keep hiding places down to a minimum. They had no speakers which at first seemed strange. But then, I pictured seventy-two televisions all blaring at once in this giant cement, echo chamber. This did not stop Spearzie. His black Sony head phones had cardboard megaphones firmly attached to each ear piece with several elastic bands which amplified the low output headphones nicely. Ingenuity seemed to be the earmark of the seasoned inmate. Among the pile of electronic parts were a dozen photos, mostly of cars and their owners toasting with cans of Colt 45.

"That's my last car," said Spearzie wistfully.

I was fixated on the individuals standing next to it. I couldn't pick Spearzie out. The passage of time had been cruel. Spearzie, like many inmates, did not have the best dental insurance. His friendly smile was punctuated by large gaps. He weighed in at close to 300 pounds. The people in the photo were young, handsome, and vibrant.

"170," Spearzie tapped the photo with his huge index finger.

Back in my cell, I began doing multiple sets of sit-ups and push-ups. "Food is the enemy," I kept repeating.

"Do you play chess?" said a voice at my door. It was my neighbor. Dwayne was in his forties and he looked more like a high school English teacher than an inmate.

"I do," I said, remembering his *Checkmate in Two* book.

"C'mon," he turned on his heels.

Dwayne worked in the library. His room was strewn with books.

"I'm reading all the classics," he grabbed Dostoevsky's *Crime and Punishment* along with *Demons*. "You can read these if you want. I'm done with them."

He tossed them on the bed where they made an excellent foundation for the flimsy cardboard chess set with its small plastic pieces. We played right thru chow. A strange desire to fast had come over me.

"The food in here will kill you," Dwayne dumped a bag of peanuts on one of his many chess books. "I'll help you until you get on your feet."

Again, the strange offer to help.

"You got anyone on the outside?"

"No," I responded.

"No worries," he said.

We were evenly matched. Neither of us was too disappointed when the guard yelled "Five minutes to count. Five minutes to the major standing count!"

"You'll be a challenge," remarked Dwayne. "Just what I've been looking for. We'll have to get you in the library with me and Doc."

"Who's Doc?" I took Dostoevsky from Dwayne's outstretched hand.

"Ohh, he's gonna like you."

Although a stark improvement from the east wing, the mundane nature of A-1 began to sink in. The day room resembled a louder, more volatile version of *One Flew Over the Cuckoo's Nest*. The pool table was a revolving version of "who's next" as was the ping pong table. Checkers, chess, domino's, dice, and card games lay scattered across the metal tables. The young Latino guys played a game that involved a torn bed sheet scrawled with crayon symbols and a great deal of theatrical posturing. Animation was the common denominator in all games. Trash talking bravado celebrated every sunk shot or trumped card. Dominoes slammed down on the metal tables demanding acknowledgment like a judge's gavel. The strangest by far was angry chess. Chess, in my book, was supposed to be a quiet game of regard and dignity. Here, pieces were snatched off the board with violent precision. Moves, or lack thereof, were narrated with insulting comments and disrespect-ful slurs. The wild gestures and petty squabbling got louder and louder as the game's outcome became certain.

Other inmates dealt with their boredom in a more practical manner. One in particular had developed an elaborate exercise regime which consisted of running the six sets of stairs that made up the three tiers, doing pull ups and abdominal crunches on the bars of the third tier, before traversing the opposite staircase down to the flats where he would perform ascending sets of push-ups followed by leg lunges down the entire length of the block. Every third trip he would duck into his cell and do multiple sets of curls and triceps exercises with his mesh laundry bag which he had filled with books. I began to emulated his routine daily.

Most of the lifers kept to themselves except to use the micro-wave. It was forbidden to glance into their cells.

Not every lifer was touchy. In particular, there was O'Mal-ley, the Irish Mafia Guy, who lived in the top corner cell and ran the laundry. He had a minion of workers to run his errands, loans, and gambling.

Laundry was on Tuesday. You placed your mesh laundry bag in bins alongside of everyone else's soiled garments. I cringed at the thought of my clothes being so intimate with those of my neighbors'. Inmate laundry workers jammed as many bags of laundry as possible in industrial-sized washing machines and then dried them in enormous dryers. At the end of the day, your bag would be returned to you in much the same state as you sent it, except everything including your underwear now had a pro-nounced gray, wrinkled tinge to it. There were alternatives if you were willing to pay. For the right price, O'Malley returned your laundry folded in nice white, neat piles. I had no need to im-press anyone with sharp, crisp prison attire, and I wasn't about to pay someone for a job they already got paid for, so I opted for the gray damp version. This was preferable to the overcooked bag reserved for those on O'Malley's bad side: undershirts extra wrinkled with brown armpits.

Canteen was one of the most highly anticipated days of the week. After filling out the proper forms, I eagerly looked over the list. I could order up to seventy-five dollars' worth of food or personal grooming items.   This was inconceivable to me. Seventy-five dollars' worth of extra food a week? To my surprise, the majority of inmates would max out on their orders weekly. Most of the lifers worked in the plate shop as it paid the best, but there was a waiting list. When you considered that half of your prison pay was automatically deposited into a savings account and that the highest paying job might earn you about twelve dollars a week, it became clear to me that you had to have someone on the outside underwriting your prison needs. TV's were $250. Sneakers $50. I was lucky. I showed up to prison with my last paycheck in my wallet. That $750.00 ensured that I could purchase a TV, a small radio, and all my basic needs, at least for a while. There were others that came in with nothing. Without outside help, these men were hard pressed to purchase anything to make their bid more bearable. No matter how bad I had it, someone had it permanently worse.

RUPERT

The next few days were spent learning the ins and outs of my new home. The C.O. was right. It was much like dog training: stand in a line, sit on command, and your reward was food and shelter. Punishment followed misbehavior. The hierarchy was simple. I was at the bottom.

Chow offered the same set of problems I faced in Green block. I refused to sit at the Worcester table. Drug dealers, bank robbers, and tough guys, PJ held the top spot. He was young, in his twenties, and carried the bulk of an avid weight lifter. I guessed from the looks of his physique that steroids played a prominent role in his program and suspected an explosive temper was a likely side-effect. However, I found him amiable enough. He had a small entourage of subservient tough guys. Curiously, the man they called Doc also sat at his table, his gentility dwarfed by giants on all sides.

I took a deep breath. The back of the chow hall had several tables that always appeared to be sparsely populated and I thought I'd lay low there.

Every day the order that blocks were called to chow alternated. There was A-1, A-2, and A-3. These other two blocks were filled to capacity with inmates awaiting moving papers to their next stop. Some would be going to a medium security unit, others to minimum, a place I was informed I would never see.

Three times a day we all joined in the "gray shuffle" as I called it. We were the only block in the prison that was considered permanent. This granted us a sort of stature that, I must admit, I liked. On the days that our block was called last, the chow hall was nearly filled to capacity and seating disagreements erupted. On these days, I often skipped chow. The stress of figuring out where to sit made me lose my appetite. When I got up the courage or the hunger to go to chow, I sat in the back. There was a guy from my block that seemed to always sit at the back tables, and I figured that was a safe enough place.

Rupert was in his late sixties, in excellent shape, and had the guarded look of a lifer. His fixed facial expression and total disinterest in his surroundings served as a deterrent to conversation. He never looked up when I sat down or acknowledged me in any way. After several days of silence, I received a small nod when I sat down followed by, "Rupert" in a low voice.

I responded in kind with "Ken," as if we were Indians from different tribes. Normally my propensity towards nervous conversation would have resulted in "I come in peace," but I thought better of my lame attempt at humor. As it would turn out, Rupert was part Indian.

After a few days of this solemn ritual, Rupert spoke. "I have two rules," he said. "First, are you a "ripper" or a "skinner?"

"No," I said haltingly.

"I don't sit with no rippers or skinners. And you ain't never to sit with one either or let one of them sit at our table. They sit over there." Rupert pointed to a lone table closest to the door and more importantly, closest to the guards.

Three men were hunched over, eating with an urgency that guaranteed they spent the least amount of time possible in this hostile environment. I would come to find out that rippers and skinners were rapers of young women and purveyors of small boys, respectively. The visual images brought to mind when I considered the literal meaning of these terms made me wince. Their presence was met with isolation by both inmate and guard alike.

"Second," continued Rupert ,"if someone is sitting in my spot when you get here, then remove them. I'll do the same for you. If someone is in your spot when you get here, then you got to take care of business. I ain't getting hemmed up over you. Agreed?"

I was pretty sure that this was more than two rules, but I was not about to argue the math. I simply said ,"Agreed."

The next morning, there was a large guy sitting in Rupert's seat when I arrived with my tray of artificial eggs and dry toast. I didn't recognize him and figured he was a new arrival from the East wing. I swore to myself as I sat down. Rupert did not specify the proper removal procedure. When I looked up, there was Rupert walking down the aisle looking more annoyed than usual. Panic set in. I did the first thing that came to mind. I laughed out loud like I always did when I got nervous.

"You don't know me for shit," I said. "But you're sitting in a lifer's seat. He has nothing to lose. No need to hem yourself up over a seat."

He didn't look up. As Rupert approached, he gracefully slid over one seat and never missed a bite of delicious artificial egg product.

Rupert looked at me in surprise and said, "Good morning, Ken."

"One down and 999 battles to fight!" I proudly said. This was met with complete silence.

The following day, the roles reversed. Someone was sitting in my seat as I arrived with my congealed oatmeal and florescent morning beverage. Rupert busily spooned his corn flakes. If Rupert couldn't get this character to move, then my first prison fight was now inevitable. But like yesterday, this interloper didn't know me. I went right into character.

"Jesus Fuckin' Christ!" I said loudly. "How many times do I have to get lugged over my fuckin' breakfast. I've been sitting here for twelve years. Have some God damn respect!"

Instantly, the guy stood up and walked away. He dumped his half-eaten breakfast into one of the trash barrels and left.

"Thank you," I feigned indignity, as my heart raced. Rupert just kept eating.

This trend continued.　Every day, I entered the chow hall prepared to do battle. Each encounter got closer and closer to actual combat.　I varied my indignation with colorful descriptions of the imprint my ass had made on the chair, a result of the years I'd spent sitting here. My message: beware the old guy with nothing to lose. I began to think I was tough. I got so carried away with my performances that I stopped asking myself why Rupert was letting all these people sit in my spot in the first place.

"I got this," I slammed my tray down.

"Enough" said Rupert.　"I can't take it anymore. Although I love this new version of you, you've got to stop. There is no assigned seating here. You take the seat that's open. You'll get lugged for strong arming someone out of a chair. Everyone is waiting for you to get your ass kicked. Second, I can't be responsible. Man, you are gullible. You keep walking around here like this and someone will eventually oblige you. So, knock it off."

Rupert had just made about nine different points. What's with the multiple topics defined by two parameters?

"I thought you were my friend."

"I'm not your friend," said Rupert. "No one is.　And get this straight, don't ever imply you're doing a life bid. You don't know shit about it."

I went to speak but his glare silenced me. It felt like the hand of Darth Vader around my throat. He was right of course. I was claiming to be someone I wasn't.

As I was leaving the chow hall one of the guards grabbed my name tag from my shirt.

"Baxter, that seat isn't yours. You have no right to anything in this chow hall. Understand?" he said flicking my name tag to the floor.

"It won't happen again sir," I replied sheepishly.

I felt like an idiot, but on the bright side, I survived Rupert's hazing ritual.

DOC

Doc leaned over the railing from the third tier. He was easy to spot. He looked like one of those actors with perfectly sculpted features in the photo that comes with a picture frame. Sophisticated, almost gentlemanly in his prison garb which, on him, seemed more like surgical scrubs, Doc emanated an unmistakable air of education. To me, this was the most intimidating thing. Strange. Sociopathic miscreants, mob bosses, shank-wielding drug addicts all had less effect on me than this slight, physically unimposing man. Superior intellect made me nervous. I wanted to be that way.

Many inmates went to his cell for help, attention, or relief from a variety of ailments, real or imaginary. He never turned anyone away. He was the closest thing to real medical attention that most inmates ever received.

Your typical inmate was, in the eyes of the staff, a hypochondriac, a remorseful drug addict feigning any injury or condition in the hopes of acquiring medication. The basic standard of practice, when it came to healthcare in the D.O.C., was a budget-driven formula of deny, delay, and disavow until the inmate was either transferred, paroled, or dead. In other words, someone else's problem. This protected against the commonly held inmate's creed of get everything you can, needed or otherwise. This made it difficult for someone in actual need of medical attention to receive anything more than a disinterested brush off. Although Doc could not write prescriptions, he had a way of making people feel like he was really listening to them. If you had a legitimate medical need that required more than the typically dispensed advice of "pray and drink more water" then you were sent to the "Shattuck." The word alone induced shivers in the most hardened criminal. The Shattuck was a training hospital for financially-challenged medical students, often from far-flung places across the globe. These students toiled in a dank, crumbling hospital populated with the indigent and the poor, the complete opposite of the better-known Tufts and Brigham-Young hospitals of the greater

Boston area. Some inmates disappeared in the night after complaining of stomach pain never to be seen again. The few that did return had a World War II prison camp look to them: thin with a pale complexion and empty stare accompanied by a new compliant attitude. The word "lobotomy" was whispered around the card tables. I watched inmates line up outside Doc's cell on a daily basis. This was not how I wanted to meet him. It was imperative that I made a good first impression.

Doc jogged every other day, not too fast, not too slow, checking his heart rate methodically every few laps. He was one of the few that ran on a regular schedule. To me, running was a form of meditation, everything around me just seemed to melt away.

I didn't see Doc the first time around that day. He was shielded by Ron, who could obscure the view of most objects with his arms alone. Ron would say, "I'm a black man from Missouri, that's all you need to know."

Ron could talk the food off your tray. He knew something about everyone on the block. He was an exception inside, a guy easy to talk to. As personable as he was, he would be the first to tell you just add alcohol or drugs and stand back. His warning didn't require much imagination. He was as wide as he was tall and could bench press a small town. His agility on the handball court amazed me. The thought of Ron under the influence and the wrong circumstances made me glad I was meeting him in a sober setting. His appealing inquisitiveness made us instant friends.

I jogged up to them. Ron's voice bellowed in the crisp winter air. The words "God" and "Anthropology" in the same sentence warranted a pause in my run.

"Doc, this is the guy I was telling you about. Ken, this is Doc."

Doc nodded in my direction. I nodded back.

"I was just telling Doc about that Burgess Shales discovery you were teaching me about where there were lots of shells and stuff. Right?" said Ron.

"The Cambrian Explosion," I replied. "Fossils from 570 million years ago of animals with hard shells."

It was the perfect introduction. Ron was the perfect ambassador for my intelligence.

"I said you were telling me this was way before God was

invented," continued Ron.

Not knowing Doc's religious inclinations, I quickly side-tracked with, "I told you that about 1.6 billion years ago Eukaryotes, which are us, came into existence when bacteria made its home inside a single cell organism, thus separating themselves from the Prokaryotes."

Ron wouldn't let it go. "So, you're an Atheist?"

"I'm an Agnostic, but that's irrelevant."

"God's irrelevant?" Doc interjected.

"A topic for another day," was what I should have said before confidently jogging away. But I didn't. I did what I always did when I got nervous. I began to babble. The subjects ranged from the number of religions on the planet with story lines similar to the Bible to childhood catechism classes and church collection baskets. I couldn't shut up. At one point, Ron added that God put him in prison to save his life. I followed that if there were a God who put me here, then it wasn't for my benefit, but for the benefit of everyone around me who deserved a better life, one without me in it. I couldn't stop myself. I threw in statements like "I've done all that I wanted in this life and I'm quite satisfied." I rambled off a list of my accomplishments: my music career, black belt in karate, heroic firefighting acts, marriage, children, all to impress Doc. My voice crescendoed.

"If I die tomorrow, I'm happy with that!" I sprinted away, running a little faster than normal, my knees pumped higher. My superior athleticism an exclamation point to my impassioned monologue.

Later, I sat on my foot locker feeling pleased with myself. I believed I came off looking smart. I started to wonder why that mattered to me. After all, Doc was an inmate too. I knew he was in for perjury. After all, no one was in here for littering. When I looked up, Doc stood in my door.

"Do you practice that story in front of a mirror?" he asked. "I'd really like to hear what lies behind all that drama. I'm up in #52." With that, he disappeared only to reappear just as quickly. "Unless of course you'd rather kill me for calling you out, but I'm betting you won't. By the way, the first cells with nuclei appeared closer to 1.9 billion years ago."

"Drama?"

It took a couple of hours before I could rally the courage to accept Doc's invitation. I politely knocked on the wall above his door. He was reading a book on Matrix Energetics.

"Death for me or Enlightenment for you?" he asked.

"Too much advantage, your Dojo." I responded. We both laughed out loud.

This was the first time I laughed that genuinely since I arrived here weeks ago.

Doc instantly remarked, "Did you feel that? Something just shifted."

"Something good?" I asked.

"Something new."

We talked for a while about the adjustment to prison life and its perils. Doc had been here nine months. Over the next few weeks, there wasn't a day that I didn't stop by Doc's room or he mine. He kept close tabs on the books Dwayne was bringing back from the library for me and started to supplement them with books on chemistry, biology, and Buddhism. Doc had a Vanderbilt education and his idea of fun was reading and educating himself on well, everything, especially on healing and spirituality.

I was intimidated and excited, all at the same time. We were so different. While I was playing music on Martha's Vineyard or recording a commercial in my studio, Doc was doing his residency and then a Fellowship in Endocrinology at Tufts. While I was fighting fires in Worcester and disentangling people in three car pileups, he took over the medical practice of his mentor and partner, Deepak Chopra. If I didn't already feel like an underachieving moron, it turned out he was also Chief of Endocrinology and then Chief of Medicine at New England Memorial Hospital and, in his spare time, studied Ayurvedic and alternative medicine. He meditated daily without fail. I was sick with achievement envy. Doc's curiosity with me was endless.

"Tell me what it's like to be on a stage in front of so many people? What's the worst fire you've ever been in?"

At first, I couldn't tell if he was being polite or if he could sense that I was feeling overwhelmed by his stellar life. It was neither. Doc was genuinely interested in me. When I tried to explain that my over-the-top lifestyle was more than likely the driving force behind my current living situation, he was unfazed. He wanted to hear it all. Every detail. Every indiscretion. He was fascinated by my outlandish behavior especially in the world of music. It occurred to me that spending the majority of your life in school followed by endless hours in an office or a hospital might leave someone wondering what a wilder life could be like. Yet, there was a deeper motivation behind his line of questioning, as if he were in search of something, or someone.

"If you're really serious about learning, it's going to require a new mindset and sacrifice," he said.

"What kind of sacrifice?" I asked, intrigued.

"Avoid the nonsense," he replied, "the useless conversations, the day room, chess. All of this is a waste of your time."

CHECKMATE

"How can chess be bad?

"Are you planning on making a living playing chess?" Doc asked

"No, but it has to be good for your brain."

"The greatest chess players in the world will tell you that games are decided well before the ending. Most games are a foregone conclusion. You're made for something different."

"Playing chess with Dwayne can't be all that bad a break from studying. You consider Dwayne smart."

"I'll give you Dwayne, but he's leaving soon. Flipped his case. He'll be gone by the end of the week."

"He's leaving?" I was surprised this upset me. Dwayne was an international drug dealer with loads of money. He could afford to spend a fortune on a legal team that worked around-the-clock on his behalf. Dwayne was savvy enough not to put his fate solely in their hands and devoted his time in the library to endlessly researching the legal aspects of his case, looking for cracks he could pass on to his army of defense lawyers to exploit. His relentless legal Blitzkrieg must have exhausted and demoralized the prosecution.

Dwayne and I discussed his case over our intense chess games and while power-walking around the track. Dwayne could speed walk me into the ground with his manic energy. We talked a lot about our latest classic novel critique. Our current book was *The Catcher in the Rye*, which we both found extremely dull. We agreed that society had changed so much since the publishing of this book that it was tame by today's standards. Doc pointed out that Plato and Einstein were also outdated, but still relevant. Fiction was a waste of time in Doc's estimation, better spent on science and philosophy. I was going to miss Dwayne, our discussions, and chess. He did however leave me his treasured checkmate in Two book on my bunk when he left.

Our last game was memorable. I had set up the chess board on an empty table outside of Dwayne's room and waited. Soon, one of the "loud chess" players sat down. Tommy was a thirty-three-year veteran of the Massachusetts Prison system. He was serving time for a murder he committed as a young man. He killed a drinking buddy for the seventeen odd dollars in his pocket. Thirty-three years in here could do a considerable amount of damage to anyone. Tommy's mind was far from sound. He had a hair-trigger temper that usually resulted in nothing more than verbal outbursts although he had beaten someone with a cribbage board once. Although about six foot four, he was unimposing until you pushed his button. Dwayne had warned me about engaging him in any sort of game. Tommy repeatedly challenged me to play chess with him. He taunted me, accused me of being afraid of him, prodded that I couldn't handle the embarrassment and humiliation of losing to him. When he sat down, I didn't even look up. I said I was waiting for Dwayne. "Let's just play till he gets here," Tommy prodded.

What could be the harm, I thought. "Speed chess. We're done the second Dwayne gets here."

"Agreed."

Tommy rubbed his hands together. "Prepare to be destroyed."

Considering Dwayne was no more than a couple of minutes out, I tried a high-risk Queen's Gambit, not something you normally get away with against an experienced player. My gamble instantly started the verbal theatrics.

"The firefighter's gonna try to be fancy. You won't get away with this shit. Take that!" he slammed down his piece. It was the wrong move.

I could see Dwayne walking down the flats from the day room and by the time he reached us the game was over.

"What the fuck!" Tommy yelled "Let's have a real game, none of this speed crap."

Dwayne didn't even bother stopping. He just motioned that I should bring the board to his room. I left Tommy loudly complaining that he'd been cheated.

"Are you nuts?" said Dwayne. "I told you not to play him."

Within thirty seconds, Tommy was in Dwayne's doorway.

"I got next," he demanded.

"Go away," said Dwayne without looking up.

We both did our best to ignore Tommy standing in the doorway.

"I'd never fall for that," he spat out after one of Dwayne's moves. "You know what I'd do?"

"We won't be finding out," Dwayne shot back. "If you're going to stand there, then be respectful."

In the next few minutes, Tommy resorted to juvenile exasperation. He focused his disdain on me. Sensing I might be distracted, Dwayne offered, "Do you want to finish later?"

"Go on," I said, and Dwayne promptly removed my Bishop from the fray with a clever move I didn't see coming.

"I knew it!" Tommy shouted. "I can't believe you didn't see that coming! You're a poser!"

"I beat you in eight moves," I replied flatly.

There was a short pause as Dwayne's eyes closed as he placed his chin on his clasped hands, his head moving slightly back and forth as if to say "Noooo."

Tommy began spitting and jumping up and down as he backed out of the room. "Nobody disrespects me, you fucking punk."

I knew a fighter when I saw one and Tommy was no fighter. He only had crazy going for him. But in here, crazy was a formidable weapon. "I warned you," sighed Dwayne.

"We're not done," I said.

"Oh, we're done," said Dwayne. "Now you have to finish this with him."

Dwayne gathered up the chess pieces.

I'm not gonna fight this moron," I said.

"He just called you out," Dwayne said standing up.

Punk, apparently was one of the worst epithets in here. PJ and Spearzie suddenly appeared in the door.

"Firefighter, you have to go deal with this now, he just went into his cell. Go after him. You can't let that stand." PJ's voice was stern.

"I got your canteen," said Spearzie.

"What does my food have to do with anything?" I was confused.

"If you get into a fight, you're gone," explained PJ. "They lock down your room and you go to solitary in Ten block. All your stuff is packed and your canteen gets tossed, so give it to us. At least that way your friends get it."

"You guys are my friends?" I asked.

"Well, we're not calling you a punk to your face," retorted PJ. "If he backs down, we'll return it, promise, but you gotta go now."

Everyone stared at me. I got up and walked to the stairs.

"Pretend you're going into a fire!" yelled Spearzie.

My years of karate training were still at my disposal. In truth, I hated pain and confrontation. In a normal world, I would have avoided this idiot. In here, the rules of a civil society did not apply.

My paced quickened. Close quarter fighting. I had this. In fact, I could teach this. An inmate leaned on the rail across from Tommy's cell and nodded his head slightly, indicating he was in there. Tommy was on his bunk reading when I burst in. I was at the foot of his bed before he knew it.

"Are we going to have a problem?" I yelled. I wanted to give fair warning. I was unsure of the proper etiquette.

Tommy jolted up, dropping his magazine on his face. Temporarily blinded, he smacked it away, arms flailing. Leaping off the bed, he tripped over himself, knocked his half-filled coffee off the desk. The cup sailed through the air and deposited its contents on the front of his perfectly white tee shirt.

"We don't have a problem," he stammered, "get out of my room." He strode towards me with all the confidence he could muster.

But this was over. It was over the second I entered his cell, but I wasn't going anywhere. Tommy glanced over my shoulder as he teetered on the balls of his feet, trying to tower over me. It was the only advantage he had left. A small crowd had gathered across the tier and I was invigorated by it. I realized I had a long way to go before I could claim to be the person that Doc thought he saw in me.

"You made your point. You called me out. We don't have a problem," Tommy stammered.

I did what I had to do and it was over, but I didn't leave. I got louder.

"You think you can call me a punk and get away with it?" I shouted.

"Lower your voice," he whispered loudly.

"I don't care who hears me," I snarled. "I can't even play a game of chess in peace and now you want me to be quiet. I jabbed my finger in his face and with that, I turned and walked out of the cell. I pretended to be surprised at the crowd nodding their approval at my performance. Doc leaned against his doorway. Tommy was his next- door neighbor. His arms were folded. He cocked his head and looked at me disapprovingly.

"Nice," he said. "One step forward, two steps back," and with that, he retreated into his room.

I walked down the stairs; my feelings mixed. On one hand, I took care of business and did it within the parameters defined by prison life. I simply played the hand I was dealt and I played it well, but there was the bigger picture, the one Doc was shining his harsh light of reason on.

My brain was flooded with adrenaline and cortisol. The only solution was to exercise until the chemicals dissipated. "Control your process," Doc had taught me, and if you can't, then put the resulting chemicals to some productive use. With my hands still shaking, I wrapped ten of my books in a blanket and stuffed them into my laundry bag. Doc's lectures emphasized that the key was to control your environment by anticipating outcomes. Practice successfully predicting the future in real time. Your brain needed to be ahead of your actions was one of his mantras. It seemed so simple in theory, yet time and time again, I was stuck resorting to hindsight and here I was again.

My arms burned as I performed set after set of tricep and bicep curls. My knuckles reddened as the laundry bag scraped against them. It took me awhile to calm down. When I did, I thought growing up was hard, especially when you start at 50.

THE VISIT

I fidgeted in my itchy grays waiting to be patted down by the guard posted outside the visiting room. Like a third-base coach signaling the batter, I tugged first on one sleeve, then the other, pulled at my collar, ran my hands through my hair, adjusted my waistband.

It hadn't occurred to me that anyone would bother to come see me. I had purposely faded out of my own life in those months before my trial. The notice delivered by the CO informed me that Timmy and Shawn, twins and my long-time friends, would be braving the gauntlet to visit me. Timmy was a fellow firefighter and Shawn, a musician and videographer. They operated a re-cording studio near the Quabin Reservoir where we engineered countless music projects together.

Shawn jumped up when I entered the cramped room. He grinned and waved. My insides ping-ponged between excitement and dread as I picked my way between the rows of visitors to get to them. Timmy shook my hand hesitantly, glancing at the guard seated in a high chair at the end of the row. Shawn gave me a bear hug. I sat down and they followed suit, sitting side by side in the plastic chairs across from me. For a moment, the three of us sat in a bubble of silence while all around us the room was engulfed by hushed, urgent voices laced with every possible human sentiment.

I exhaled, realizing I was happy to see them and with no prompting, launched into a travelogue of my prison experiences. I told them about the size of my cell and all the characters I met, about my soilet and playing endless games of chess. I described yard time and chow hall brawls and reading books I'd never even heard of before. They sat there in stunned silence as I barreled on.

"Are you high?" whispered Timmy.

"No, this is me not on drugs."

My exuberance for all things prison aside, I was still me.

"Who's the big guy?" nodded Shawn, looking down the row.

"Which particular big guy?" I replied.

"The scary looking one."

"Again, you're gonna have to narrow that down," I laughed.

I spied Ernie sitting across from a stern-faced young woman, two whimpering children clinging to her. She seemed to be lecturing Ernie who seemed to be eyeing the clock on the wall. I strained to refocus on what Shawn was saying about their latest wedding video business but was distracted by the torrent of Spanish volleying back and forth between the two parents sandwiched next to Shawn. The mother sat steel-rod straight and avoided looking at her inmate son who couldn't have been more than twenty. He slumped in his chair; tattooed arms crossed in defiance. I had not considered until that very moment that prison destroyed the lives of entire families. It was easy to see how the domino of bad choices turned lives upside down beyond the victims of crime. There were mothers, fathers, wives, girlfriends, siblings, children – all these people left in limbo waiting: waiting for their loved one to do their time and come home, or worse yet, fearing their loved one would eventually be coming home.

"Sit back!" yelled the desk sergeant.

Timmy flinched, "Is he talking to me?"

"You're leaning too far forward in your seat," I whispered, "toes behind the yellow line."

"I wasn't even close to you," Timmy said.

"Just one of the endless rules," I said.

"So we don't pass you a shiv?" said Shawn.

"Actually, even more desirable than a weapon: food," I said.

"Actual food?" Shawn said.

"You'd be surprised what inmates would do for an apple," I smiled. The three of us laughed and then abruptly stopped.

"This has got to be tough on you," said Timmy.

I looked at him and remembered the two of us dragging a line up the staircase of some rambling old three-decker with a kitchen fire. I had an overwhelming feeling of being lost. My exuberance evaporated.

"It's hard to hear," Shawn filled the silence. "My hearing's not what it used to be."

"Mine either," I grinned.

"Too much rock and roll," Shawn said. We laughed.

With-out warning, the guard scraped his chair back from his desk and made a beeline to a couple by the window. Everyone in the room hushed as the guard grabbed the inmate by the arm and shoved him towards the door.

"Geesh," said Shawn.

We could all hear a muffled one-sided tirade out in the hall. The guard returned sans inmate and escorted the young woman from the room. Shawn and Timmy looked at me.

"Let that be a lesson," I said. The din returned to full volume.

"Who's that?" questioned Timmy. "She doesn't look like she belongs here."

About five seats down on my right, perched on the edge of her chair, an act bordering on a violation, was an elegantly dressed women too sophisticated for these drab surroundings. Blond haired, blue-eyed, she sat there, hands in her lap, as though she was waiting for a college lecture to commence.

"I don't know," I said, intrigued.

At that moment, Doc walked through the door and her whole being came alive. I watched the woman throw her arms around his neck soaking up his entire being in that permissible five second embrace, completely immune to the grim chaos echoing around her. Doc stood apart from the rest of us. He sported what prisoners of means called *visiting clothes*: black dress pants, a perfectly ironed white dress shirt neatly tucked in at his waist, and out-of-the-box-new shoes. They made my Bo-Bo's look like they belonged in a garbage dump. I looked down at my feet.

"Do you need shoes?" Timmy asked. "We can send a pair of

sneakers. Maybe even a guitar or piano so you can play."

I choked on his generosity. No one had sent me anything.

"It's not allowed," I said quietly, "but thanks."
I explained that sending anything to an inmate beyond a letter was forbidden, even birthday cards were considered contraband if adorned with so much as a sprinkle of glitter.

"Maybe we could donate the instruments to the prison," Shawn said.

That was an idea I could explore. Surely things like musical instruments could be donated to the prison. I made a mental note to ask the C.O. My Bo-Bo's and I would have to make do for a while longer, but I didn't mind. There was a part of me that thrived on having so little.

Out of the corner of my eye, I watched Doc and the woman talk, holding hands across the aisle. I couldn't take my eyes off her. She seemed completely absorbed in Doc. The full range of human emotions tracked across her face. She was the most transparent person I had ever witnessed. Her body arched forward with a loyalty of devotion. She glowed with it. This place had no power to tarnish the love this woman beamed at Doc.

Our visit came to an abrupt end. Timmy would be the only firefighter to come see me or write to me. For a long time, they were the only ones who dared cross into my world. I felt like a leper, locked away and shunned by those who knew me. Yet, so many of my friends and family didn't understand why I was here. I struggled with the truth of that decision also. For now, I was content with the outside world remaining on the outside. It was easier and harder all at the same time, a paradox of punishment.

Back in A-1, Doc asked how my visit went.

"It was good to see them. It took a lot for them to come. But they don't know the whole story. I felt shackled to my past."

Doc listened and said, "No lie on your soul."

I repeated his words, confused.

"It's not what you're thinking," Doc replied cryptically.

It was just one other thing I'd have to wait to understand. It felt like that had become my entire existence, waiting and wondering about the twists and turns my life had taken to bring me here. I was even more confused and unsettled after the visit than before. The lies of my past haunted me. What other truths evaded me? In his quiet, observant way Doc knew more about me than I knew about myself. I walked out of his cell in deep thought and forgot to ask about his visit.

PHILOSOPHER KINGS

"What is knowledge thru the five senses?"

"Empiricism."

"Rationalism is?"

"Attaching reason to the equation, compiling information."

"The study of being?"

"Metaphysics. The who we are and how we got here disputation."

"Excellent," said Doc.

I sat on the footlocker that had become my classroom chair during my re-education as Doc called it. On any given day, I would spend hours sitting, listening, answering questions, mostly listening. Subjects would vary from math formulas to the biology of the cell. I once spent an entire afternoon listening to Doc explain the wonders of evolution through the marvels of carbonic anhydrase, an enzyme he claimed had evolved to aid in the process of water and carbon dioxide formation. I'm not sure. Sometimes I strained to stay awake.

"Most learning is attached to emotion," Doc began. "You remember the girl that sat in front of you in school. The teacher you didn't like. I believe that if we can isolate the neuronal pathways, we could create a dedicated area for learning unattached to emotion."

This was the premise behind the Pi experiment.

"Once a day, I would like you to recite Pi to as many digits as possible," ordered Doc.

The trouble with this was we didn't have access to the number Pi. Doc found it written on the cover of a book, but the digits trailed into infinity as the numbers got smaller. We could only discern about fifty digits. Once I committed these to memory, reinforcements came via Nicholai, whose first letter included several hundred digits of Pi printed on the back. It was gold.

"Why don't you just Google it?" asked Nicholai on one of our few and far between phone calls.

He never seemed to get that prison not only kept me isolated from society, but from information as well. There were no computers, no I-phones. Doc rummaged through the library to find adequate teaching material, mostly outdated or remedial. He resorted to purchasing learning courses and text books to supplement my education.

After a while I imagined the number that defined the center of a circle to infinite was a gateway to a sacred place, where I could sit in total isolation. I would write the numbers on the wall of my secret cave in groups that I could remember.

"You sit in a cave when you recite Pi?" asked Doc.

"The bigger the number, the deeper I go. It's all written there."

"Anything else written there?" asked Doc, half-kidding.

"Scratched in the stone above the numbers is the phrase 'We are what we repeatedly do.'"

"Nice. Who said that?"

"Aristotle," I replied smugly. Oh, my God, there was something Doc didn't know.

I relished these teaching sessions though the pace, volume, and complexity of the incoming information made me question what Doc's true motivation was. He seemed surprised by my level of enthusiasm on the one hand and frustrated when I floundered over the more esoteric topics. At times, I believed his intelligence proved an impediment to his teaching ability. It reminded me of the accomplished musician who struggled with slowly progressing students. It was as if they couldn't be bothered with people unable to grasp technique as quickly and proficiently as they could. There seemed to be no end to the subjects Doc could espouse on.

"The general consensus on the origins of religion coincide with written language some five thousand years ago approximately 3200b.c.e."

"What do you think of religion," I interrupted, just trying to slow the rate of information down.

"That depends. Are you referring to organized religion or to acts that are associated with beliefs? There does seem to be evidence of intentional burials around 300,000 years ago. Then there are the appearances of symbolic artifacts during the Stone Age. You also have Darwin who attempted..."

"I mean you. What do you think of religion?"

Doc seemed puzzled by what I was asking.

"Explain," he said.

"It seems to me that once you start discussing faith, then logic and fact take a back seat to belief, so, I am asking what you believe in?"

Doc grimaced. The moment hung there between us.

"Opinion is not fact," he stuttered. "Knowledge and opinion are separate issues." Doc paused like a computer stuck in a loop.

I could see his brain searching for a way around my intrusion. He had no qualms about pushing everyone who came to sit on this footlocker into their uncomfortable places, whether they came seeking advice, medical or otherwise, or knowledge, my impassioned quest. He deftly coaxed people into revealing themselves whether they wanted to or not. I wasn't sure sometimes if this was entertainment on Doc's part, or if he had devised some psycho-sociological study he was gathering data for. He stood up nervously though there was really no place to go and he sat back down again, his eyes trained on the wall behind me.

I had never honestly addressed religion myself beyond the occasional desperate prayer when I was in a tight situation and needed to make a deal. Yet, I found myself wanting him to explain what he believed versus the text book versions of what he knew. An ardent, life-long meditator I suspected Doc, having spent a lifetime letting go, was now desperate to find something to hold on to. Everyone in here was. I assumed his attempts to maintain the facade of being an unprejudiced observer collided with the brutal realities of coming to prison.

He took a deep breath.

"Religion does not offer Enlightenment. When I came here, I considered believing in God."

Doc described the same scene of dropping to his knees that

I had experienced on my first night. The hypocrisy of this tableau was not lost on him either. The humiliation and uncertainty of prison overwhelmed even the most hardened.

"I thought with forty years of meditation, I could shut all of this out."

I imagined the harsh reality of prison life eroded Doc's sense of knowing, And, not knowing was something he was completely uncomfortable with. In prison, A+ B was beginning to no longer equal C.

"I went to church for a while, even got baptized," he went on. "But then it just blurred from something I needed to do, to just something to do. I realized that most of my life was spent in a state of spiritual arrogance, that all that discipline isolated me from my family, from everyone. My first night here was a near-death experience. My life flashed before me and I didn't like what I saw. It was like my eyes were open for the first time and it consumed me."

Doc went on for a while about his frustration of seeing things so clearly that night and realizing that none of this had to happen. The gut-sinking realization had him sizing up the air vent and his bed sheet. He recited an in-depth description of how long he calculated it would take to hang himself, the burning in his head as the oxygen drained from his body. I was riveted.

"And then there's you," he said looking at me for the first time in ten minutes, his voice quivering just slightly. "You knew this before you came here and still you chose this. Why would you do that?"

In that moment, Doc was revealed. He and I had found common ground in our shared experience of having everything stripped away. It was in this brutal unmasking that gave us a glimpse of Enlightenment, the unfettered connection that made us all equal. Doc didn't need answers or a student. Doc needed a friend, and here in this godawful place, designed to confine, we were untethered. The wall between student and teacher dissolved and the real learning began.

We spoke for a while about our hopes and fears. Even discussed religion – not the history or the controversies, but our actual knowing and not knowing. "Not knowing" could be a subject all on its own. It gave us license to come up with crazy theories. Why couldn't we be the ones to uncover the next step, the next paradigm shift. That afternoon left us both fired up with a new sense of purpose.

"Have you ever heard of Philosopher Kings?" asked Doc.

"Philosopher Kings?" The words piqued my attention.

"Yes. I believe we may have found your major."

THE THREE REASONS

I spent the next two months reading and contemplating the never-ending stream of information Doc deposited on my desk. My current assignment in my crusade to understand the Philosopher King was to come up with an original thought. This task left me questioning whether I had the mental capacity to sift through all of this. Doc encouraged me to combine epistemologies and write about something in my own words, something that rang true to me.

"Become a maven," he challenged.

Of course, I had to look that one up. A maven was someone who accumulated knowledge.

"How?" I sighed, tossing another book on the ever- growing mountain of reading material crowding my tiny desk.

I read *The Dialogues of Plato*. I combed through the lines of The Republic making a Herculean effort to discover a morsel of misinterpreted information I could set straight, anything I could claim as my own. I started to ponder what was worth knowing. What was worth the test of time.

One afternoon, totally exasperated, I barged into Doc's room and demanded. "What is the point of any of this!"

"Good afternoon to you, too," said Doc. "What seems to be the problem?"

"If your point was to distract me from the fact that I'm in prison, then I must say I'm a little disappointed. Granted, I've sat through meals where I can't recall what I just ate which is probably a good thing. I look forward to being locked in my cell at night. But I did not come here just to survive. I had a goal. I had a vision. But let's face it. No one's going to hire me as a theoretical physicist or a philosophy professor. My future, if it exists at all, consists of Burger King and Home Depot, and that's if I'm lucky."

Doc stared at me over his glasses, unflappable as usual, taking in my tantrum. He closed the book he was reading, carefully marking his place with the pencil he was using to underline passages and settled in for what was to be a colossal venting on my part. It was as if he'd been waiting for me to hit the wall, even hoping for it.

"Write a paper with original thought? No one in here, maybe even including you, can do that. It occurred to me this morning that even describing Plato's version of the three elements of the soul, as interesting and insightful as it is, proves that no one has apparently learned anything in twenty-five hundred years. His insights have eluded the majority of the so-called intellectuals who profess to teach them. Our society not only doesn't adhere to Plato's logic, but it almost seems as if we've chosen to deliberately ignore it. So, explain to me how writing in my own words about our ass-backward perversion of Plato's theories isn't just some clever form of plagiarism? How is this twenty-year old ,worn out college textbook not just another form of pseudo-intellectual, plagiarized mental masturbation?" I stopped to catch my breath.

"Are you done?" Doc asked, trying not to smile.

I was about to say no, feeling I was really on a roll when Doc recited: "The absurd is a consequence of the encounter between a rational human being and an irrational world. Who said that?"

"Albert Camus," I responded smugly. "Would you like me to plagiarize *The Prisoner* for you?" I was not backing down.

"You have an interesting point," Doc conceded.

"I what? I have a what?"

"This place is a testament to absurdity," Doc continued. "I suggest you put your self-pity about your imagined bleak future aside for now. It's not on the curriculum. Your plagiarism diatribe has merit. Not that it's an original thought, but intriguing just the same. How do you know we haven't followed Plato's insights? On what grounds does your experience show you this?"

"Well…" My mind fished for some witty retort in my defense.

"Write it down," Doc interrupted. "Become Socrates. Become Plato. Show me a path to becoming a Philosopher King. Make me understand what you think you've learned," he challenged. "Make me see what you see," he said with a satisfied smile.

Walking back down to the flats I started thinking. Become Plato. become Socrates. Show the path to a Philosopher King. I wondered if I'd just come up with that or did he. It's difficult to tell sometimes. Back in my cell, I realized part of my frustration was the long list of notable scholars that had taken this same journey before me. Did I even have the right to pretend to be on par with these icons of generations past? My philosophy textbook with the missing cover defined philosophy as "the systematical, critical examination of the way we judge, evaluate, and act, with the aim of making ourselves wiser, more self-reflective, and therefore, better men and women."

Philosophy, by its literal definition, was "the love of wisdom." I seriously doubted that simply "loving wisdom" would be enough to make me a philosopher any more than watching *The Shawshank Redemption* three times would give someone actual insight into the reality and dangers of prison. You kind of had to be here. But that was the thing about prison; you were freed from the burdens of a work-a-day life and instead, bestowed with prodigious amounts of time to read and study. In the past, the task of pondering the why's and wherefores of life and science was a luxury afforded only to the leisure class. Incarceration awarded me entry into a modern- day leisure class minus the wealth and privilege. I had an opportunity here, opportunity being the key. I could sit in prison and begin a downward spiral of self-pity and despair and spend years worrying about the dark horrors of a dim future, or, I could re- frame it as a scholarship to a prestigious university where I was the only student. The professor lived upstairs and was available at a moment's notice to answer, in extraordinary detail, any question on any subject I wished to learn. What was I complaining about? Sign me up! I decided to simply start where Plato began.

"Baxter! Stand for count!"

"I'm sorry!" I snapped to attention. Damn! I broke into a nervous sweat. Not standing for count was a ticketable offense. How could I not hear count time? I needed to remember: I'm in prison.

"Baxter! You know you can't have more than ten books in your cell."

I looked down at the twenty or so books strewn about my room and panic set in.

"I need all of ..."

"Don't worry. I won't take your friends away from you. You look like you're almost enjoying yourself."

"I am. Thank you."

"You think you're going to become a philosopher or something?"

"It's not about becoming anything." I answered quickly "It's the attempt that makes you better."

"Whatever. Just pay attention to count time. The next guy might not be so lenient." He shook his head in disbelief and walked away.

He was right. I couldn't let a stupid indiscretion screw up my plans. Things changed in an instant in here. One minute you could be studying, the next you're moved to a new facility, or, shanked in the kidneys. There was no room for error in here, and that's how it should be: Structure. Confinement. Fear. The perfect setting.

I looked down at my notes. Become Plato. Become a philosopher king. What better way to learn, or live for that matter, than by embodying a philosophy that rang true to me. Don't memorize the words of Plato. Emulate them. Then, and only then, can you own them. The walls of my cell melted away as I wrestled with whether the three elements of the soul were Socrates as interpreted by Plato or a revelation by Plato himself. But then, I didn't care who invented ice cream, I just knew I liked it. For clarity's sake, I decided to refer to them as the "Three Reasons of Plato."

"All information is out there." I heard Doc's mantra. "The past, the future, everything that has ever happened or ever will happen is all out there."

Doc explained that I would understand this as I learned to

meditate more efficiently, that I too could tap into this compendium of knowledge. But Doc's stillness meditation seemed more like torture to me. But maybe if I could master these techniques, maybe I could travel back in time and listen to Socrates lecturing at the Lyceum. I would raise my hand and explain that I was from the future and that I wanted to surprise my teacher by bringing back the secret to becoming a Philosopher King. Plato would interrupt and speak for Socrates, as usual.

"Tell him you had it right. Tell him it's not about becoming a Philosopher King, it's what you told the guard. It's about the attempt."

Didn't I just say that? How did Plato know. Maybe this meditation stuff actually works.

I envisioned listening to Plato as he differentiated three distinct elements of the human spirit. First was *Reason,* or the power to deliberate, compare alternatives, suppress impulses, and thus, inspire sensible choices. Second was the *Spirited Element* or *Spirited Aggression,* the willful part of the personality, in Plato's time, the literal warrior. And third, the *Appetites* and *Desires,* which were self-explanatory. Each one of these elements had a purpose and a role to play in what Plato called the Virtuous Soul. The Virtuous Soul, Plato expounded, had learned to orchestrate a concord among all three elements thus attaining a state of virtue. Reason restrained Spirited Aggression from destructive pursuits and tempered Appetites and Desires. Plato proposed that true wisdom sprang forth from this parity among the elements of the soul; only when freed from internal discord, could one diligently pursue worthwhile goals and contribute positively to society. Not only did this ring true with me, it was something that I could immediately implement in my life. The beauty of Plato's theory was its simplicity. At least it sounded simple.

Looking around at my current neighbors, it was immediately apparent I was living in the midst of a case study on the effects of the unbalanced soul. It took little insight to determine which of the three elements led the decision-making processes of my fellow detainees and which element had been gagged and bound. What became even more obvious was that no one in here would be considered a candidate for a *Philosopher King.* It seemed to me even that Doc struggled getting anywhere close to this state of internal justice, to borrow Plato's terminology, this perfect internal balance among the three elements, infused with respect and ultimately governed by logic. Plato postulated that Philosopher Kings, though few and far between, had the ability to place the needs of society above their own interests and would therefore make the wisest and most benevolent rulers. I was immediately struck that in today's society, the last thing governments or corporations wanted was a Philosopher King making decisions based in the best interests of its citizens or employees, but before I got caught up pointing out the flaws of society, it seemed only right that I corral my own soul into balance. Such an ambitious aspiration would be challenging, especially in here, where leading a life of virtue, by means of reason, was, well, in the words of Albert Camus, absurd. My paper for Doc boiled down to a singular sentence: It's about the attempt.

Doc added, "to implement this understanding within yourself."

"That was implied," I defended.

"I see you're learning how to learn. A piece of advice: before you race on to the next topic leaving this pearl in your wake, learn to combine your subjects. Find the next piece of the puzzle and continue to build on this. Never replace what you can combine. Let me repeat this: Never replace what you can combine. Great start though," he said holding up my paper. "I particularly like that you understand it's not the time to build a soap box and claim ownership of knowledge that is not fully yours."

"I saw enough of that on the fire department," I agreed.

I had witnessed first- hand the destruction it left in its wake. The ready, fire, aim mentality of certain individuals caught up in something they didn't quite fathom.

I felt a twinge of pride as I walked back to my cell. *Never replace what you can combine.* I had just spent months lost in a swirl of information and intrigue that I never would have equated with reading or studying. How had I missed out on the absolute thrill and sense of achievement offered by learning? Somewhere early on, I missed that blinking neon sign that advertised *"this way to awe and understanding."* How foolish I felt in moments like this. Why did I never choose this? But choice was all part of why I was here. This was not a weekend course in philosophy. This was a conscious commitment to a life I never before thought possible. Oddly, I was becoming fully invested in discovering what I was capable of, of what lay ahead of me if I stayed focus and disciplined. I hugged my philosophy book against my chest and smiled at the sight of the sun setting behind the west wall, the pink and gold rays waving goodbye for another day. A day well spent. A day where not a single moment was wasted. I had a glimpse of how a life could be led as a Philosopher King now and I accepted this quest. This was a life worth pursuing.

ONE STEP FORWARDS, TEN YEARS BACK

On Dec 3rd, 1999, I walked into the communications room of the Park Avenue Fire Station. No one looked up. The small group of mutual aid and off-duty personnel stared blankly at a silent radio.

"We're missing six."

I heard the words, but they simply didn't register. "What?"

"Six guys unaccounted for. There's been no communication. It's been too long."

From behind me came a familiar voice.

"Ken, I'll give you a ride. I can get you close enough."

It was my Dad. Although a retired lieutenant now, he spent most of his time here, drinking coffee, diligently at work on a pile of scratch tickets. On our way to the scene, I asked who was missing. There were over three hundred of us. This was a lottery no-one wanted to win, and as far as anyone else knew, all our names were in the hat.

As we approached the scene, there were cars parked everywhere, hastily abandoned along the roadside. Barriers were being set up by police and Department of Public Works crews. Ambulances and firetrucks lined up as far as the eye could see.

"This is as close as I can get," my Dad said. "They abandoned inside operations a while ago. It's a surround and drown now."

Entering the staging area, a wall of heat stopped me in my tracks. Even from this distance it was obvious that no one could survive this. No-one could recall when the last firefighter was lost in the line of duty, but no-one had to look through the records to know we had never lost six. The windowless Worcester Cold storage building with its eighteen-inch-thick brick walls originally designed to keep cold in, now doubled as a furnace. All we could do was watch.

"Baxter. It's about time you got here! Where were you?"

"Just found out," I said.

"Kirk and Sterling still haven't shown up."

"As if that's a surprise," cracked another firefighter.

"Little good they'd do," came a comment from behind me.

I passed off these comments as people feeling frustrated and powerless, yet they continued.

"I heard Sully left his guys in there."

"Figures," someone added.

This angry back-and-forth ridicule kept building. I was grateful when a lieutenant from my station approached me.

"Kenny, the scope needs relief. You up for that?"

"Absolutely," I replied.

As we made our way, he divulged the names of the firefighters that were missing. Two I had never met, one I came on the job with, and another was a close friend. My stomach turned over as the Lieutenant lay out the circumstances. When the first companies arrived, there was confusion over whether there was anybody still trapped in the building. All the S.O.P.(standard operating procedures) were carried out without delay. Heavy two- and one-half inch lines were deployed immediately. A second alarm was requested. Firefighters searched the floors above. Sometimes even with all the correct steps taken, there are situations that simply spiral out of control. Sometimes even the best intentions prove futile. Being a firefighter is a dangerous job. It's a roll of the dice. It's the chance you take. It's the life you choose.

The Arielscope was parked on the highway directly adjacent to the building, parallel to the upper floors. The crew we relieved nodded in silence before we piloted the bucket to its fully extended position. As we opened our gun my already queasy stomach lurched again under the strain and recoil of the water cannon. Over the next several hours, we dumped thousands of gallons of water down with little effect. The upper floors had pancaked into an impenetrable barrier which only added to the fire's reluctance to being brought under control. At one point the lieutenant said a prayer for the families of the men we lost. I bowed my head. "The next few weeks," said the lieutenant, "that's when we'll see how this city handles tragedy. I have my doubts if we're ready." In hind sight, we weren't.

It took eight days to complete recovery operations. The next few weeks were crowded with funerals, ceremonies, a presidential visit, and country-wide media attention. We were given the chance to become as close knit a community as you could imagine. What we became is still a topic of debate.

Everything Worcester became magnified. A small group of individuals succumbed to what I called the "Tragedy Pathogen," a virus that infected their words and actions in ways that nobody could have predicted. It left our community disabled.

A full year after the fire, I was playing a show in Atlanta. The nightclub owner came over during a break to introduce me to a battalion chief who was watching our performance. He bought me a beer.

"Firefighter from Worcester?" he asked

I nodded.

"I just got back from a Chief's Convention in Houston. Worcester was used as an example of what not to allow happen to a city after a tragedy. I hope you're not offended, but the stories are outrageous. What happened up there?"

I explained that most firefighters and their families had a grip on the situation. We spent the next hour discussing the mismanagement of funds allegations, the systemic marketing of a tragedy, unqualified union members making asinine financial decision with no oversight. Liaison's to Families moving in with wives of fallen firefighters.

"In short," I said to the Chief, "Worcester had an addiction to tragedy that had no end in sight."

Looking back now through the lens of logic, I see how things changed, differently.

It was a rainy Saturday afternoon. Doc and I were walking back from a class we both attended on the effects of incarceration. Doc had just gifted the psychologist who ran the program with a ten- minute refutation on the theory of sociopaths, claiming an artful opposition to the amount of crimes conveniently attached to this, in Doc's words,"erroneous affliction."

"Sociopathic behavior is a learned response," Doc lectured "Not a pathological condition. An armed robber, for instance, learns to put his feelings aside to increase the odds of their success. A victim is more compliant when he or she believes the criminal assaulting them is void of emotion and capable of anything. It is a practiced behavior and, for the most part not a neurological disorder."

As we entered A-1, Doc invited me to come upstairs and have popcorn.

"Alright," I said, hoping Doc wouldn't notice my hesitation.

Normally I loved popcorn, but Doc smothered his with cayenne pepper and the fish oil he drained out of a bag of mackerel purchased through canteen. He took great offense if you hinted it was less than deliciously healthy. Considering that chow that night was the pink slime product passed off as a hamburger, I accepted his offer.

As we walked the stairs to the third tier and into Doc's cell, he said, "So, the city that wants to be a town, I think you called it. Tell me about Worcester."

Someone had made reference to the city of my birth during class and just from the tone in Doc's voice I knew this was a set-up, but I jumped right in anyway. I started with a diatribe on the dead- end main street, the failed mall, the airport with its own climate. I declared how I wanted to be proud of the city of my birth, but I couldn't. I raged on, my voice echoing off the cement walls as I systematically ticked off every mis-managed, misguided, miscalculation wrought by the city Worcester. There were arm gestures and dramatic facial expressions. I claimed that I understood that finding fault with the city I grew up in and served, was some form of displayed aggression, but implored him to look at the evidence. I was a well-rehearsed one-man show straining to win over my audience. Worcester was my windmill. I was Don Quixote fighting the injustices of a cruel world.

Doc extended his bag of dead-fish-eye-burning-spiced pop-corn in my direction. I debated whether this was a reward or a punishment for my performance.

"You're a contradiction." he said.

"You don't like being told what to do, yet thrived on the fire department with its military chain of command. You thrive here in this structured environment. You're smart enough to avoid confrontation, and yet you invite it. You could have secured a future away from all of this and instead you chose a courtroom as the first time you finally decide to take a stand and end up purposely putting yourself here. What is going on with you goes a lot deeper than windmills."

Doc sat on the edge of his bunk. I took my normal seat on the footlocker which at times doubled as a psychiatrist's chair.

"Worcester was easy," I said. "I was the medium-sized fish in the mediocre pond. The fact that I lived in a city that couldn't get out of its own way almost helped. I never had the courage to venture very far. Boston was intimidating. New York and Los Angeles were for real talent. I convinced myself Worcester was enough."

"What changed?" asked Doc.

"The warehouse fire. It changed everything. The tragedy amplified everything. My lifestyle. My marriage. My thoughts of mortality. My indiscretions."

After the fire I did the two things that most firefighters did. First, I thought: it could have been me. Then I asked how can I help. It was amazing to watch for a short time anyway, how we as a city could pull together and share our grief and support those families who lost so much. Fundraisers and benefits were set up and millions of dollars were raised. I was approached to write songs for compilation albums, record a children's choir, and put on shows at local concert venues. It all seemed very healing. I didn't think much at first when certain fire department union leaders started making decisions that seemed beyond their pay grade or intellectual capacity. I grimaced when union liaisons moved in with the wives of our fallen brothers. I got annoyed when informed that any show or benefit I was involved with would have to be approved of beforehand and that all funds must be deposited into sanctioned accounts under union control. In truth, I was never much of a union guy.

Before the tragedy, a fire department union meeting consisted of seven guys looking for a night out away from their wives to drink and discuss the merits of what style dress-hat we should wear: an eight point, versus the traditional round bell cap. Not really my thing. When I chose not to cooperate with union guidelines, I was warned to fall in line. It was also suggested that musicians had no business being firefighters. Then there was the message left on my answering machine accusing me of making a career off the deaths of six firefighters and should watch my back. My children heard this. This was a city where not much happened. Every day, every newscast, every event became inflated and some people liked it. They soaked up the attention. It was an addiction.

At a large music show, a woman who sat on the newly formed fire department Women's Auxiliary stomped up to me and accused me of stealing her husband's moment.

"He was on the Rescue Squad and you weren't," she barked.

Now, I knew her husband well and he wasn't even on duty the night of the fire, so I was pretty sure he was alive and told her so. She would have none of it. All this music stuff was taking attention away from her husband, she screamed, before storming off.

The women's auxiliary formed with the best intentions. It started out with 264 women, my mother and my wife, Joy, included. After it was infected by the tragedy pathogen, most of the women jumped ship until the group consisted of only twelve members who I called the "Twelve Appostlelettes." I suggested their motto should be "Hate in the name of God."

I think the final straw was when the actor Dennis Leary, a Worcester native, came up to me in a crowd at a memorial service to thank me for all the work I was doing. The wrath and outraged indignation aimed at me from my fellow Worcesterites could have ignited a fire all on its own.

"Who the hell does he think he is?"

"Rock and Roll drug addict."

We moved out of the city after that hoping to escape the spread of the disease. I had glimpsed a part of humanity I found disgusting. I worked for a department I no longer respected. But what was I doing? The objections to my carefree lifestyle were somewhat justified. Yet, I was laughing it off, still partying, letting my family down. In short, I was part of the problem.

On the day the planes hit the twin towers in New York I was building a house in the country, a house I would never live in. My wife wanted to move away from Worcester, start fresh. She offered me one last chance to get my act together, which I ignored.

Some weeks later, the nation still in shock and mourning, a union official from Worcester walked into the station holding a piece of paper claiming that he calculated, based on the size of each department, that we technically lost more men than the New York Fire Department which proved our tragedy was still bigger, that Worcester was still number one. I should have gone right out the door, gotten into my truck, begged my wife to forgive my attitude and left, but I didn't.

Although I had gotten used to the sound of a prison door closing, a bolt of panic surged through my body when Doc's cell door slammed shut, I was still sitting on his footlocker. Doc and I were so engrossed in a Worcester memory I thought I had learned to live with that neither of us heard the announcement of five minutes to lock in. God! I'm going to get lugged for this. Fear prickled though every cell. I scrambled up and started yelling frantically out the tiny widow in the door.

"Open 52! Open 52!"

I think Doc even broke a sweat.

The door clanged open and I hurried down the stairs towards my cell, trying to be invisible. I passed a guard on duty who looked at me with complete incredulity.

"I forgot I was in prison," I shrugged.

He threw up his hands as he opened my door.

During count, the guard stopped at my door and said, "Really?"

What else could I say. I could hear him repeating the phrase as he walked the block. "Baxter forgot he was in prison."

But I did forget sometimes. There were however, things I couldn't forget. The loss of a loved one or the death of six firefighters.

The majority of people in Worcester felt the same as I did about those individuals clinging to their fifteen minutes of tragedy-induced fame. Most people retreated to the safety of their homes and focused on their families and the things that truly mattered. I sat on my bunk well into the night staring at the wall lost in one singular thought.

Why didn't I?

On Dec 3rd, 1999 six firefighters died in a warehouse fire.

On Dec 3rd, 2009, by no coincidence, I was sentenced to state prison.

SHIRLEY STREET

"Childhood memories are clear indicators of where your decision-making process comes from as an adult," said Doc as he handed me a blank piece of paper. "Without thinking too hard, I want you to write down three childhood memories. You have thirty seconds."

"I don't have a pen."

Doc reached for a peanut butter jar filled to capacity with assorted writing utensils carefully choosing the one he felt he could do without.

"Who comes to class without a pen," he tossed it in my direction.

I cleared my head and saw an image of a large Christmas present that turned out not to be mine.

"Psychological implications aside," he said as he paced the length of his cell, "whether your memories are good or bad, it's how you choose to use them, or how they use you, that will define who you become."

"This would go a lot quicker if you stop talking," I said.

My second memory was my first day of school. I saw myself standing in a disproportionately large hallway dressed in uncomfortable clothes.

The final image was a puddle of orange juice, streaked with blood and broken glass on our kitchen floor, bare feet, and my father's strained look as he attempted to staunch the flow of blood from his wrist caused by the bottle that had just exploded in his hand.

"Excellent," said Doc, "write about that." His finger tapped on my macabre childhood description of blood and shock.

We lived on the third floor of a three-decker on Shirley Street. At the age of four, the borders of my world extended not much further than my home, my yard, and on bold adventurous days, the neighbor's yard. These confines, defined by parental law, were a universe in size to me, and I was an explorer, an archaeologist to be exact. Given any opportunity, I would set off on an expedition (much to the dismay of our landlords, the Dowd family), armed with an empty can of the jolly-green-giant variety as my trusty excavating tool, determined to uncover what was buried below the ancient wall that surrounded our home, referred to as a "foundation" by less imaginative adults. Obvious structural needs aside, I wondered why someone would put a wall underground if not to hide a vast treasure.

One day, by fate or by laziness, my father left the garage door open granting me access to actual shovels. I was not about to pass up this opportunity. It was critical to dig up the treasure before being caught. With expediency in mind, I enlisted the help of a cohort.

My sister Jodi was two years older than me which, in my mind, made her nearly an adult at the age of six. This served a dual purpose. Our goal could be reached twice as fast and, if we were caught, she would be more culpable because of her advanced age. Of course, I had to agree to relinquish half the treasure.

We dug at a furious pace. After an hour, we were surprised by how far down this treasure- concealing wall called "foundation" really went.

This was where memory got a little sketchy.

As I recall, I saw the treasure first. Partially submerged, it was shiny and of ancient origin, and it was mine. Jodi recalled it differently. What we both did agree on was that irregardless of why I jumped into the hole, it was directly into the path of her downward arching hoe. I remembered the treasure. My sister remembered the blood.

Both of us recall, much to our horror, that the hoe actually stuck into the top of my head. Although the dent was still there to this day as a reminder of our adventure, this unsurprisingly, was where that particular memory ended.

I was carted off to the emergency room. The dig site was buried. The adults involved claimed there was no treasure. I maintained to this day that they kept it for themselves. Jodi was given a thrashing the likes of which still haunted her today.

After the excavation event, it was decided, on the insistence of the landlords, that I was never again allowed outside unsupervised. My parent's solution to this over-reactionary decree was to tie me to the garage with a rope thus permanently relegating my hierarchical family standing to that of an unruly house pet. I wouldn't have minded so much except in this particular instance, it was like tethering a lamb to a pole on the African savanna.

The residents of the second- floor apartment were the Lubens. Both parents taught romantic languages at Clark University. The Lubens had a single child, Henry, who was way older than Jodi. He was six and a half. He was smart. My father used to say,

"I can't understand a fucking thing that kid says."

Henry was an entrepreneur and ran a toll booth on the back stairs. If you didn't pay the fee, you were promptly pushed down the stairs. Since I was unemployed, I suffered this indignity on many occasions.

Now in Henry's defense, running a business was grueling on a young Republican, so I completely understood his need for some form of stress relief. Unfortunately, his second favorite pastime was untying the rope from the garage door and dragging me around the driveway. I didn't mind so much because when he was done playing with me, I was free.

One afternoon two travelers from the forbidden zone appeared, grabbed my rope, and took turns playing with what I think they called the human yo-yo. Ronnie and Shelly lived two houses away through the side yard. You never went two houses away, hence the tag: forbidden zone. My knees already bloodied and my pants torn as a result of my early encounter with Henry compelled me to make a stand. When I say make a stand, I mean cry loudly. This resulted in them stuffing me underneath a burn barrel, a fifty-five-gallon drum used in the sixties for burning rubbish. They threatened me with imminent death if I dared try to escape. After what seemed like forever, I heard my mother's muffled voice calling me for dinner so I decided to risk it. To my surprise, there was no one there.

As I trudged my way up the back-apartment stairs past the toll booth, which fortunately was unmanned during the dinner hour, it occurred to me that torn, bleeding, and radiating the aroma of baked cat food can ash was going to require an explanation.

"What have you done now?" gasped my Mother.

Me, I'm going to get blamed for this? Me?

The trip to the hospital after the hoe incident had kept me clear from encounters with my Dad's belt (my sister was not so lucky), but that card could only be played so many times. My mother continued in a more agitated tone now.

"Your new pants are ruined!"

Might I point out the pants weren't new. They were hand-me-downs from my brother Tom who was at least a foot taller than me and remained so my entire life.

So, the phrase "you'll grow into them" was a biological impossibility. I was about to remind her of this when my heart stopped.

"What's the little asshole done now?"

My father was home.

There he stood, beer in one hand, cigarette in the other, looming in the hallway between the living room and the kitchen and boy, could my father loom. Eight feet tall and 372 pounds of loom-ability. At least it seemed that way. Everything seemed out of proportion when you're not much bigger than a common house plant, and that's exactly how I felt, my feet firmly rooted to the kitchen floor unable to move. I must have looked like the kid who forgot his lines in the school play because my mother, now sensing that she had inadvertently hung me out to dry, attempted to intervene.

"Now, Wal. Let's hear what he has to say."

Wal was short for Walter. In our house, it was hit-first-ask-questions-later, and Wal liked to hit. Not that my father would normally be bothered to put down either the beer or the cigarette before commencing his attack, but in this moment, as I watched him place his can of Schlitz on the table while simultaneously balancing his smoldering cigarette on the edge of the stove, I had time to think. The problem was, nothing was coming to mind.

"Well?" he taunted in almost an amused tone, already invalidating anything that could possibly resemble a worthy excuse.

My mother's eyes widened now as she began to comprehend what she was becoming an accomplice to. Her telepathic message was crystal clear.

"Say anything!" she screamed in her mind.

But it was too late.

My father muttered, "that's what I thought," as he began to move towards me.

I grew up in a generation where domestic violence was simply part of the curriculum, part of the excuses we would use later in life to validate why we turned out the way we did. This would not be one of those times.

Out of nowhere, a voice stopped my father cold in his tracks. I recognized the voice, but not the words being used. The voice was mine. And the words were the truth.

Speaking in full, precise sentences, I told them how Ronny and Shelly made me play hide-and- seek under the barrel. I described how Henry re-enacted old western movie scenes where I played the disgraced cowboy being dragged behind a horse. I told them about the tollbooth and being repeatedly pushed down the stairs. I told them everything. I threw everyone under the bus, and it worked.

My father worked part time at a service station which explained the scent of gasoline as he charged by me. He thundered out the back door with such a bang I thought he went right through the screen door. It never again functioned correctly after that day. I presumed he went downstairs to have a "chat" with the neighbors because I could hear the roar of his voice through the floorboards over the sound of the bathtub being filled for the purpose of removing the day's festivities from my body. I don't believe he ever found Ronny and Shelly. They lived two houses away, and you never went two houses away.

A couple days later I was hung by the neck in our garage. It seemed my rope had another use after all. Flipped up over the beam and wrapped tightly around my throat, it proved very effective. After all, Henry was a smart kid.

White light, gagging, the rumble of my father's black Rambler pulling in the driveway. The incredulous look on my dad's face as the image of Henry pulling the rope taut came into focus were the last things I recalled. It's funny the things you remember from being a kid.

The swinging screen door and the discarded cup and fork lying on the hardwood floor of the now abandoned second floor apartment were the only clues as to what happened to Henry and his parents. It was never talked about again. A couple months later, Ronny and Shelly were playing with matches in their bedroom and set their house on fire. They were promptly removed from society as the story goes. J.F.K was shot. The Beatles came to America, and everything seemed right in the world according to the memories of a four-year old.

"When does the orange juice bottle blow up in your dad's hand?" asked Doc, turning over the paper.

"I don't remember. I only know it was on Shirley Street, so I wrote you this."

"Well, "he said, holding up my story. "This does explain a lot."

CRIME SCENES

"It's time for you to tell me," Doc said.

I paused for a moment, because I knew exactly what he was asking. "Do you remember Kurt Russell as the hero in the movie, Backdraft?"

Doc frowned.

"A real firefighter doesn't walk out of a fully engulfed warehouse no helmet, no respirator, coat unbuttoned carrying a small child in his arms who looks like he just woke up from a nap. Cause who needs oxygen, right?"

Doc stared at me and didn't say a word.

I kept going, "Even though it's fake, I still love it. Like everyone else, I enjoy that rush of a good rescue, everything working out just perfectly. Movies do that. They tie everything up in a neat package, fully delivered, and we know what we're supposed to feel."

Doc looked down and straightened the blanket on his bunk. I squirmed in my seat. I would rather discuss anything else but what Doc was asking of me. Anything. I had not spoken aloud the true details of the events, choices, and decisions that had led me to prison. Like that false hero, I had entered a building without any protective gear. Now, I had to exit this secret the same way.

"Start at the beginning," said Doc.
Doc crossed his arms and leaned back against the wall, "Don't tell me what you remember. Tell me what you can't forget."

That morning, my mind was fixated on the kitchen cabinets I was going to install. A hundred other construction details floated through my thoughts as I neared completion on this latest house-flipping project. Helen, my girlfriend at the time, and I had entered the house restoration business. She had the money. I had the know-how.

As I climbed out of my truck, a familiar odor caught my attention. I stopped in my tracks. Firefighters can detect the nuances of smoke. We can sniff out the differences between a fire in its infancy versus one that's been extinguished. The smoke I detected on that morning was of the non-threatening variety.

I calmly walked inside and immediately identified the smell of gasoline. I traced the smoke to the cellar. As I descended the steps, I could hear the sound of gushing water. The newly soldered water pipes had quickly heated to their melting point, burst, and had essentially extinguished the flames. The water poured out the basement door and had carved a canal through the lawn down to the street. I turned off the water main.

I soon found the other intended ignition sites on both the first and second floor. The amateur arsonists had soaked paint tarps and old clothes in gasoline. They would have been successful if they had thought to turn off the water main prior to their attempt. Still, the damage was extensive.

"Why would you be blamed for this?" questioned Doc.

"I wasn't. Have patience." I said, "It's complicated."

I felt defeated. This house was supposed to be my fix-all project. After my last injury on the fire department, I was informed by a city Doctor that I would not be going back to work. What started out as numbness in my left hand, turned into me needing an operation to repair vertebrae in my cervical spine. Nearly a quarter century of firefighting, not to mention playing music were taken from me on a single afternoon. This was a sobering reality, that when piled on top of a failed marriage and an ever-increasing habit of self- medicating, created a level of depression I had never experienced before. If I wasn't a firefighter or musician, then who was I? All I had left was this house and now the fire ruined that.

"Wasn't it insured?" asked Doc.

"Only for what we bought it for. It was too expensive to fully insure an unoccupied house, and we were so close to finishing."

This particular house had needed a tremendous amount of work. It was a great opportunity for Nicholai to make some good money while he was going to school. He was there for the new roof and the replacement of all the windows. His myopic attention to detail had him painstakingly painting every room in the house. It seemed like the perfect solution for everyone. It even offered a chance to engage Alex his younger brother, in a new adventure. Alex had not fared so well after his mother's and my divorce, and much like myself, required diversions from his actual feelings. Alex's latest diversion was heroin.

Joy was a good mother, but this drug was beyond the scope of anyone's best parenting skills. To escape, Joy moved to the Berkshires in western Massachusetts. Both she and Nicholai suggested strongly for me to move away from Worcester. Even though I had no real reason to stay, my stubbornness for the man I used to be, tethered me to this city I had grown to resent and in turn, this city resented me back.

Alex's behaviors scared me because I understood him all too well. He, at sixteen, saw through the facade of the American Dream and the vacuous promises of the world's religions. I understood this angry young philosopher because I was simply an older version. I ranted just like he did about the false democracy of capitalism and the simplistic answers to unanswerable questions. He didn't fit in and I still didn't. He rebelled against a life and a system that cared little for him. Like me, he turned to drugs to escape and to alter the pain of living. As a first-responder, I had seen the devastating effects of heroin. It was a beast of another nature with its own agenda. It took whatever it wanted, and it wanted my son.

That afternoon, the air was bitter as Doc and I walked the track. We settled into our familiar quiet. He sensed I needed some time to walk and breathe before continuing with my story. I watched how the wind whipped up the dirt from beneath our feet and how it settled around us. My throat clogged.

"What did you do?" he asked.

"I flipped over a five-gallon bucket and sat down in the basement. The water covered my feet to the ankles."

"You just sat there." said Doc.

"Drowning in five inches of self-pity."

"What else did you feel?" he asked.

"Angry."

"Because of the destruction of the house?"

"Yes and no."

He nodded for me to go on.

Alex had been living with Helen and me for a short time. Soon, however, Alex's drug use was not something Helen would tolerate. Against her specific orders, I let him live in the house we were rehabbing. I was out of options and I thought it might be good for Alex to have to take care of something for a change. I gave him chores to complete during the evenings when other people were not working. I thought it would be better if the house wasn't left vacant since the rate of crime in Worcester was high. For a short while it worked well. Alex followed through and worked hard.

Then one night I arrived unannounced and found Alex in the cellar with two older Hispanic men cooking crystal meth. After a short altercation, I convinced his two friends to leave. They threatened to return, warning this wasn't over. Alex knew he was in trouble. I could tell he feared the repercussions of ending the drug operation, but his Worcester experiment was over. I sent him back to his mother and her rebound husband who were planning to move to San Francisco. Keeping tabs on Alex's problems were about to get much harder. Everything was.

"So, you just sat on a bucket?"

"For a long time," I said. "In the middle of the crime scene. All I had to do was call the police."

"Why didn't you?" asked Doc.

"I sat there thinking there was a slim chance someone else set the fire, but it was pretty obvious by the amateur attempt following their threat that it was Alex's business partners."

"Occam's razor," said Doc.

"Exactly," I nodded.

"When all variables are taken into consideration more often than not the simplest and most obvious answer is your solution."

"So how did you feel?" said Doc in a tone that suggested he was beginning to understand the gravity of the story I had been holding on to.

"Mostly angry at myself. I failed him. I failed my family. I failed my career and my true passion. Now I failed at the only potential source of income I had. The insurance would not cover the damage. I made a bad decision to leave Alex alone in the house. I knew better, and I still did it."

"Regret and self-blame," said Doc, "Is a game you can play forever."

In hindsight, I did sit and play that game and the process lasted a while. The longer I sat there, the longer the secret was mine alone. There was no fire in this world. There was no knowledge outside these walls of this unmitigated disaster. All consequences held motionless in the air like the wisp of white smoke that remained trapped between the floor joists of the ceiling rafters. Almost on cue, I was distracted by a familiar sound. The sound a dripping faucet makes in the middle of the night when you're trying to sleep. That relentless Plop, Plop, Plop.

In the dim light, I saw the source. The water looked alive.

One by one from above my head termites were emerging from the center beam that supported the house and belly-flopping into the water below. One of them landed on an empty box of Ephedrine that was floating by, a remnant of Alex's business venture. The irony made me laugh out loud.

"I laughed so hard I nearly fell off that damn bucket. Then it dawned on me. The termites were my momentary stay of execution."

"How so?" said Doc

"I could easily cover up Alex's meth lab, claiming instead the termites were the reason to end the project. Helen would be so disgusted with me that she'd never set foot inside the house again."

"Quite the unintended consequence," Doc said.

"Exactly."

"So, you never reported the fire?" said Doc

All I could do was nod as we continued walking. I noticed how much time had passed. The sun dipped down over the horizon earlier on a winter day in prison than in the rest of the world. The thirty-foot cement wall created a new horizon of sorts in this man-made reality.

Helen and I had numerous arguments about next steps. I told her the termite infestation would make selling the house impossible. I didn't lie. Granted, leaving the Arson and the Meth lab out of the story was a large omission, but it was a discretionary move to bide time. None the less, we agreed I was to blame and left it to me to find a fix. Apparently, Helen had discussed the situation with her mother and her mother offered, "Maybe it should just burn down."

I had to laugh at the truth of her words, but Helen began to seriously consider this as a possible option.

"Who better to burn down a building than you?" she said.

Even a vacant house with no exposures was a dangerous situation and difficult to control. I could not put anyone at risk. But still, it would tie things up nicely. It would have to be clean and simple yet get the job done. I needed it to be bad enough to get condemned so Helen could claim the insurance. 18 days I went to the house and sat on my bucket. 18 days, and I still couldn't do it. When Helen said she would hire someone else I decided to act. This one would be on me.

On a hot August day, I prepared the house I worked so hard on for its end. I was devoid of emotion. Sitting on a bucket in the basement for nearly three weeks had given me plenty of time to contemplate myself into a coma. Maybe this gesture of a father protecting his son would be my one singular noble act in my life. Maybe it would change everything for the better.

All I had to do was create a vapor expansion that would be quick and efficient with only residual fire damage. The remnants of gas from the first fire would assist the second fire. I closed the doors and windows creating a tight seal. As I went through the steps, it reminded me of the patience of a baker, mixing just the right ingredients, setting the oven at the perfect temperature, and allowing the cake to rise at its own pace. It would be large enough but not too large. From a firefighting perspective, it wouldn't amount to no more than an exercise for a well-trained crew.

I left the house to pre-heat and drove to my parents' home. I did this every day. My mother was far along in her dance with Alzheimer's and my father's aortic aneurysms were taking a back seat to his lung cancer. I spent three hours with them. She repeatedly thanked me for coming to help prepare dinner. In fact, she had not prepared a meal for several years and I always loved that she thought it a coincidence that I just happened by as she was struggling with what to make. When I left, she would always thank me profusely. In hindsight, I may have gotten that part of my life right.

When I returned to the house it was easy to see that my plan had worked. The windows bowed ever so slightly. It was early enough in the day that the response time would be quick and over in minutes. I felt the difference in pressure as I stepped through the front door. I closed it quickly. My eyes began to burn. I went downstairs to turn on the water, replicating the first fire.

I skipped back up the stairs and felt light-headed as I went up to the attic. The air was unbearably hot. I was dressed in my bathing trunks and flip-flops, not exactly the proper attire for blowing up a house. I was sweating profusely and breathing became difficult.

I emptied my mind of thoughts. I emptied my heart of feelings. I lit the MEPPS burner and marveled as it left my hand. I watched in slow motion as it fell.

"Good-bye," I said as the burner hit the floor.

"How can you be sitting here right now?" Doc asked.

I looked at him. Our walk around the track was hours ago but it felt like it was taking years to tell my story. After break for chow, we sat in Doc's cell. "That part I am still a little sketchy about."

Doc encouraged me to go on.

"It was like I stood inside an exploding Hologram. Everything was wavy and distorted. The heat was intense. The sound felt like it came from inside of me. Somehow, I got to the stairs and began walking down. I felt pushed from behind, like the fire was shoving me away from itself. I stumbled out the front door and felt like I had just been on the receiving end of a hard right-cross."

"So that's when got you arrested," Doc said.

"You'd think so, wouldn't you?"

Doc looked confused.

"None of the fire fighters could believe I was standing there waiting for them. It was too ludicrous to believe I would commit arson and then wait for police and the fire department to arrive. In fact, I was the one that called it in. Everyone assumed I had the expertise to wire a house to blow with a cell phone from Wyoming if I wanted to."

"How could you walk away from that unscathed?" asked Doc.

"I had serious burns on my foot and arm. How I didn't have worse, I still don't know."

"Sounds like you didn't care."

"I only started to when I got to the ER and the shock began to wear off. They had to treat my burns and gave me morphine against my wishes. Anything stronger than codeine makes me nauseous. I saw the doctor walk in with a catheter kit and the reality of what I had done began to sink in as the pain got a head start on the medication."

Doc nodded. After all, he was a physician. He knew what I was in for.

"You tried to kill yourself," he said quietly.

I stared at a spot on the wall just over his right shoulder. All I could see were the pieces of wood and shards of window glass that lay around me. There wasn't a single wall that wasn't damaged by the concussive blast. The muffled sound of sirens surrounded me as I stood in what used to be the front picture window frame in the middle of the road. I watched as the residual fire was put out in short order. Water lines and equipment and men bustled around me, but no one seemed interested in me. I stood alone among the wreckage until the paramedics forced me to sit on the tailgate of the ambulance.

My eyes refocused on Doc; he looked back at me, "You wanted to die in that house."

Did I? I still wasn't sure.

"I simply didn't care." I finally said, "Either way was fine with me. One way or another, everyone would get what they wanted, and it would be over, or different, or something."

"It sounds more like you were punishing yourself again," Doc said.

"No. I was evening up the score on my own accord before somebody else did it for me,"

Doc nodded, "You took control."

"I did it to protect Alex."

"Is that all?"

"Ok, I seized the moment as an excuse to end my shallow existence. Is that what you want to hear?"

"I want you to hear it." said Doc.

I paused.

My seemingly sacrificial act for my son was nothing more than a selfish opportunity to punish myself. I choked on this truth and couldn't bring myself to speak.

Doc seemed to understand my silence. "Now, my friend", he

said, "There's no lie on your soul."

We sat until the familiar call to end the day was announced. I stood, and though my bones felt heavy, my heart felt light. I cleared my throat to speak, but again no words came to mind.

I walked out of his cell and turned back.

Doc smiled. "You have no more stories holding you back. Now, we can move forward."

RESPECT AND THE PAUSE

In prison, the only true respect you got was the respect you gave yourself. Many a battle began over the demand for this daily requirement. The need for respect outranked the basic necessities of food, clothing, and personal comfort.

Webster's defined Respect as: *A feeling of deep admiration for someone or something elicited by, and in accordance with, one's abilities, qualities, and achievements over time.*

Demanding respect from others in here seemed ridiculous. It seemed analogous to demanding you be drafted by the New England Patriots because you happen to be holding a football.

One of my first realizations in prison was that being physically tough was not as important as simply being willing to engage in confrontation. As it turned out, almost all inmates understood this unwritten law. It mattered little whether you were physically outmatched. All that mattered was your immediate response to any act of perceived disrespect. Whether you won a victory or a hospital bed, both were admired as standing your ground.

Respect boiled down to this: the simple requirement to carve out and maintain a personal boundary that others acknowledged and did not encroach on. It occurred to me that my practice of considering a *pause* in my own reactions to the daily stresses of confinement, the times when my patience and logic and better judgment frayed, could prove an unexpected benefit of my incarceration. This practice could become a martial art of the mind. Prison could become my training ground.

Doc quickly pointed out that the concept of the "pause" that I claimed to have discovered was not mine to lay claim to. Apparently, the Buddhists had been talking about this for a millennium or two but, on the bright side, it was another indication that my mind was starting to share ideas with better company.

Thoughtfulness and sensitivity towards others were something that was clearly missing in an inmate's repertoire and, for that matter, what was sorely lacking in most of the outside world as well.

Yet as much as society claimed to possess this seemingly obvious knowledge, it was seldom applied. This lack of follow through was akin to someone proclaiming to understand their dietary requirements while eating a bag of Doritos. What we espoused to know and what we actually did were two very different things.

Another key factor in understanding the dynamics of respect in prison life was personal space. In prison, the deprivation of personal space was part of the punishment. To drive this point home, a lifer once told to me he'd give up a pardon for a single cell. I had yet to endure the cozy experience of a cellmate since one of the benefits of the permanent work force was the sought-after one-man cell. I imagined that being forced to share the confines of a 6x8 with another person redefined the meaning of "invading my space." The day room, the chow hall, even the outside track already forced inmates in too close proximity to each other.

With this constant battle for space, I had to learn to apply a *pause* to my every moment, before reacting to any situation. If I practiced this, I could achieve *balance*, which was the brass ring Doc and Plato dangled in front me. I could make some headway at attaining that elusive concord of the Three Reasons. I felt like I was finally beginning to embody Doc's philosophy lectures. All the reading and studying was beginning to trickle down from the theoretical to the practical, from the cerebral to the cellular. Cool.

Martial arts however, taught me the opposite. Hesitation was the enemy. It took years of training to make my reactions bypass my thought process so that my blocks and strikes happened automatically. Any athlete required developing a level of hardwired reflexes that transcended the brain and reacted instantaneously, like hitting a 90-mph fast ball. A well-trained athlete had the ability to tap into this – to be in the zone, where your body did what was needed in the moment and where your brain only became a hindrance that slowed you down. Athletes dreaded getting "stuck in their head", which usually translated to missed catches, fumbled balls, falls on the ice, unblocked strikes to softer parts of the anatomy.

Once an athlete achieved these seamless, automatic reflexes, something very interesting happened. Time slowed down. Ted Williams, the legendary hitter for The Boston Red Sox, claimed he could see the stitches on a baseball as it was thrown and could predict its rotation. It occurred to me that the pause required attention and the zone required trust. I was about to be given an opportunity to test my theory and like most opportunities in prison, I had to be willing to see it.

"E=Mc2 is nonsensical," Doc was saying. "It only holds true for a single particle in an isolated system at rest which doesn't exist."

It was during speeches like these that I started to think Doc had greatly overestimated my ability to understand him.

"The math is not important right now," he went on. "What you need to consider is..."

"He needs to consider the end of his life!" exclaimed PJ, bursting into Doc's cell.

"We're busy," sighed Doc as PJ lunged at him with blinding speed, stabbing him repeatedly with an imaginary knife.

"Punctured your lungs!" PJ yelled "You're dead again!" he laughed.

A small band of cohorts lingered outside Doc's cell door. This regular death ritual had become a staple of Doc's day. But this time, PJ redirected his attention to me.

"You're coming with us. Time to introduce you to hockey."

"Hockey? What? Where?"

"Under the weight room," said Mason, one of PJ's groupies.

Now I thought, without a doubt, I was about to be killed. I had come to grips with this possibility. But hockey?

The guard seemed not all that interested when I answered, "To play hockey, I guess," in response to his query about where I thought I was going.

He simply chuckled and said, "Good luck with that, Baxter."

I followed PJ and company down the stairs towards the weight room. My throat tightened as we descended. The passage was narrow and winding and with each step I began to realize that maybe I wasn't as prepared to die as I thought. As we emerged from the dimly lit staircase into the bright lights, I felt that classic reaction to a surprise party.

"No way," I said out loud, inhaling the moldy air.

"Way," said PJ and Mason in harmony.

This ancient basketball gym looked like the inside of a cement gray whale. The old crank down basketball hoops mounted on cracked walls straining to hold them in place. The protruding cement support structures every twenty feet made up the ribs of this ocean giant. The high ceilings created an illusion of freedom so foreign after the months I spent in low slung, cramped quarters. The floor was marked with the usual outline of a full-size basketball court. I laughed at the foul line which seemed a mixed metaphor. The floor was not one of those shiny coated ones you find in most modern gyms, the kind that squeaks at every twist and turn of an athlete's movements in his Air Jordan's. This floor was the actual bedrock under the prison. But none of this was as shocking as what was happening around me. The ugly painful version of street hockey with that god-awful orange rock ball. There were full sized regulation hockey nets. The sticks were sturdy. I hadn't played street hockey since I was a kid where you actually played in the street, carrying away the nets every time a honking car went by. I had a visceral memory of the smell of the storm drain at the corner of Reed and Norcross as I laid face down on the blacktop, my arm stretching to its limits as I reached with the twisted coat hanger, I had shaped specifically for retrieving the tennis balls. It was in that moment, as my eyes fixed on the net on the other side of the gymnasium, that I experienced what I have come to understand as a defining moment.

"I'll play goalie," I said out loud.

"What?" said PJ. "We were just kidding. You don't actually

have to play. We just wanted you to see this. You can stand over there," he said pointing to a place along the wall where the second and third lines of players were lined up along with a small collection of frightened onlookers.

"No." I reiterated. "Your Goalie flinches."

"Hey, Ernie!" shouted Mason. "The firefighter just called you a pussy."

"I didn't say that," I defended.

"What did you say?" Ernie shouted back yanking off his helmet and lumbering over to where we stood.

"They're called Air Plane reactions," I said slowly, my heart racing as I desperately searched for a way out of this mess.

Ernie reminded me of Ron, only larger. I had seen him in the weight room using two spotters to lift the 400 plus pounds he was benching off the rack. He was a lifer. We hadn't had the opportunity to make acquaintances up until this point.

"What the fuck does hockey have to do with airplanes?" he growled still moving towards me.

This was good. Words were good.

"That's an excellent question," I said. "What would you do if an airplane was about to crash into you?"

"What?" said Ernie, looking more annoyed.

Shifting gears, I searched for another analogy.

"Say Mason here was running from the cops and he turned a corner directly into the path of another oncoming cruiser speeding right at him. What would his first reaction be?"

"To claim he didn't do it," said PJ, which brought a chuckle from the others. Ernie smirked. I seized the opening.

"Not his outward reaction," I said, "but his unconscious reaction."

"He'd shit his pants," deadpanned PJ.

"Very funny," said Mason.

"No, he would extend his arms to fend off the impact," I said exaggerating the motion to make my point.

"Little good that would do," laughed PJ.

"That's the point. It's an involuntary reaction. Thing is, if you have time to put your arms out..."

"You had time to do something else," Ernie, finished my sentence.

He began to take off his flimsy goalie equipment.

"Let's see if you can do any better. Theoretical physics still has to be tested by someone else's experiments," quipped Ernie showing the book knowledge he had acquired in his many years in prison.

I surveyed the meager protective clothing in a pile on the floor. Uncertainty swept over me. Someone in the corner mumbled under their breath, "This ought to be good."

I was about to turn and say at least I'm gonna try, when I realized the comment came from one of two C.O.'s sitting on a chair in the corner. I hadn't noticed them when I came in. They had placed two benches on their sides to create an out of bounds of sorts, protection against what was about to take place. Mason ran over to help me secure the mylar plastic goalie pads I was fumbling with.

"Kneel down," he ordered, pulling the straps tight around my exposed calves. "You're sure you want to do this?" he asked in an almost apologetic tone.

I got the feeling he was having second thoughts about the part he may have played in my impending death.

"You're going to get killed."

"Don't care." I said, "I played goalie in the cellar of our house on Reed street when I was a kid."

"Well, you're not in Kansas anymore, Dorothy," he grimaced, pulling the last strap so tight it burned into my exposed skin.

My brother Tom would blast tennis balls at me from twelve feet away. I would put on my dad's fire boots as pads and wore a baseball glove. We had a plastic goalie stick and an old Boston Bruins Jerry Cheever's mask. Tom taught me everything I knew about sports. He was better than me at everything. By sixteen, he was a high school sports star. Football. Baseball. Track. Tom had, in football terms, what they called a canon for an arm. When he came home from practice, he'd send my friends and I out for a pass. We'd take off running up Reed Street veering right onto Norcross in an attempt to catch the football that came magically soaring over the houses into a vacant lot half-way down the street. By the time we jogged back, breathless with the ball, he was gone. It was a tradition my friends and I looked forward to on Fall afternoons.

Tom also played street hockey in a league at Crompton Park. Sometimes I would go along to watch. On one occasion, their goalie was late and there was no one left to fill his place. My brother called out for me to come over and right then and there, I was pressed into service, against the wishes of most of the team.

"What's he like, ten?" someone complained.

"He's twelve," my brother insisted, "just small for his age. He'll be fine." Tom turned and looked at me hard. "You let me down and I'll kill you," he whispered.

I was scared, but I would rather have died than let my brother down. The first shot knocked the air right out of me. The tears came involuntarily, but I didn't care how much it hurt. I might have been small, but I was fast. I threw myself in front of that rock-hard orange missile like some crazed kamikaze, scrambling up without a whimper and steeling myself for the next lunge or body block. For me, this was the Stanley Cup finals and I would make Tom proud!

We were ahead two to nothing and I was the hero. Or, so I thought. As the game neared the end of the second period, their real goalie showed up and I was unceremoniously dismissed without a word. No high five from my brother. No good job. Nothing. I was devastated.

Back on the sidelines, I felt a sadistic glee every time the other team got that ball past my replacement. They came back easily winning four to three. I would have cheered out loud if I thought I could've gotten away with it.

As he left the court, the referee looked over at me. "They get what they get."

I would never forget what that felt like. The betrayal, the lack of respect. But, more importantly, in this moment, I instinctively knew I could do this.

"Alright, old guy," said this giant of a man they called Big Steve. "Don't fuck this up."

"Old guy?" I said, "I'm twelve. Let's do this!"

A quick shoot-around to warm up proved painful as I got my

feet underneath me. My glasses fogged under the helmet which was difficult enough to see through in the first place, so I took them off. I walked over to where the guards were sitting and asked if I could place them behind their protective barrier. The last thing I could afford to do was break them. Reading was my life. The guard begrudgingly agreed with a half-hearted nod. I placed them on the floor behind the bench and ran back to the net.

"A blind goaltender," griped Joe, one of my new teammates, "just great."

Joe was the premiere runner at Walpole and one of but a handful of people I couldn't outrun in all my years in prison. He was in his early thirties and not someone you wanted to tangle with. Joe was also the best hockey player on the floor. He was serious about hockey and even more serious about winning. I wasn't going to be intimidated. I needed this. This wasn't about the roar of the crowd or some trophy. I figured that no one would ever hear about this game outside this gym. This was exactly the kind of opportunity I was looking for. I needed to earn my own kind of respect. But more than that. I wanted to be all in. I needed to be all in. I wanted to make this moment the most important moment in my life. I was gonna play this game as if it was the last thing I'd ever do. In reality, it very well could have been. I needed to be reminded of all the moments when I did not give my all, when I shied away from a challenge. No more. Never again. I picked up my goalie stick with my garden gloved hand. A piece of cardboard in the shape of a goalie's blocker had been securely duct taped to the glove. I smiled. The more absurd, the better. And so, it began.

From my place between the pipes, as they called it, I had the best view of the cavernous playing field. Over the course of my fifty years, I have played my fair share of sports, but nothing would ever equal what I watched unfolding in front of me. This was hands down the most brutal event I ever witnessed. Full check, full speed, all-out mayhem. Convicted criminals wielding sticks. The rules were self-governing. The harder you hit, the harder you got hit. If you wanted to chop and hack with your stick, you were chopped and hacked back. Dirty players were dealt with harshly, double teamed into the corners and assaulted out of view of the guards. Everything was in play: the walls, the basketball hoops, the fans. There were no out-of-bounds, no stopping a play, except after a goal or by the goalie holding onto the ball after a save. Many inmates cowered on the sidelines, preferring to be spectators than risk the carnage, though spectators had to move quickly since there was virtually no place to hide when the game barreled in their direction. I watched in horror as inmates slammed opposing team members into the giant cement ribs of the whale skeleton eliciting oohs and ahhs out of even the guards, who watched with morbid fascination. It was a primal, barbaric, gladiator free-for-all. There were no penalties. There were very few fights. Fighting would result in a lifetime ban from the sport not to mention the instant lugging by the guards. This was a world until itself and I was right in the middle of it.

Basically, it was A-1, our unit, against the other two blocks. They had an advantage with a greater pool of willing participants and fresh replacements. The rivalry was longstanding. As for me, I was good. Not as good as I wanted to be, but I would get better. Much better. It felt so natural. Cut down the angles and don't flinch. All of this was in direct contrast to what Doc and I had been studying these past months. The *pause* and Plato's Three Reasons were great models for achieving inner strength of character. This was its total opposite. This was unbridled reaction, allowing the mind to separate from the body and the body to act instantaneously, completely freed from thought. This was a violent, high-speed version of a walking meditation. It was the answer to what was missing in my schooling.

The world of nature works under the premise of opposites. It's the plus and minus charges that bind matter itself. Now I was beginning to see a new opposite: the thoughtful, reflective, curious mind of the student philosopher in contrast to the lightening reflexes, pain, and punishment of the elite athlete.

With every acrobatic save, my confidence multiplied. The other team started yelling at their goalie to make saves like him. When the next orange ball whipped by his cardboard blocker, he was relieved of his duty and limped off in disgrace.

When I took my helmet off at the end of the game, I heard one of the guys from the other block say, "Jesus, he's an old guy." I peeled off my goalie attire. Everything was soaked completely through with sweat. My elbows had begun to swell from the repeated impact with the cement floor. My knees were the worst. The plastic pads separated when I dropped to the floor providing no protection against the unforgiving bedrock. I was noticeably limping when I made my way over to the guards. The same guard who had all but ignored me originally was extending his arm out in my direction. As I approached, I could see he was holding my glasses in his hand and smiling as he handed them to me.

"Un-Be-Fucking-lievable!" he said.

"Utterly amazing!" said the other C.O., laughing and shaking his head.

As I was putting my glasses on, one of the disgraced goalies from the other team looked at me in disbelief.

"Can you see without those?"

"Not really," I replied smiling. "I just get in front of the orange blurry thing."

Sitting on my bunk later that night I had a feeling of immense satisfaction despite being crippled and broken. I had made a break through and it was glorious. I had begun to re-evaluate my need for respect and the "way of the pause" when I heard a voice.

"You're an idiot."

It was Doc's voice. I'm sure of it, but it took so long to turn my head in any direction that when I finally did, there was no one there.

PROPERTY

The morning started like every other morning: Count time. Count time. I put on my grays and faced the day. Jose, my neighbor, stuck his head in my room and asked me how to spell "firstavule."

"Firstavule. Firstavule? Use it in a sentence?" I prodded him.

"Firstavule baby, she didn't mean nuthin to me."

"Writing your girlfriend again, Jose? I'll help you when I get back from work."

The line for breakfast was quiet as usual. Only a few of us were morning people. Sock puppet guy in cell two on the flats was in his dressing room rehearsing what I gleaned was *Fiddler on the Roof.* I swear I heard one of those hand-made performers singing *If I were a Rich Man.* Strange though, he usually only gave performances on weekends. I think he worked in the plate shop. I didn't really talk to him. His shows weren't very good and nobody paid much attention to him because, well, he was crazy. Just another example of someone who could have benefited from a mental health facility.

I marveled at how quickly I had become desensitized to everything around me: the noise, the anger, the dehumanization, the crazy guy locked in his cell doing Shakespeare with hand puppets. When I was called into the job assignment office after chow, it was with the same abruptness that everything happened in prison. One minute I was washing the floor talking to a sergeant in the East Wing corridor about the benefit of the interlocking golf grip, the next I was standing in front of a lieutenant who was informing me I was re-assigned to Property. My fear of all things new rose in the pit of my stomach. I recognized it more readily now. Plato's reason would intervene.

"Hold the gate," I yelled to the guard.

I had to cut through the hospital to gain passage to the underbelly of the prison which housed New Man's Land and Property. I had flashbacks to the first night I arrived here, numbed and in shock. Instantly, the visceral sensations of being separated from society, having orders angrily barked at me as I was strip-searched, humiliated, and made to feel as insignificant as possible flooded my senses. This was the well-practiced induction ritual that marked the exit from my human life and my initiation into being W95521.

"You don't remember me, do you?" asked the process sergeant. "You look much better firefighter. Getting it in?"

"You know it!"

"Getting it in" referred to exercise and was a compliment.

The last time I saw the sergeant, I was twenty-five pounds heavier. Now, I was approaching fifty-one and in the best shape of my life. Prison did have its benefits after all.

The runner from New Man's Land glared at me as I approached the heavily fortified entrance to my new career. Apparently, he had had his eye on the Property job and was none too happy about being bypassed.

When Penelope opened the door, the first words out of her mouth stunned me. "Where the fuck have you been? Your first day and you think you can wander in any time you god damn feel like it? This is not a good start for you."

I stood there unable to respond to this petite, pretty woman.

"What are you looking at inmate? You got no business looking in here," she snapped at the New Man's runner. She yanked me inside and slammed the door shut, leaving him speechless in the hallway. "What are you smiling at?"

"I ... I..."

"Great! He's illiterate," she sneered. "Just keep him away from me. He won't last a week," she said to a C.O. who appeared to be holding back a smile.

"You'll get used to her, although her bite is as bad as her bark," he warned me.

The name on his uniform said "Rourke," but he introduced himself as Tommy. This was the first time any guard had used their first name with me.

"C'mon, I'll walk you through it."

Tommy escorted me over to a large room where my new boss was flipping through paper work. The nameplate in front of her read: Sergeant Baudoin.

Without bothering to look up she growled, "Do what your told. Don't go anywhere without someone with you. Don't lie to me or steal anything or you're done. No second chances. Get it?" She looked up and stared at me. I must have nodded, because she nodded back. "Good. And no talking to Lacy. She has enough trouble concentrating as is."

"Hey," cried Lacy, who appeared to be a civilian secretary. "Be nice."

"Be nice," mimicked a young C.O. who had just walked in. "Sargent's right. Do you even remember who you slept with last night?"

"I bet you wish it was you," said Lacy with a wink. "In your dreams, pig farmer."

"Not in front of the new runner," said Tommy, entering the fray. "We don't want to damage him just yet." Tommy turned to Penelope and said, "Go show him where the cleaning shit is."

"Jesus Christ. I have to do everything around here," she snapped.

"That's because you're black."

"Oh, it's on," she said, and lunged at Tommy.

I stood there dumbfounded, unsure if I was so supposed to intervene or help Tommy. She was ferocious.

"Follow me," sighed the younger C.O.

I followed him down a long corridor that stretched the entire length of the underbelly of the prison.

"They call me the Rock. Welcome to Property."

TIME AND THE ORIGAMI PARROT

I watched from my goal crease as Doc edged his way along the damp wall, trying to escape the brutal hockey melee. He came down to the gym one Thursday night to observe the now infamous weekly hockey game, a staple of prison entertainment for both inmates and guards alike. He didn't come to cheer or place bets. His soul purpose was to gather compelling evidence to prove to me that this whole obsession with violent sports was counter-productive and did nothing more than feed my ego. Philosopher Kings did not play goalie in prison.

The following afternoon, I limped up the stairs to Doc's room to get his opinion on my swollen, black and blue elbow and knee. Before I could get a word in, he started his dissection.

"What do you get out of killing yourself on a weekly basis? Is it a form of self-punishment?

"I like that it hurts."

"So, you need to prove something to someone. Yourself, maybe?"

"You never played a team sport?"

"I exercise. I don't have time for games. I did notice though, that some guys, ones I thought were really tough, seemed out of their element down there."

Doc didn't understand that honor was at stake in these hockey matches. In short, a player was judged and exposed based on his performance or lack thereof. Only the most sadistic came back week after week.

"It reminds me a lot of the fire department," I said, avoiding his initial question.

"Why the fire department?" asked Doc.

"A three-alarm fire has a way of separating people."

"Never witnessed anything on that level," said Doc as he examined my knee. "You do know you have a cracked knee cap. I can stick my fingernail in the separation."

I flinched and then slowly lifted my elbow which had swollen to the size of a soft ball to be examined.

"Feels like you have a bone chip floating around in there. So again, why?" he pushed.

"So, it hurts," I replied defiantly.

"You understand that punishing yourself is not the same as seeing something through."

"I do, but this is different. I discovered something about myself down there. I just can't explain it."

"I saw it too," he nodded. "Quite something you've tapped into." He looked over his glasses at me.

I didn't know if it was the savage intensity of the game, the whole life and death scenario, or if it was *me*. I thought back to fires I had been in, the fear and excitement, but this was different. This I could control. I could see the player's moves before they did, the trajectory of the ball before it was hit. My body knew what to do out of instinct which seemed to be coming from some place I couldn't quite determine. I wasn't sure if it was a place in me, or a place I was tapping into.

"It's like a violent walking meditation," Doc offered, "but I still don't approve."

"All in the name of science," I winced as I wrapped a tee-shirt splint around my throbbing elbow. I looked up and Doc was staring at me.

"Now, the trick is, what else can you do with this."

On my way out, he handed me three books and a bag of candy.

"Is this a reward?" I tossed the candy in the air and caught it.

"It's a test. In one week's, time, I want you to show me that you still have some candy left."

"Yes, sir," I said, understanding immediately the reference to my impulse control problems.

"I've already read these books." I said looking down at the binders.

"The human mind lacks the concentration to grasp anything on one reading. I want you to read everything twice. It's not like you don't have time."

"Do you read everything twice?" I asked.

"I can skim with more focus than you can intentionally read on your best day. Re-read these and come back to me with something new."

And with that, I was dismissed.

As usual, Doc was right. I had little difficulty applying the prolonged and consistent effort approach to exercise and sports, but the less glamorous pursuit of studying was a wholly different challenge.

The three books he assigned to be re-read were on physiology which left me wondering his motive. That night, I read about the body's reaction to injury, about phagocytes and leukocytes, about white blood cells manufactured in the bone marrow then directed by the immune system to areas of swelling or infection. I had no memory of reading any of this before. Also, I ate all but one of the pieces of candy and put away the last piece to show Doc next week.

Days later, I walked up and down the flats reviewing my notes in anticipation of Doc's pop quiz on this week's reading assignment. As I passed by Rupert's cell, he called out my name. Now, I didn't normally go into Rupert's room because, like many lifers, he had developed some O.C.D. issues over his many years of incarceration. Everything in his room was arranged to perfection. White clothing hung on handmade drying devices. All extraneous items were stored out of view in his footlocker or under his bunk. His TV and radio sat on his desk in symmetrical alignment. I had once had the misfortune of stepping backwards in Rupert's cell and inadvertently brushed up against his face cloth. My carelessness sent him into a rage that frankly scared me. With this in mind, I stepped cautiously into his room. Rupert was very carefully placing a life-sized, multicolored origami parrot onto a matching stand.

"What do you think?" he said.

"It's awesome," I marveled.

"Really? You think so," he grinned.

His unvarnished display of pride struck me. Rupert was typically a well-rehearsed stoic. I was enthralled with his handiwork. The parrot was astonishing in its intricacy and color and was certainly the pinnacle of Rupert's origami endeavors.

"How long did it take you?" I asked respectfully.

Rupert opened his footlocker and carefully took out several books, some more worn than others, and a very neat pile of colored paper of different thicknesses.

"Time is irrelevant," he said placing the pile of teaching manuals on his desk reverently. "Patience is all that's required."

He began to flip through each book pausing along the way to show me important milestones of his journey. There were insects, butterflies and birds, horses and giraffes. In the final section of the newest book, the painstakingly detailed directions for the parrot and stand took up what appeared to be an entire chapter.

"Very impressive," I repeated.

"Let's have you make something." He challenged.

I reached for one his bright purple sheets. He handed me a plain white one.

"How much time did you get?" Rupert asked suddenly.

I hesitated. The length of your bid was not something you usually discussed with lifers. Prison etiquette deemed it inconsiderate because no matter how long you thought your bid was, you would eventually be getting out.

"Five to seven and a half."

"You can do that," he said, handing me a book. "Try this one."

I looked down and saw directions for a blue butterfly.

"You have the right attitude. Done wrong, time can do you, especially when you get out."

"How so," I said making the first fold.

"What do most short-timers talk about?" he quizzed.

"What's your definition of a short-timer?" I asked.

"Anyone without a life sentence. Don't be an idiot," he snapped. "Most guys find ways to make time go faster. Stay up late watching TV. Sleep in on weekends. Plan entire days around meals."

I had noticed this tendency myself. "Tuck flap A into fold C," I whispered to myself.

"They can make weeks go by without ever looking up," Rupert continued. "Problem is, they lose the ability to do anything productive. Their focus is entirely on making their sentence go by as fast as they can."

"What's wrong with wanting to get out?" There is no flap D.

"They lose the ability to slow time down."

I glanced up from my crumpled moth.

"And before you say anything, yes, you can slow down time," he answered my unspoken question. "You do your time differently though. Keep reading those books. Don't stop questioning Doc. Stay on that track," Rupert looked down at my wanna-be-butterfly. "That looks like one of those paper-finger-things that a sixth-grade girl would make."

"This is harder than it looks," I sighed in defeat.

"Much like everything," he said. "But listen, if you can keep this up, maybe when you get out of here, you'll be able to slow time down on demand. That's a skill worth mastering."

Sitting in my cell that night, I started thinking about everything Rupert said and how it dove-tailed perfectly with the work Doc had me doing. I understood the dedication required to apply the knowledge of how the body heals itself through the active meditations.

Every few days, piles of library books magically appeared on my desk, specifically hand- picked to point me toward some constellation of ideas that formed a theory or posed a question. The pop quizzes at chow or the monologues I was expected to recite as we slow jogged around the track kept me studying late into the night.

"Make the information your own," was Doc's incessant mantra. "Connect the dots."

There were days when I just wanted a break. I wanted to play chess or watch TV like everyone else, but Doc seemed driven, even impatient at times. He was adamant that I stay focused, that learning and the desire to know and understand become hard-wired into my brain. I began to wonder if I was just something for him to focus on while time went by between visits from his daughters and his girlfriend, or if there was something he needed to achieve, something born out of his self-inquiry, his silent drama, his need to be relevant in here like everyone else.

THE CATEGORICAL IMPERATIVE

Placing a pause in my decision-making process, let alone in front of my reactionary impulses, was a Sisyphean task, nearly impossible to achieve on a consistent basis. Doc explained that to become a true Philosopher King, I would also have to define a personal set of rules and values that transcended the laws of society.

"Sounds like your basic criminal philosophy. Make your own rules. Take whatever you want. Put your emotions aside and do whatever it takes to keep your victims in fear. Oh wait, that's governmental policy. It's hard to tell the difference sometimes."

"That's funny. You're a funny guy," deadpanned Doc. "I was referring to Emmanuel Kant's Categorical Imperative which states that when you expect more of yourself than the laws that govern society, those laws never need come in to play."

"And then I walk on water. I've seen that movie and it doesn't end well," I tossed back.

"I love movies," puffed Ron as he slowed his jog to join our walking classroom. "You can't handle the truth!" he yelled. "I could have played that part."

"I believe you could have," I said.

Doc nodded in agreement.

"Who would you play, Doc?" asked Ron.

"Gregory Peck," replied Doc without hesitation. "To Kill a Mocking Bird."

"Never saw it," said Ron.

"It was in black and white," I replied.

"Oh, so it's a racist thing."

"Yes, but that's not the point," I laughed.

It was a beautiful fall day, a Sunday in fact. Planes circled above trailing banners that advertised unnecessary products to the large crowds gathered about a mile away as the crow flies in Gillette Stadium, the home of The New England Patriots in Foxboro. I pictured Tom Brady warming up, tossing passes to the Gronk.

"Today we will discuss your court case," announced Doc.

"I thought I wasn't supposed to spend too much time reliving my past."

"True," he said, "but in your case, I think you need to see how far you've come and that you were already on the right track before you even got here."

I recalled numerous occasions sitting in Doc's cell discussing my court room drama and they never ended with me feeling good about myself.

"So why now? Why are we going over this again?" I sighed.

"Because at the core of your foolish act is the origin of the Categorical Imperative. Besides," he grinned, "it would have just fed your ego to know you were right."

"I was right?"

"Yes, for all the wrong reasons, you were right."

"Doesn't sound like much of a compliment," laughed Ron.

"You take what you can get. Go back to the part where I was right," I perked up.

"When you look back on those days during your trial, can you describe what you were feeling?" Doc asked turning serious.

"Nothing. I was feeling nothing."

I explained how within a period of a few months, my father, my son, and one of my close friends all died. My dad went first. He lost a battle between an aortic aneurysm and lung cancer. The lung cancer won. Aaron, a childhood friend, succumbed to pancreatic cancer and died while I was at my son's memorial service in San Francisco.

"So, you were feeling so much, you shut down," injected Doc.

"I tried to feel. I felt guilty for not feeling. I acted the way I thought I was supposed to, but everything seemed muted. I kept thinking why don't I feel the way I should."

"How did your son die?" Ron asked quietly.

"He threw himself off the Golden Gate Bridge."

Silence echoed off my blunt pronouncement.

I sighed. "That's my point. Shouldn't I be crumbling into a ball. The last conversation I had with my son – he told me he was coming back for the trial to set the judge straight. He wanted to help me. I told him no. The culpability lies with me."

Neither Doc nor Ron said anything. In the distance, I could hear the stadium crowds cheering, which suddenly seemed ironic.

"I told Alex that every decision has ramifications. That there is a ripple effect that can't be reversed. I told him I was disappointed that he still hadn't straightened himself out."

Hearing myself explain this to Doc and Ron, I began to wonder who I was really lecturing: Alex or myself.

"And those were the last words I said to him except a phone message he never heard."

"Jesus," said Ron. "That's awful."

"Back to the courtroom," redirected Doc. "In that moment, when you realized they were going to let you walk, what went through your mind?"

"Wait a minute," said Ron, grabbing my arm and stopping me. "Are you telling me you were given a deal to walk and you didn't take it?"

"I thought you knew that," I frowned.

"I thought you meant walk away from your responsibility. That I get. But you're saying the DA offered you a chance to go free?"

I nodded.

"Jesus Christ. No offense, but you're a moron."

"Ya, I get that a lot."

"So, you punished yourself?" pressed Doc.

"It had nothing to do with punishment. It had to do with starting over. Prison seemed so terrifying, so irreversible. It was a commitment I couldn't renege on. It was the calmest I'd felt in years."

"Not my experience," said Ron.

"They had worked out a no-contest plea and my first thoughts were that I'd won something. That this was a great victory. My court-appointed-joke-of-a-lawyer was at the bench negotiating the rest of the charges be downgraded to misdemeanors. I stood there looking around the courtroom. None of it felt right. The voice that speaks to me on occasion took this moment to speak as loud and as clear as any conversation I ever had: Go to prison. Nothing scares you more. Do this and it will lead to something extraordinary. I actually said out loud "Really, we're going to have this conversation now?'"

The voice was right though. Everything in my life up to that moment had been mostly about me. Things always worked out without a whole lot of effort on my part. And here I was again, dodging responsibility. Where was the self-respect in that? I could do what I always did and promise that I would straighten up, do better, turn over the proverbial new leaf. But who was I kidding? How long before I outsmarted myself. Prison! Think about it. I was a firefighter being convicted of arson in a city whose claim to fame was the tragic death of six firefighters. Me going to prison would be the ultimate humiliation.

"I would tear myself from the fabric of my life once and for all. How awesome is that!"

"State prison. How awesome is this," said Ron laughing.

"But it is. Don't you see," I said.

"Take me into that moment. The moment you're standing there making that decision," said Doc.

"The court room became a comedic theater. I had already moved beyond any decision they could make. I didn't want a deal, some get-out-jail-free card. I wanted to do my penance as I saw fit. I wanted there to be no way out, no way to fool myself, or renege on the agreement. I would take responsibility for my life and either become something new or perish. Both were acceptable."

"The Categorical Imperative in a nut shell. Emmanuel Kant

would be proud!" said Doc. "You never realized that what you were doing was putting more responsibility on yourself then anyone could ever demand of you. The court's punishment disappeared. Its verdict superseded by the punishment you chose for yourself. Best of all, you never even made the connection. You simply applied a philosophy that resonated with you and that," declared Doc, "is relevant and worth pursuing."

As wonderful and heroic as Doc's words made me feel, there was more to it. Alex's choice to take his own life was no surprise. When Nicholai called me to tell me Alex was missing, we were both calm. We both knew. I flashed back to the last conversation Alex and I had where he asked to come back. I had told him I would take responsibility. Responsibility for what? Who was I kidding? Maybe he wanted to come home. Maybe he was hoping I'd say "just you and me Alex, let's just drive off somewhere and go camping." We could have saved each other. The truth was, I wasn't ready. It was me that wasn't ready to grow up. Out of all the people that tried to help Alex, they all did their best. I didn't.

"I'm sorry about your son," said Ron, throwing his arm around my shoulder. I saw myself in Ron. He was just a guy that wasn't raised to understand the world's pitfalls and dangers. He had no one to turn to when he discovered that drugs and alcohol could take over his life despite his best intentions. He still maintained a childlike enthusiasm that everything would turn out okay, next time. Next time. There was no next time. That was the truth of my court room decision. It was not some insight into a philosophy. It was the knowledge that my son needed me to be ready and I wasn't. He needed someone to turn to. But there were no Philosopher Kings. For me, there was at best, A philosophy born of arson, and with that knowledge, I was exactly where I should be.

MORE PLEASE

As winter turned to spring, life seemed almost agreeable. I settled into an institutionalized routine that, as it turns out, I was quite well adapted for. Up early to meditate and fill my journal with thoughts and questions for Doc. Then, read a chapter on whatever book was next in line; today was biology, photosynthesis to be exact. I understood how Doc wanted me to learn. If I couldn't explain it, I didn't own it. Nothing should be beyond my grasp. Knowledge was not hiding itself; it was for everyone.

At chow that morning, we discussed the second part of the learning process: choose an idea from a particular field of study and discern a connection between this idea and whatever other current issue we were studying. He believed that combining different fields of study was the key to new thinking. Today's topic was photosynthesis and its correlation to the visible spectrum of light.

"The frequency that carries what we perceive as the color green is the photon that plants resonate with. The conversion of light energy to chemical energy first occurred when cyanobacteria separated out the hydrogen in water molecules to create energy, releasing oxygen as a by-product, though we humans believe it was created just for us."

"Actually," Doc interrupted, "photosynthetic organisms probably employed hydrogen sulfide as a reducing agent first, but go on, without the sarcasm please."

"Whatever," I shrugged.

My correlating subject was physics; Einstein to be exact. I went on to explain how Einstein was aware that green photons separate carbon dioxide molecules into their constituent elements, absorbing the carbon and releasing the oxygen. The larger blue photons were able to interact with certain metals, dislodging electrons that could then be harnessed.

"This is what he got his Nobel prize for, not the Theory of Relativity," I declared proudly.

I looked over at Rupert who was nodding his approval at

my early morning triumph. Doc had moved to our table in the back of the chow hall a month or so earlier and breakfast proved a good time to review the previous day's readings before we headed off to work.

"You took the easy way out. I was hoping you'd go with chemistry," said Doc without looking up from his pancakes.

"Jesus," said Rupert. "Tough crowd."

I nodded in agreement and turned back to Doc.

"I can rattle off the structure of six carbon sugars, ATP production, and the importance of redox functions, but that's a little heavy for breakfast."

Rupert laughed out loud. "You created him."

"Okay smart guy," said Doc, smiling slightly, "we'll begin quantum physics next."

"Really?"

I had been asking for months only to hear the same answer; In due time. All in due time. I wondered what it would've been like to have this much enthusiasm for learning as a child. It pained me to think of all the possibilities I missed out on.

"Have you considered quantum healing?" asked Rupert, turning serious.

"I have," answered Doc.

"Quantum what?" But no one was listening to me.

Rupert had been in so long that some of his thoughts drifted into the realm of magical thinking. I saw a lot of that in here. But on the subject of meditation, or what you could achieve with meditation, even Doc perked up when Rupert chose to share some of his insights on the subject.

"You've seen him play hockey, the injuries he gets. You have to wonder what's possible," mused Rupert.

"I'm reserving my opinion. I still don't think the tradeoff of serious physical injury in exchange for potential metaphysical investigation is worth it. So, if you choose, it's on you," Doc challenged.

"When night yard begins," nodded Rupert, turning to me.

I had heard about night yard. It coincided with the end of hockey. You got to go out after chow as the days grew longer and warmer.

I welcomed the promise of Rupert's healing techniques as my injuries were mounting and we still had several games left.

"Hey Goalie, you playing tonight? We're gonna be watching," yelled a guard as I walked back from chow.

The guards streamed our game live via the cameras in the gym.

When I arrived in A-1, I found a set of socks on my bed. On closer examination, I discovered the socks were fitted with elastics on each end. In the middle, double stitching secured a pair of thick winter socks folded in two creating a thick padding. These retrofitted socks fit quite nicely in place when pulled up over my elbows. The craftsmanship obviously took time and care, and I was most appreciative to whoever had that left these for me.

The next week, the more elaborate knee-pad versions of these handcrafted marvels showed up, made with the same high quality and functionality. The thing was, no one ever admitted to making them. My new hockey equipment would be considered contraband as they were "altered" items and could easily earn me a "ticket" according to prison rules. The very first time I wore them, the guard performing the pat down at the entrance of the stairway to the gym, hesitated when his hands ran over them. He looked up at me and then allowed me to proceed.

"Clever," he said before adding. "Good luck tonight, Goalie."

Knowing my knees and elbows were now marginally protected from the harsh impact of cement-on-bone allowed me to play with a reckless abandon which did not go unnoticed. A few days later, Big Steve came to my cell and simply said: "Come with me."

I followed him to the day room where he motioned to a seat. "Sit there and shut up," he growled and walked towards the microwave ovens where there was a line of inmates waiting for their turn to warm their ramen-noodle-based-artificial-meat stick meals. He stood, arms folded, and appeared to be waiting for something. When the bell went off, the first in line removed his bowl. The next inmate ran over quickly with his bowl, pressed the digits on the pad to two minutes, and then returned to his pool game. Steve deftly reached over and recalculated the time on the pad to read seven minutes and returned to his previous arm folded position against the wall. Two young Spanish guys sitting at the table next to the microwave playing some ridiculous dice game looked up when Steve performed his covert re-timing act. He glared at them.

"Either of you have a problem?"

They quickly shook their heads.

"Not a fucking word," Steve hissed.

I couldn't for the life of me imagine why I was chosen to witness this random act of mischief. I watched in fascination, waiting to see how long it took the pool player to notice that time was not flowing at the correct speed. He never did. When the bell finally went off, he came dancing over with anticipation. I cringed.

"Son of a bitch!" he yelled, tossing the baking hot dish onto the counter next to the microwave and vigorously shaking his hand. "What the hell?"

He looked around accusingly, but no information was forthcoming. He wrapped his hand in his shirt and picked up his late-night snack, examining the melted, warped cover that at one time sealed nicely over the top of his bowl.

"Fucking great, that's just fucking great!" he muttered, tossing the cover in the garbage.

I could hear him swearing all the way down the block. Steve, who hadn't moved an inch from his position up against the wall, calmly reached down and took the misshapen cover out of the trash and motioned me to follow.

As I trailed Big Steve back down the flats, I couldn't help wondering what the point of all this was. Was he trying to show me his grasp of thermodynamics or did he just like witnesses to his acts of cruelty? He was bending and shaping the still warm cover in hands as we walked. A bowl cover weapon, perhaps?

"Do you have a pair of tightey-whities," he asked when we reached my cell.

"Yes," I hesitated, now nervous, "but I don't wear them. I prefer boxers."

"Really? Do you think I give a shit about your preference in underwear? Listen up. Before you play tomorrow, and you are playing, put on your boxers first and then pull your tightey-whities on over this." He handed me the still slightly warm re-shaped plastic cover. "You're welcome."

"Brilliant," I said out loud, but by that time, Big Steve was gone. It was perfect. The whole thing was brilliant. In fact, I had never been so honored. The very next night after a particularly hard slap shot echoed off my soup bowl-protector I was certain I saw Big Steve smile.

Days seemed to flow effortlessly now. My cell was organized. I had all the things I needed: coffee; a TV that I didn't watch as much as I thought I would; pencils and paper; books; actual sneakers, courtesy of Timmy and Shawn putting money in my account. I was at a loss for words at their generous gift. I was in the strange position of relying on the compassion and generosity of others to survive in here, to create a small semblance of the feeling of home. Gratitude was becoming a familiar emotion that I now readily embraced.

The newness of summer yard was a welcome change of pace, the only drawback being that everyone was outside. The running track looked like a Los Angeles freeway during rush hour with most inmates shuffling at a snail's pace with the occasional high-speed runner erratically weaving in and out. I met up with Rupert on the first evening of night yard. He was walking slowly around the track and I was eager to take him up on his promise to discuss what would become known as Meditational Sounding.

Rupert had read a hundred books on meditation. His philosophical understanding was complimented by years of dedicated practice. He claimed meditation was useless unless you combined it with other disciplines which he believed paved the way for a new level of understanding, much like Doc insisted from me in our educational pursuits. Rupert offered to teach me how to heal myself. Healing, as it turned out, was much like his theory on levitation. It was merely a side effect of deep meditation.

I was skeptical of metaphysics. I believed them to be a flight-of-fancy-sort of wisdom, but I had come to learn that most great breakthroughs were accomplished by someone often labeled crazy by their colleagues and society at large. So, open-mindedness was my new motto. Thus, began the Ping Pong ball experiment.

The rules were simple: just give it an honest effort. Rupert supplied the working parts of the experiment in the form of a paper pyramid which he placed on my TV along with a white ping pong ball that fit perfectly in the top of the pyramid where he had cut out a small wedge. The goal was to move the ping pong ball off its perch with my mind. Of course, it was!

"Call it telekinesis. Call it whatever you want," said Rupert. "Every night, try a different technique until you get that ball to move. Be sure and document your work."

Rupert left his prized origami parrot on its custom-made stand as a proctor to make sure I stuck to my commitment. I didn't need the parrot. I was going to take this assignment seriously, put in the work. I was going to meticulously document every attempt. I was going to form a relationship with this ball. I was going to make it want to move for me. I would bend its will to my own.

I held up the ping pong ball and told it my plans before placing it back in its perch. I decided to call it Wilson. Wilson would learn to trust me. We would become best friends.

I first tried Doc's analytical meditation to enlist Wilson's cooperation, focusing all my energy directly on him and nothing else. Then, I tried ignoring Wilson and focused instead on all the things that were moving, mostly outside my window: the distant tree tops, birds, the cardboard coyotes swaying in the wind that had been arranged in the yard by prison management to dissuade geese from colonizing the inviting green lawn. I tried to coax Wilson into finding a better life, a more pleasing existence filled with movement. I tried to persuade him to give up his attachment to inertia. Yes, inertia! Newton's Laws! Maybe this was the key: a body at rest stays at rest until acted upon by an outside force. A force of will was not enough. Maybe I could summon the wind outside to blow the ball from its perch. I tried surrounding Wilson with my own energy, reaching outward and enveloping him within my peri-personal space. When I stood up, the ball would be compelled to move with me. Nothing. I tried everything. I would have to dig deeper.

I understood that every object hums at a certain frequency from my study of atoms, all of which can be identified by their unique frequency and wave function or intrinsic spin. Neil's

Bohr! Where are you when I need you? What if I hummed with Wilson?

"You and me, Wilson. Hummmmm."

I hummed in different keys noticing that each one seemed to affect me differently. That was interesting. Different tones seemed to affect different areas of my own body. So, if I just found the right key signature, a combination of Pythagorean length perhaps. Wait a minute, what if I sped up the atoms? Friction created heat and more importantly, heat rises. Yes! Heat rises. What if I spun the electrons faster and faster combined this with a tone that would lift the ball from its mooring. Heating, burning, faster, faster. Maybe I could scare it off its Egyptian throne? I could throw my hands up unexpectedly trying to release the stored-up energy I was creating in my own body.

I didn't notice the guard in the doorway watching my antics. When I did turn towards him, he simply said.

"Telekinesis, Baxter? I thought you'd last longer than this."

Damn you ping pong ball! Move! Damn you, Wilson! MOVE! Nine Block and the crazies were calling my name.

The seventh day came and I was broken. I had tried my best. There were a couple of moments where I swear Wilson moved, a tiny quiver, but I had no tangible evidence. Rupert appeared as promised and asked for my notes. The parrot, I assumed, had told him of my failure since he never asked if I had succeeded. As he read through my well-documented defeat, he smiled.

"Wilson, I like that."

Was he mocking me?

"This is extraordinary. You're ready to move on," announced Rupert.

"Move on? Move on with what?" I stammered.

"With healing."

"Healing? What about the ping pong ball?" I cried out, exasperated.

Rupert reached over and flicked it off the paper pyramid with his index finger.

Now, it was not that I didn't expect that all along, but I harbored a glimmer of hope that maybe he could actually move the ball with his mind. I wanted it to be true. Who wouldn't, but c'mon, he could have left me with something.

"With all these tactics and techniques, you've documented, especially this one," he said tapping my day four experiment on humming, "answer me one simple question. What is more plausible? That you could get the ball to move or that you could elicit some reaction from your own body, your own cells, your own molecules?"

"My own cells. My own molecules." I smiled. "My own body! Of course."

"Let the healing begin!" Rupert nodded. He looked back over his shoulder as he headed out the door. "The parrot said he wants to stay. He thinks you're fucking hilarious."

SELF-INFLICTED PAIN

There was no actual baseball diamond at Walpole. After some prodding, we were allowed to remove some small areas of grass and replace them with gravel, creating bases. The uneven surface made fielding a ground ball or running the base path an adventure all on its own. In fact, the first time I was up, I slapped a ball to right center and much to my embarrassment, I fell coming out of the batter's box. My mind was ahead of my feet. It had been about twenty years since I had tried to sprint around base paths. I would argue that when it came to throwing a baseball, it was the first-time many inmates had thrown anything with the exception perhaps of a rock through a window. Hockey Joe had warned me to avoid softball entirely as it never led to anything good. Every strike, every safe or out call ignited explosive arguments.

As usual, Doc stood on the side lines shaking his head at my daredevil athletic endeavors. I played softball much the same as goalie, diving at anything hit near me. Like with hockey, the more I let go of my thought process, the better I became. It was in a word euphoric. Doc called it squandering my Chi. The truth was, I liked the attention, the notoriety. The old guy that could hit a ball a mile.

One afternoon I hit a ball that rolled all the way to the fence stopping on the fringes of No Man's Land, the barren stretch of asphalt that separated the fence from the wall. If entered this restricted area, you risked being shot from the guard towers. Rounding first, I admired how far my ball was traveling. I was so caught up in the applause that I failed to see the hole. The sudden loss of forward motion wrenched my body to the left. Searing pain. Everything went white.

I had dislocated my hip, yanked the ball joint right out of the socket. Panic stricken, I instinctively began hopping on my good leg and repeatedly thrust the injured leg forward with as much force as I could muster, trying desperately to pop my hip back in place. Surprisingly, it worked. When it snapped back in, I was momentarily blinded by the pain. I gasped, unable to take a breath. The crowd, unaware of my predicament, yelled for me to keep running, their whoops and cheers pulling me back into myself. I somehow managed to hop to home plate and then collapsed off to the side. I waited for Doc. He would know what to do.

Eventually, he appeared over me and leaned in. "You wanted something to heal, good luck with this." And with that he was gone.

It took every ounce of strength I had to limp back to A-1. I declined the offer to go to H.S.U. The thoughts of the Shattuck Hospital were incentive enough to keep moving. I could fix this. I had to. I had suffered through cracked knee caps and swollen elbows, but this seemed more than I could bear. Every movement, every breath was greeted with stomach turning agony. I managed to lay on my right side for a few minutes, but there was no escape from the relentless throbbing. I struggled to get back up. I couldn't roll over. I couldn't bend my knee. I couldn't control the pain. Breathe. Find the tone. Vibrate the hip. Communicate with my cells. I knew the procedure, but the nausea prevented me from concentrating.

"Count time. Count time."

Are you kidding me? If I wasn't on my feet by the time the guard peered in my cell, I was out of here. I grabbed at the window sill and reached for the corner of my desk. I willed myself upright just as the guard approached.

"You alright, Baxter? You don't so look good."

"Fine," I managed to get out, barely looking up. "Just a little sore."

I had to get up and I did. That's what it took. Sheer willpower. Indefatigable determination. I hobbled over to the sink and splashed water on my face. I could do this. I had to do this.

For the next eight hours, I took turns supporting myself upright then laying on my side. I tried twice, unsuccessfully, to get my pants off and gave up. The pain never subsided, but I adapted to it long enough to breathe and hum. I turned on the TV to mask my tonal hip singing, my ballad of phagocytes and leukocytes. Ever so slightly, I put weight on my injured leg, first for seconds, then longer. I tied a tee shirt around the injured area to make sure my hip knew to stay in place. I applied pressure with the palm of my hand as I attempted to limp to the cell door and back again to the bunk. The night guard warned me that he had left a note on the desk informing the day shift that I was injured and required medical attention if I was not up and moving come morning. About five in the morning, I dozed off momentarily half-sitting, half-leaning against the wall. I felt something shift. I had reached what Rupert had called the quantum level of healing. I was on the other side of this. I had seen more early mornings than I cared to remember fighting off a night of music and partying to make it into the fire station. This would be no different. Both were self-inflicted abuse. God, you'd have thought I'd learned by now.

After skipping breakfast, I braced myself for my work shift in Property. There was no option to call in sick. Still dressed in my grass-stained pants from the day before, I slowly limped down the hall, sweat beading off my forehead. I got this. Breathe. Hum. Repeat. Don't throw up.

Normally, I loved Penelope's vile use of the English language, but I barely managed a smile when she opened the door into Property.

"What the fuck, douche bag," she backed out of my way. "Did you sleep in those clothes."

"I'm having some issues."

"You think, dim-wad," she responded, without missing a beat.

As I gimped toward the office, I could hear The Rock and Lacy in the middle of one of their classic back-and-forths over Lacy's tardiness.

"I had trouble with the shower," Lacy explained.

"It's always something," chided The Rock.

"Whose shower was it this time?" came the follow up jab. The room fell silent.

"Was that my outside voice?" I said quickly, but it was too late. Everyone erupted into laughter.

"He can't say that," Lacy said, half-shocked, half-smiling.

Sergeant Boudain, (who recently granted me permission to call her by her first name, Mary Ann) was already reaching for her phone and dialing. I was certain she was calling the Move Team to lug me away.

"You're not going to believe what Kenny said to Lacy! Yeah, my runner," she continued almost crying with laughter now.

The Rock was trying to explain the details to Tommy who had heard the commotion from the other room.

"So, where were you? Do even know?" prodded Tommy.

"It's none of your business." She turned her attention to me. "I want you to beat up the runner."

Maybe it was sleep deprivation. I couldn't help myself.

"Why are you mad at me?" I said in mock disbelief. "We have so much in common."

"Like you're a firefighter, and she likes hoses," laughed Tommy.

"No, we're both wearing the same clothes as yesterday."

Everyone turned to look at Lacy.

"You are. You are wearing the same clothes," gasped Mary Ann. "Lacy's wearing the same clothes as yesterday," she reported into the phone.

The Rock stepped up the assault. "The convict's right. They both have grass stains on their knees."

"I'll kick your ass," squealed Lacy, looking down.

"Oh my God! She looked," crowed The Rock.

"Tell us where you were," baited Tommy.

"I told you. I had trouble with the shower," giggled Lacy.

"You'd be the last person I thought would have trouble with some guy's plumbing," laughed The Rock.

The room descended into complete hysterics which stopped on a dime when the Superintendent threw open the door.

"Well, if this isn't the happiest department in the whole prison," she said surveying the room.

"What's your secret?"

"Lacy's love life," said Tommy and the laughter erupted again.

"I came down to see you," the Superintendent pointed at me. "I heard you were hurt and won't go to the H.S.U."

"Nothing I can't handle, Ma'am. Just a dislocated hip. I'll take care of it."

"You will, will you? And how do you plan to do that?"

"I have my ways," I smiled.

"And one of them is Doc Stryker, I take it. I hear you two make quite a pair," she said.

"He teaches. I listen."

"We'll have to talk about that sometime, carry on then," waved the Superintendent as she turned and left.
"What's that's all about," asked Mary Ann.

"Got me," I shrugged.

The rest of the day Mary Anne let me roll around in an office chair working on the filing system since even she couldn't bear to watch me hobble. My duties had increased significantly over my time in Property as I proved myself quite resourceful. I was amazed how much of my day was improved by my new way of being as Doc described it.

I spent the next few days immersed in my self-healing regime, rehearsing and repeating the techniques that most effectively stimulated my body's ability to heal itself. Deep breathing and the proper hummed tone vibrated into my hip socket and the surrounding tissue. Sleep did not come easy. My goal was not to ease the pain. The pain kept my mind laser-focused on the afflicted area.

"You seem to be enjoying your predicament a little too much," observed Doc, appearing in my doorway. "I can't help but think you're using this to once again castigate yourself. I don't approve. No matter how much you punish yourself, it's not going to bring your son back."

Doc knew how to cut right to the point. I have to admit I was tempted to see this as a sign more punishment was still pending.

"I hope I'm around to see the day when you stop hating yourself." He walked over to where I sat propped on my bed, leaned up against the wall. "So how is your experiment going?"

"Fine and dandy," I hummed.

"It's unlikely that you actually dislocated your hip. You wouldn't be moving around this soon. In fact, your hip would be so badly discolored by now that it would probably scare you."

I paused a moment for effect, then struggled to my feet. "You mean it would look like this?" I said, pulling my pants down.

Doc stared at the large yellow-green bruised area that extended from my hip down to my knee and half way around my butt.

"Yeah, it would look just like that," he said suddenly intrigued.

I sat down almost proud. "And that's the only time I'll ever take my pants down for an inmate."

In the subsequent days, Doc monitored my progress. He wanted to hear every single detail of that first anguished night, which combination of techniques coalesced into my breakthrough. He sat and watched me hum and breath, making comments, asking questions. It occurred to me that whatever I had tapped into confounded Doc and that made him not only curious, but a little uncomfortable.

"You've got to be more vigilant if you're going to continue this all-out assault on your body. How long do you think you can last?" he warned.

"With no lie on my soul, I'd say indefinite, as long as you're here to help out, that is," I added quickly.

Doc smiled at my impertinence.

"Remember, and don't take this as a deterrent, but who you want to be doesn't always win."

"Why Doc, it almost sounds like you're rooting for me."

"I'm doing more than that my friend. Now get off that leg for a while. You're not Superman you know."

4:30

I watched as snow started to fall outside my window, glistening and reflecting the light spilling from the guard tower. Its steady tranquil pattern was soothing. I had learned to find peace in the silence of a day just beginning. I was seldom bothered anymore by the thoughts that drove the unconscious in the quiet serenity of a winter morning. I breathed in time with it. I didn't even respond to the guard who paused at my door to shine his flashlight off the back of my head. I did not allow the intrusion to distract me from my meditation. He lingered just a moment too long, annoyed that I didn't turn around at his insistent stare. It was not in defiance or disrespect on my part. I was simply lost in the sheer beauty of the moment. I thought of Alex and winced at the irony of how such an absurd situation could be made so wonderful, how the knowledge of embracing any opportunity to breathe in a particular moment was all that was required for happiness. I had a momentary glimpse of a future where I forgave myself.

I paused and contemplated the influence my new-found philosophy might have had on him and a twinge of regret grabbed at my heart. I was still annoyed at my failure to learn these lessons years ago, but I no longer pushed these feelings away. I wrapped myself in them, and as I did, the snow changed direction ever so slightly, perhaps an indication of its acknowledgment and approval of this connection. I smiled and my eyes watered.

"Never waste a single moment," I whispered out loud. "Give as much of yourself as possible, every day. Make it count."

I turned, eyes closed, and took the four equal steps to the door. The perfect symmetry of distance that had become my life and the extent of a night time walk. I peered across the way and saw the flickering of TV sets glowing in half the cells on the block. Some inmates stayed up all night watching TV. Others just needed the comfort of any distraction from their own thoughts.

I was filled with a sense of sadness at the frustration emanating from the spaces around me. In just a few hours, the chaos would begin again, fueled by the false bravado born from insecurity and wielded as the weapon of choice. The endless insanity of this place.

I turned back to the serenity of the silent crystalline dance outside my window. Fresh snow means I would get to chase my own footprints around the empty track. No one but myself and possibly Hockey Joe would go running on a day like this and that suited me just fine. Losing myself in these perfect solitary moments in the dark, I felt invincible, as if I could predict and control the world around me with nothing but my will. I knew this arrogance was an invitation to the universe to remind me this was a delusion and that the real wisdom came from knowing I was completely powerless.

The sound of a cell door opening in the night was unusual. It could wake you from a dead sleep because it meant something was happening. On occasion, an inmate might be on his way to an early courtroom appearance or was being shipped off to another prison, even lugged for some unknown indiscretion. But as prepared as I was, I panicked. I knew exactly what this meant the moment I heard it. It was four-thirty and I would never see Doc again.

It was not as if we weren't expecting this. It was the second time Doc had been taken to the hospital in the middle of the night.

One evening we were discussing anatomy and physiology, a subject that he insisted I study in order to foster my new-found healing technique which I was practicing regularly on the many injuries I incurred weekly from hockey or softball. He asked me to feel the rotation in his shoulder as compared to mine. We were discussing rotator cuff and AC joint injuries.

I put my hand on him and immediately pulled back. Before I could stop myself, I gasped out loud.

"You have cancer."

He paused for a moment and said, "I see you're constantly learning."

"It's bad," I wavered. "Why aren't we addressing this?"

Immediately, a cascade of thoughts tumbled through my mind. Doc had been making plans for the future. He was mapping out the best way to earn good time to shorten his sentence. He was preparing his request to be sent to Pondeville, the mini-mum- security prison, in the Spring and to eventually marry his girlfriend.

Doc's eyes watered as he spoke in a hushed tone. "I thought if we kept progressing with your ability to heal, I could learn to use the technique on myself, but..." He paused and sat down on his bunk. "There won't be enough time."

"Why would you hide this? Did you see the Doctor?"

Doc laughed. "Drink water and pray. By the time I convinced her to get an MRI, the hole in my hip was the size of a quarter."

Doc had stopped running a few months earlier and we tried stretching exercises to correct what I thought was middle-aged hamstring issues.

"We were wasting our time on karate stretches and you knew?" I said.

"I suspected."

"Why wouldn't you tell me? Does Jenny know?"

"No."

Doc and I had passed the student-teacher relationship months ago and he was fast becoming the best friend I had ever had so I had a right to disagree.

"You're planning on getting married? When are you planning on telling her? She has a right to know."

Doc explained in his usual slow, thoughtful way that he hoped against hope that he was wrong.

"Remember what we discussed about having no lie on your soul as the key to any self-healing journey," he said looking at me intently, "Remember that I made you promise to adhere to this as if your life depended on it."

"Are you saying that you did this to yourself," I said quietly, understanding all too well where he was going with this.

"That's exactly what I'm saying. I've gone too far."

"That's bullshit," I said, only half meaning it.

"I've known for months it was beyond the stage of curing. I'm guessing it had passed the tipping point before I even came to prison."

"But Jenny," I said again, questioning his logic.

"She has her own practice in Pennsylvania and would have dumped it all the moment she found out. She would've spent the remainder of my life sitting and waiting for every visit and refusing to believe that she could not heal this and, as you and I know, I don't have the tools to justify a miracle at this point."

"Why in the world," I said, suddenly dumbfounded, "are we sitting here talking about shoulder rotation when all this is going on."

"Because there's so much you need to see, so much more for you to learn. You're so close to becoming something, something I've searched for all these years and never found until I came here."

Doc looked at me. I held his gaze

"What can I do?" was all that was left to say. "What do you need? I'll do whatever you ask."

"I'll start needing some help," said Doc as he turned to look out the window. "It's going to get much worse in the coming weeks. I hope I can count on you."

Those next few weeks were difficult. Doc could barely make it up and down the stairs. On our way to chow, he would place his hand on my shoulder just to walk. This did not go unnoticed. Guards questioned it and other inmates, especially in the chow hall, tossed around demeaning comments about two men in their fifties walking slowly, side-by-side, one supporting the other. These sideways looks and snide comments weighed heavily on me. I never did well with humiliation, a throw- back to my Dad's less-than-stellar-parenting techniques and after all, 'do your own time' was the customary saying. In that moment, I realized what a selfish asshole I was being. He had given me so much, in fact, he had changed almost every way I looked at, thought about, or dealt with life. There was no way I could ever repay him. I did not want to look back on this wishing I had done more.

As time passed, it became impossible to hide Doc's struggles from staff. He requested he be allowed to stay here as long as possible and was told that it was a working block. If he couldn't work, he couldn't stay. I was given permission to take care of him as long as it did not interfere with the running of the institution.

Now I stood here at 4:30 in the morning, locked in my cell, unable to say goodbye to my best friend. Kicking my door brought one of the night guards running along with some angry comments from inmates I had woken up.

"Just let me out for a minute," I begged. "Just to say goodbye.

He's going to die."

The guard stood firm saying he wasn't about to let me roam around on camera at four-thirty in the morning so I could say goodbye to another inmate.

"I'm sorry. It's not happening."

"But it's Doc," I pleaded, knowing the respect people had for him.

"I know, but it's not happening."

When the doors cracked several hours later, I fully expected I'd have to deal with the grumpy inmates I had woken up with my tantrum, but nothing was said. In fact, it was the opposite. In the gray shuffle down to chow, several comments were directed my way about how much everyone admired Doc. "We're all gonna miss him," said PJ. "You're not alone in that."

But I was alone. I felt abandoned and vulnerable.
Then I wondered what Doc was feeling.

Act Two

APPETITES AND DESIRES

THE CRUELEST THING

"Of course, he's here. Where else would he be," I turned my attention from the filing cabinet as Mary Anne continued, "It's who? No kidding! Well, this should be interesting," as she hung up the phone, she said, "You have a visitor. Its Doc's girl."

I made my way up the back stairs, with each step the heaviness of uncertainty pulled on my work grays. In order to make this climb I had to shed the weight of my silent anguish. Doc had asked me to take care of Jenny. How? I had not yet come to terms with my own feelings, and now I was meeting this woman for the first time.

I spotted her instantly. I had only seen her once and had never spoken to her in person, but I knew her right away, as if I'd always known her. I could see from across the room that she'd been crying.

The desk sergeant said in a low voice that I did not have to see her if I didn't want to. As I approached, her hands drifted towards me. The short, hug turned into a release of emotion that was unparalleled by anything I had ever been a part of. It was as if she had been holding back this flood of tears and could no longer bear it. The prison visiting room lacked the intimacy for such an act of liberation. The sergeant looked uncomfortably in our direction and could not seem to bring himself to yell out the order to separate, though the allotted time for contact had been surpassed by a considerable margin. It was with every ounce of restraint that I sat down across from her. Our hands took forever to separate, finger tips hooked together in a last- ditch effort to hold on like the desperate act of lovers boarding a train in the final scene of a tragic movie.   This whole visiting room protocol designed to purposely restrict contact, had never seemed so wrong to me until now.   It was so obvious that she just needed to be held. But there she sat, perched on the edge of her seat trying desperately to stay as close to me as possible. The sergeant busied himself with the papers on his desk. He couldn't bring himself to utter the command to sit back.

"I didn't know where else to go," said Jenny in a broken voice.

Even as I sat there, witnessing her grief, trying to energetically embrace her, I couldn't help but notice my own emotional response to the loss of my friend. I didn't cry when they came and told me Doc had died. There were no tears. Had this place hardened me against emotion or was it something much worse? In fact, the only emotion I recognized in this moment was the uncomfortable feeling of embarrassment I was trying to control as the other visitors stared at us. I knew this was a selfish reaction that I should be mature enough to set it aside, but still, there it was nagging at the fringes of my compassion.

"Why wasn't I told?" pleaded Jen.

Doc and I had argued over telling her about his illness, and I reluctantly dropped the issue when he assured me that she would disregard all other aspects of her life and set aside everyone else that relied on her, her parents and her clients, to be here for him. Doc was not going to be responsible for that. When he could no longer hide his condition, his short phone call simply stated, *"I have metastasized bone cancer. I have three months."*

As expected, Jenny threw herself into her car without hesitation and headed from her office in the quaint village of Lemont, Pennsylvania to the unsympathetic bureaucracy of Walpole State Prison nearly 500 miles away.

She was driving in the middle of the night, two cats sleeping in the backseat along with whatever she managed to toss into the car in her hurried departure, and pulled over immediately when I called. The grief and fear in her voice was palpable when she realized it wasn't Doc. He had talked about me so she relaxed when I explained that I was being allowed to care for him and was fully qualified to do so. I assured her he was not alone and that I would keep him as comfortable as possible. I told her that our goal was to keep him here at Walpole as long as possible versus going to the Shattuck Hospital where we feared all control and accessibility would be forfeited. Her voice changed as she thanked me, the fear replaced with a sense of purpose implying, "I'll take it from here."

Just like Doc described, Jenny had an indefatigable will and un-wavering determination that she aimed at the Massachusetts prison system hierarchy pushing through the mounds of red tape and bullshit. She had an amazing talent for getting people to do what she needed by simply not accepting no for an answer. She wrote letters and made endless phone calls. She didn't care who she had to cajole, flatter, or out maneuver. She fought for every consideration, comfort, or the removal of senseless protocol that would obstruct Doc getting the best care and the most access to her and his family that she could she finagle. She was, in a word, Impressive.

The girl that sat across from me now seemed broken. With nothing to fight for anymore, she seemed without purpose and the emotions she had set aside flooded over her. She looked at me intently, tears rolling down her cheeks, and thanked me for the other calls I managed to make with my limited funds. They always seemed to arrive, she said, at moments of extreme turmoil when she was feeling like she'd lost the battle and needed to talk to someone who knew exactly what she was up against, who knew how horrible it was to die in prison. She smiled and thanked me for encouraging her to persist even when it seemed hopeless. She told me how Doc struggled to hold on that last day until she was permitted to see him at the prescribed visiting hour and how he died shortly after they made her leave, after all rules are rules and visiting time was over. Her voice choked into a whisper as she ex-plained how he died alone while she wailed her grief outside the hospital in the falling snow. She described parking her car near the Alewife T stop in Boston when she got the call from the doc-tor who was gentle and kind and assured her that Doc stopped struggling to breathe after she left, that he surrendered to his life ending. When she mentioned the snow storm, I realized that we both must have heard the news about the same time. I was watch-ing the snow fall when the guard came to my cell to inform me Doc had passed away.

The desk sergeant came over with a roll of toilet paper and placed it next to her without saying a word. As I felt this woman unravel, I knew that somehow, we would both get through this together.

The how was a mystery.

Would anyone miss me this much? I struggled to pay attention for Jenny. I had more than enough time to contemplate my insignificance later.

Sitting in my cell that night, I thought of the pain Jenny was going through and wondered if we didn't cheat her out of precious moments she could never get back. It took extraordinary effort to dress Doc for her visits and help him down the hallway where he would pretend that he was just feeling under the weather or simply tired. After those visits with Jenny or his kids, even the guards gave him a break with the strip searches, fearing he would collapse trying to get in and out of his clothes. At least now there was no more pretending.

Jenny returned several times over the next couple of weeks, although the crying never actually subsided, we both got a better view of each other's world, hers from the outside, and mine from this strange place of isolation.

"He couldn't stop talking about you," she said, "the studying, the stories, Ken this. Ken that."

I hadn't thought of that. Here's an attractive girl with what Doc insisted was a superior mind holding on to the only thing that was left of Doc, me.   Think of the absurdity of the situation. Doc was a well- known, if not infamous, figure with a life of service and deep-rooted secrets, and I was a disgraced firefighter with my own personal demons lurking just below the surface. Why would any sane person get caught up in such a dead-end friendship, especially after what she'd just been through? A sane person would never return to a prison again as long as they lived. They'd go out and embrace life, go to the beach, fall in love again, not spend dreary afternoons in a drab visiting room talking to someone they barely knew. I convinced myself that as soon as Jenny was done grieving, she would be gone.

Learning had become my sole focus, the nourishment that fed and sustained me. Jenny could jeopardize that. Right now, though, I imagined there was no one else in her world that she could talk to about what she had just survived. I was the only one who could give her back the last months of Doc's life. She had been kept at arm's length about what he went through and she wanted to experience every moment, be privy to every thought, every word. I would acquiesce for now, but I was not about to get attached to some expectation of friendship that would leave me sad and lonely when she moved on.

When she came back for a third visit, I had to wonder. Who was this girl? What lay beyond her grief? It wasn't hard to imagine why people wanted to be around Doc. He was accomplished and brilliant. Even though I considered him my best friend, and I knew him in a way you only get to know someone when they are stripped of everything, beyond the success, wealth and respect, there was the unspoken side of Doc, the unanswered questions of exactly how he ended up here. I wondered how much he had revealed to Jenny. The unspoken topic was always avoided when it came to Doc. What did Jenny know and how would she react to a straight-forward question? Surely, she had an opinion about Doc's past.

Although I had been present for the outrageous taunts lobbed at Doc by PJ and others about his involvement in the un-solved murder of his one-time girlfriend, I had never asked Doc about it. I saw the "Forty-Eight Hour" special. Most people in prison did when the repeat episode broadcast one Friday night. But this was the land of the disgraced, the forgotten. I was not about to jeopardize my own selfish needs by broaching a subject that had the possibility of alienating Doc. But at this moment, my curiosity was getting the best of me. Besides, I had a few years in front of me and Jenny was bound to disappear anyway, so during our next visit I just asked.

"What do you think of the murder accusations?"

"We didn't discuss it," was her curt answer. "We didn't dis-cuss the past."

This much I knew was true. Doc dictated what subjects were spoken about, what parts of his life he was willing to share. She must have an opinion. Jenny was now visibly uneasy.

"I don't think we should talk about this. Our relationship was in the present. The man I knew and loved was kind, gentle, generous. I'm not going there," she said definitively.

He was my best friend and she was considering a life with

him, so it begged the question.

"What are you getting at?" she said, getting agitated.
She looked up at the clock, took a deep breath and turned back. She met my gaze and quietly asked, "Did he say something to you?"

As if perfectly timed, the announcement came over the intercom. "Visiting hours are over." Jenny stood up, hugged me, "Good luck," she said.

Self-preservation I told myself. Break the tie before she breaks you. The cruelest thing in life may actually be "Hope." What was I thinking anyway, that this beautiful woman was going to become enamored with *me*? That she would spend the next few years waiting for *me*? I thought I was done with delusional thinking, but it was still there, that wistful dreamer stirring the pot. Better to have nipped this in the bud before I ended up wasting my days thinking life had any real meaning other than the confines of my six-by-eight school room.

Funny how I fooled myself into thinking I no longer fell prey to fantasy, that my new found knowledge insulated my heart with facts and philosophy. Maybe this was my true punishment. The cruelest thing in life may actually be "Hope".

As I stared out my cell window that evening, I watched the tips of the trees that reached above the top of the west wall sway against the wind. I imagined what a tree felt like, my hand against rough bark, the crunch of dry leaves beneath my feet. I thought about all the things I no longer experienced. The feel of a steering wheel in my hands as I drove through the countryside, free to see as many trees as I wished, free to stop anywhere I wanted, to get out and walk for miles on a mountain trail, to hear the melody of a brook skipping quarter notes over rocks. To share laughter with a girl, to "touch", that lost sense of touching and being touched.

My eyes began to water as I realized how much I had been hiding, how much I had been avoiding, how much I still wanted to be a part of something, and how crippling this choice of mine was turning out to be.

WINNING BUT LOSING

Thoughts of the outside world could be negated by extreme exercise, and for me, that meant hockey.

There were more people than usual in the gym. With a seasoned edge and a chip on my shoulder, I informed the inmate who was going through the two piles of goalie equipment that he was trying on the catching glove that I use. He apologized. I pointed to the net at the far end of the gym indicating he could man that net if he wanted to test his skills.

"So that's him," said a guy in is early twenties, gesturing towards me.

We had become used to the next batch of wannabes. Every four or five weeks the populations in A-2 and A-3 turned over, supplying us with fresh enthusiasm we could crush. This night seemed different. Thoughts of Doc and the new distraction of Jenny tugged at my focus. These new guys were really good and I wasn't the only one who noticed.

"Fast and organized," said Hockey Joe, shaking his hand after having it nearly chopped off on a breakaway.

Big Steve yelled at a couple of teammates to step up. Not only were these new guys not backing down, they were taking the fight to some pretty tough characters not used to being challenged. Bodies sailed in every direction. We were being outplayed.

Normally, I could read shooters and knew exactly when to come out and cut down angles or to stay close and cover the backdoor pass, but these guys played like a coach was calling in plays from the sideline. If I didn't know better, I'd have thought someone had brought a team of young ringers in to teach us a lesson. As it turned out, that wasn't too far from the truth. At least four of these guys played on high school teams together.

"Did these guys win the state championship and celebrate by robbing a bank together?" I joked to one of the guards during a break

"Got me, but you guys are being outplayed," he said.

"No shit, Sarge," I grumbled.

When I cut off the shooter's angle, another player just appeared. Two, three quick passes left me grasping at air. When I came out to cut down the angle on the next shooter, forcing him to fire wide, the ball still ended up in the net. When it happened again, I couldn't pass it off to luck. I'd never seen anything like this. I was sure a shot would sail wide, ricocheting off the back wall, but it didn't. It just kept curving with uncanny accuracy into the net.

"Gotta play defense," panted Big Steve.

"They're too fast," said Dave the Fisherman, bent over at the waist.

Playing solid defense helped, but we were being out-shot three to one. Fortunately, they rotated goalies and none of them were very good which kept it close, but they won handily and we faced a grim reality: we were an aging team with our glory days behind us.

"You're good, Goalie," said one of the young guys, "but it won't be enough."

Big Steve and Hockey Joe said nothing.

"All good things must come to an end," said Dave the Fisherman.

I fumed. I sat on my bunk talking to myself till two in the morning, re-living every shot, every soft goal. I was sore and beaten. The old me would have devised a graceful exit listing a variety of excuses that were logical and well-rehearsed. The new me wasn't so quick to surrender. I was not going to quit on anything or anyone, and apparently, I wasn't the only one inspired by our humiliating defeat. Big Steve and Joe were already talking when I approached them in chow line in the morning.

"We need to hit' em where it hurts," said Steve.

"Hack' em in the ankles and double-team 'em against the wall," added Dave.

I was pleased by the show of team spirit, but worried about getting lugged or, worse, seriously maiming one of our opponents.

As we entered the chow line, comments were lobbed in our direction.

"Surprised you made it out of bed," jabbed one of the young bank robbers. "Time to retire old man."

Reservations turned into revenge.

We had to wait an entire week. Every day in the yard, the harassment continued. Every meal their self-satisfied jeering added more fuel to the fire. The energy in the block transformed from prison to locker room. Spontaneous strategy sessions broke out in the weight room. Specific plays were worked. The night of the rematch, several of our B players backed out of the game with the excuse they were leaving in a week and didn't need to get into a fight.

All around me people were leaving. Twenty-three months was about the limit for anyone on the semi-permanent work force, and there were only a dozen or so of us left. The new arrivals were not all that eager to join this battle. No matter. We didn't need that many players anyway; nine or ten would do, and as it turned out, that was all we could muster.

It was a tradition in hockey that during a long playoff series, an enforcer was sometimes deployed to throw off the rhythm of a well-coordinated team. The ideal enforcer was someone with more brawn than actual hockey skills. The theory being if you can't beat' em, then beat them. While our core group had legitimate hockey skills, we were hard to match in the kick-your-ass department. I was just glad that they were on my team.

The sounds of the night dominated the landscape. The reverb of bodies hitting cement. The grunt of air being forced out of the lungs as two bodies collided. The thud of a forearm coming in high velocity contact with someone's head. Big Steve slammed opponents into the air vent, the clanging exclamation point resonated long after the victim hit the floor. Hockey Joe was more subtle. Like an assassin, he accurately executed chops at the ankles or hands, the butt end of his stick to the ribs. Although a very accurate shooter from the point, he continually missed the net this night, his shots landing instead with precision on the back of someone's head, or worse, their face. Dave the Fisherman, his enormous forearms chiseled from years of pulling nets and lobster pots out of the North Atlantic, swept players from in front of the net like the Hulk.

Even I played on the edge of what I considered dirty. An opposing team member's attempt to screen my eye line was retaliated with a piercing stab from my goalie stick, or one of my full contact leg-whips that face-planted my opponent into the floor. Our go-to moves should have put all of us in the penalty box or had us ejected. The guards yelled out warnings a few times when it looked like a fight was on the verge of breaking out. Several players stumbled up the stairs holding their faces, blood streaming through their fingers. Our opponents, to their credit, never backed down. They were simply beaten down and, in the end, our goal was achieved. The score declared us winners, but even for prison, it didn't feel right. It lacked honor.

Not much was said the next few days at chow. In the yard, the talk of a rubber match circulated. The youngsters from A-2 an A-3 stated that the series was tied at one and there was still the deciding round. But when Thursday came, hockey was canceled, the excuse given there were not enough guards on duty. This tactic was regularly used to cancel the yard, gym, or the weight room. I understood it as a union thing, but this felt like a warning. There was no way this game was taking place. Some of the injuries were severe and I'm sure the guards were questioned as to how this could have been allowed. When the question of the cancellation was brought up the response was simple.

"Awesome game fellas, but that's never happening again."

I'M IN HERE

The sight of Rupert standing in my door caught me by surprise. I was focused on the finishing touches of what had become a month-long project: the construction of a cardboard piano. I had painstakingly replicated the proper distance between keys, the perfect length that separated the intervals between white and black. It was math after all.

"I could have killed you ten times over?" he warned. "You're way too comfortable around here."

"To what do I owe this honor, Sir," I rose and saluted him.

Rupert smiled and returned the salute. "Are you going to afternoon yard?"

I nodded.

"Okay, I'll see you out there."

Suddenly his face changed. The frown lines etched by thirty years of prison life returned to their well-worn scowl.

"They took your parrot. Bastards. I'd like to kill them all."

Rupert's flip-of-the-switch reaction was something I was quite used to at this point. It took very little to set off certain individuals, especially lifers. Structure and familiarity with ones' surroundings became vitally important in here. The slightest bump in the road was routinely met with the ferocity of a head on collision.

The life-size, colored origami parrot Rupert had made was important to me too. It disappeared while I was at work. No explanation given, none required. I had read the directive that brightly colored paper was now considered contraband along with all other displays of origami.

A new superintendent had been brought in and this arbitrary rule was just the beginning. She had to make her mark on the institution. Like a wildfire, she would raze long-standing directives, reducing her predecessor's framework to ashes, making way for her new era. These revolving-door politics seldom benefited the inmate proletariat.

In my position in the Property Department, I was privy to relevant changes in policy, the enemy of most inmates. Mary Anne, my boss, knew I would face a litany of requests and complaints over the implementation of said changes. I understood this but questioned the politics of certain choices and their ulterior motives.

The new Superintendent's first edict was that all members of the permanent work force were to be moved to new locations after serving two years. The lifers had been under the assumption that they could stay as long as they wanted, a deal worked out with the former Superintendent. Their anger and resentment over losing their security, as well as their single-cell status, percolated thru the unit. Things were coming to a boil. Being moved against your will was a constant reminder of your status as ward of the state.

I caught up with Rupert in the yard that afternoon.

"Last time I got moved, I smashed all my shit. My TV. Radio. You name it, I trashed it. Took me two years to replace everything. Guess I need to learn that Pause thing, you talk about."

Rupert was hoping to get transferred to Norfolk, a massive medium-security facility that housed 1800 inmates just down the road. His request did not have to be honored and he knew that. He would be without a job for quite some time, forfeiting his ability to purchase the few items necessary to making his life bearable. The three dollars-a-day he earned working at the plate shop would be hard to replace. Rupert was one of the many inmates with no outside financial or emotional support. He, like so many others, had been abandoned by family over time. People on the outside could only take so much shame, so much inconvenience. He had legitimate concerns about losing the stable routine he had come to count on.

"Don't know what I'll do if I get some idiot for a cellmate. No privacy, no nothing."

I had come to know Rupert only after he was removed from society. This Vietnam vet who had been asked to do unspeakable things in the supposed defense of his country, this man twisted by war and carnage, then returned to a world in which he no longer fit and did not understand was once a child, a teenager, a soldier.

As we walked around the track, he suddenly reached out his arm and stopped me mid-stride, his hand pressed against my chest, this hand that had taken the lives of more than one person when fueled by rage and alcohol.

"You have a good heart," he said. "You will write a great book."

His eyes locked on mine. The other inmates were forced to jog around us.

"I'm in here," he said, his eyes never wavering from mine.

"I know."

"No. Listen to me. I need *you* to know I'm in here. Do you understand? There is something left of me in here," his voice softened, his eyes piercing and pleading at the same time. "Can you tell people that?"

I nodded. Rupert's hand dropped to his side. He turned and started walking again. It felt like the heavy steel doors of the trap slamming shut as Rupert composed himself, tucking that moment of vulnerability away, maybe never to be shared again.

I understood him, but I had no answer, no words. How your true intentions could get lost. How the person you hoped one day to show the world got buried beneath your fears, your insecurities, and eventually obscured by your actions. I had no way to separate the man I had come to know from the actions that delivered him to this place. I only knew he was my friend.

When I had no answers, music saved me. Pythagoras saved me. I translated the frequencies that I absorbed in this tumultuous, violent world around me into notes, into chords. My emotions transposed within the bars of music. It was my way of coping, of releasing, of embodying what I was feeling. The chords cascaded down from the tiers above me, and took form in my hands. B Flat to F with an A in the left hand. Drift to the relative minor of D, a dissonant reminder of where I was, of the sadness I felt. I opened my note book and the words flowed effortlessly, burnt on to the pages. The bitter yet tender melodies, a reminder, that we are all in here.

The exodus of long-term residents happened at night. Some lifers, calculating they were next, chose to take matters into their own hands. Rupert, angry as he was, chose to leave with dignity, and I was proud of him for that. I would miss him. I would also honor my promise.

Our resident cook made a different choice, one he guaranteed would be worth watching. I had a perfect view of his cell, directly across from me one tier up. As the night guard walked past him, the cook looked down at me, flashing a sinister grin. He began.

He had laid out his plan in great detail to me at lunch. He would commence by stripping down naked in the middle of his cell and then cover his completely shaved body with shampoo, soap, toothpaste, shaving cream, and that musky smelling oil available for purchase in canteen only if you claimed to have converted to the Muslim faith. His body glistening in the fluorescent light as he jammed a broken plastic spoon alongside the button that controlled the flow of water to his soilet. Soon, the water overflowed from the tiny sink onto the floor. He then stuffed rolls of toilet paper, tee-shirts, underwear, packets of chili and lastly, deposited a bowel movement on the top for emphasis. He stopped for a moment and looked out the door, making sure I was still with him. He trashed his cell, tossing everything off his desk and out of his footlocker in a state of frenzied glee. After setting the stage he stood defiant in the center of his cell, the slippery combatant reveling in his glorious act of rebellion. Waiting.

"I will not comply," he yelled.

Strip away the last vestiges of dignity and choice, and the human spirit was broken. The Nazis understood this. Prisons understood this. It mattered little that I disagreed with him, I was not a lifer after all.

The Move Team, as they were so aptly named, consisted of six, large imposing guards dressed head-to-toe in full riot gear: black, visored helmet, steel-toed combat boots, heavy leather gloves, armed with both nightstick and taser. Like Stormtroopers, the Move Team emanated a robotic, soul-less energy as they marched en mass down the tier to their targeted destination. It almost seemed unfair as they charged into the cook's cell. Amazingly, all six of them fit. I was certain they weren't coming out in the same condition they went in. The cook, a fifteen-year veteran in for murder who spent most of his time teaching himself martial arts, was a formidable opponent, especially in close quarters, and particularly when he was slippery. He knew this would not end well for him. His injuries would be bloody and extensive. He would be charged with disrupting the running of an institution for a start, plus any and all other punishments resulting from injuries he inflicted on staff. Nothing good would come from this course of action. I was transfixed by the horrifying sounds of stick on bone, flesh smashed off cement. Echoes that receded into the darkness as the Move Team dragged him out of the block. I still questioned the long-term logic of this choice from both sides of the bars.

As the show came to its conclusion and the night drew in around me, I returned to the solitude of my own life, admiring my cardboard piano. I was ready to embark on my latest journey.

When I was young, I marveled at my mother as she sat at the old upright piano in the cellar of our home on Reed street. She read from what I imagined were ancient papyrus with titles like *Flight of the Bumble Bee* and *Theme from Doctor Zhivago*. She deciphered the hieroglyphics and translated their hidden meanings into the most wonderful sounds. As a younger man, I wished I could do that. There was no one to anoint me with the ability. The notes failed to align in any recognizable pattern, but I was not deterred. I knew this would be my calling. One way or another, I would play music.

As I sat in the dark, my hands resting on pieces of cardboard torn from the backs of notepads and taped together into a two-dimensional keyboard. The small spaces separating the white keys were perfectly etched into the cardboard. The black keys were slightly raised, an effect achieved by combining toothpaste and the black tar used in the plate shop. I would be forever grateful to the inmates who smuggled this out for my project. Eyes closed I checked the action of my keys. Now I would finally give music the respect it deserved. The walls melted away and were replaced by a wooden stage and the echo of an old concert hall. Scales gave way to familiar chords.

Pythagoras spoke to me in the dark.

"Everything is numbers, Ken. *Everything* is numbers."

The mathematical ratio between the length of the piano string and its resulting frequency vibrated under my sensitized fingertips as they hungrily worked their way up and down the keyboard, each resonating note seeking out its mathematically pre-destined companions. I knew the sound because I knew the math. The equation expanded; the music of the universe in partnership with one of its enraptured occupants unfolded in pure silence. I was lost in creation.

"Baxter!" I looked up, blinded by the night guard's flashlight.

"What the hell are you doing now?"

"I'm playing the piano."

"In the dark?"

"Yes."

"Well, turn the fucking light on. How can you play the piano in the dark?"

Several weeks later I returned from work to find my cell being tossed by new recruits in a training session. Cells were picked randomly and everything systematically torn apart. I was forced to stand, back against the wall per protocol, and watch as my room was dismantled. Two recruits flipped my mattress upside down, heaped my sheets on the floor, and branded them with boot marks. One of the recruits zealously dumped the contents of my footlocker, shaking loose my journal and notes for my book which floated in the air like giant confetti. It would take me hours to put them back in order. To my silent horror, the younger of the two recruits snatched my piano and then kicked a path through the scattered objects stomping out of the room. He smirked at me as he stood there, tearing up my companion, octave by octave, stuffing the once beautiful Steinway into a garbage bag along with the neck of a cardboard Fender guitar I had been constructing. I didn't mind losing the guitar so much as it was only a prototype. The neck was too flimsy and it felt awkward in my hands. But my piano was everything.

Anger burned in my heart. "You don't know me," I hissed in my mind. "Don't smile at me."

Just then the sergeant barked at the smug recruit.

"Don't smile at him! You don't know anything about him. That's not what this is about. They're in prison. That's the punishment. Get it! Do your job."

"Yes sir!" came the chastened reply and the smirk disappeared from the young recruit's face only to reappear on mine.

"Don't let me catch you smiling, Baxter," reprimanded the sergeant. With that, the ordeal was over.

As I was cleaning up my room, the sergeant appeared at my door. "Sorry, Baxter, can't play favorites. It's a random search."
"I know. Thanks."

My ability to place a *pause* was well-practiced, besides I had more pressing matters. My transfer would be coming soon. My next stop unknown. New surroundings. New roommates. A whole new set of challenges. I felt the butterflies in my stomach, a sensation that used to bother me. Now, it was a sign of opportunity as Doc would say. "Embrace the uncomfortable. Welcome the unknown. Create your own circumstance!"

Doc's words were about to be tested.   I focused on what I could learn and how I could grow. Music was gone for now. However, melodies were stored, waiting for an opportunity, the right circumstance. Dreams for another day. For now, I was in here. Right in the middle of this Chaotic Operetta.

The following days brought few surprises as the exodus continued. Only a few lifers remained and the rest of us were soon to follow. I didn't even recognize most of the new guys and didn't care. Dave the Fisherman was going to Baystate, a medium facility, and Hockey Joe was off to Pondeville, the minimum. Joe easily had as much time left as I did, so I began to think a minimum was a possibility, brightening my future. There was no way to hide my disappointment when Mary Anne asked me to stay a few more months to help with an upcoming audit in Property. My intimate knowledge of the ins and outs of the filing system would prove an invaluable asset, assuring the department was in compliance. The second request played on my ego. The Maintenance Sargent requested my expertise to ensure the prison was up to code in terms of their fire preparedness plan, exit strategies and the like. It was pointed out that they didn't have to ask me, that the request was a gesture of respect really not due an inmate. The irony of an arsonist planning fire exit strategies was not lost on any us. So, with absurdities aside, I agreed.

As the days passed, I found myself returning to the memory of the hockey game in my spare moments. Something about the game still bothered me. We were better than that, or at least we could have been. I hated that statement now. Could-have-been-should-have-been. The problem was there was virtually no team left. The latest arrivals wanted no part of the hockey nightmare when it was reinstated after a few weeks cooling off period. A-2 and A-3 had plenty of guys to fill two teams so they continued without us. On the last Thursday before Hockey Joe and Dave the Fisherman were slated to leave, I stopped by Joe's room and made a pitch. In honor of his departure, I would be willing to go downstairs and play one last time.

Joe smiled. "Me and you against A-2 and A-3?"

"We could just join in. No one would say a word."

"Not without me," came a voice from behind us. Big Steve had seriously tweaked his Achilles on the running track, but he was game.

Dave the Fisherman made an abrupt about face and headed back to his cell when he saw the three of us standing together, mumbling under his breath about quitting when you're on top.

Sitting on my bunk attempting to stretch, I felt like an aging veteran at the end of a long season. Sore and tired, knee and elbow still swollen, and yet, I was enveloped by this overwhelming sense of pride that only comes from finishing something difficult. The prospect of seeing something through and giving everything I had, and maybe just a little bit more. This pursuit resonated with me like a well strummed chord. Funny how I never strived for this level of achievement in life before now.

The three of us walked in silence down the corridor, dressed for combat. The rest of A-1's residents jostled down the hall towards the weight room, the prescribed activity for the evening. Moving as fast as possible without breaking into a run, they walk-raced to be sure they secured their desired weight machine first.

"Gluttons for punishment or confused heroes," questioned the C.O. as we filed down the stairs.

Most of what I was wearing was contra band from my hand-sewn elbow and knee pads down to my molded soup cover cup. A new guard looked to his sergeant with confusion as I approached him for the obligatory pat down.

"It's just Baxter," said the sarge. "We try to ignore him."

LOSING AND WINNING

It was a warm spring night. This would be the last hockey game we played at Walpole. But more than that it would be the last time I would ever be engaged in something this competitive. Probably the last time I would play a sport this violent and intense. We had come together as a unified team. As I approached the top of the stairs, I felt a hand on my shoulder.

"Didn't think I'd let my team down, did you?" It was Dave the Fisherman.

Big Steve smiled. "Let's do this."

Beads of moisture trickled down the cement walls as we descended the stairs into the belly-of-the-whale arena. I saw fifteen guys from A-2 and A-3 milling around, the core hockey team of young bank robbers were among them. Two guys were already putting on the goalie equipment. Hockey Joe walked up to one of them. "You're wearing my goalie's gear. Take it off."

Stunned, the inmate looked around not sure what to do. One of the guards nodded, "You heard the man, take it off."

From the other end of the gym, several sticks tapped the floor in unison echoing the guard's order. This sign of respect filled me with an unexpected pride. I reached behind me in an awkward attempt to strap on my goalie pads.

"I got this. Kneel down." Hockey Joe pulled the last strap tight.

"You ready for this?"

All I could think of was this was our "Rudy" moment. Meanwhile Big Steve was sorting out the teams.

"You can't play with four guys, that's ridiculous," one of the bank robbers argued.

As I handed my glasses to the guard he said, "remember the first time you handed me these?"

"Or tried to," I laughed.

"You've come a long way, Baxter." He carefully placed my glasses into his shirt pocket. "Do I need to remind you that if I see anything resembling the last time you guys were down here, I won't hesitate to pull the plug on this."

"Yes, sir," I said as I turned towards the net.

"Hey, Goalie" came an unfamiliar voice. It was Timlen, a C.O. that I don't believe I had ever shared more than a single-word response with over the past two years.

"Yes?" I said, anticipating another stern warning.

He smiled and whispered under his breath, "kick their ass."

I spun on my heels and launched into one of my trademark cartwheels. At 51, I could still do a cartwheel in full goalie gear.

Big Steve had worked out a compromise. We took a young

kid from A-3 who was arbitrarily yanked from his position leaning against the moldy wall. He looked horrified at being drafted. Steve informed our reluctant teammate that he would occupy a spot to my right and play defense.

"We'll take care of the rest. Don't fuck up." The kid just nodded, eyes wide, lips drawn in a tight line.

I thought I should say something important, make an inspirational speech, but the only thing that came to mind was "And into the valley of death rode the three hundred." This elicited nothing but blank stares.

"There's only four of us, you fucking idiot," said Dave the Fisherman. I looked around at my teammates.

"I will die for you guys tonight."

"You'd better," said Hockey Joe as he tapped my pads with his stick. "Let's do this."

The game started with a polite speed totally absent from our last match. There was no hacking, no slamming bodies off the wall, no violent collisions intended to maim. We played clean. More importantly, we played honorably which clearly favored our opponents. Individually, we were better. Steve was the dominant force whenever the play came his way. Dave was the immovable object in front of their net with a sniper's eye for scoring goals. Hockey Joe simply never stopped moving. He was, in a word, everywhere. Back on defense, charging the net, scoring with blazing slap shots, Hockey Joe fully embodied his name. And me, well I was having the best game of my life. I played with my normal reckless abandon, with a desperate enthusiasm, blindly snagging 100 mph shots from the point snow coned in my glove, or kicked out toe saves. Luck was also on our side. Shots ricocheted off my face mask that I never saw coming. Unfortunately, it wasn't enough. They were just too good. The fact that they could substitute players at will was taking its toll on us. In one horrifying moment, I took a shot from point blank range off my throat which I was sure had crushed my trachea.

Hockey Joe shouted, "Time out," as he came running over.

"I'm all right," I gasped, handing him the ball that somehow ended up in my glove.

"I don't give a shit about you," he barked. "Take your helmet off and lay down like your dead. I need to breathe."

Big Steve huffed, "Tie the ball up when you get a chance, I'm dying."

The game was still tight at this point. We were down by a goal and it was the closest we had been all night.

"I'm sorry," I whispered. "I'm doing the best I can."

"Don't you fucking apologize," panted Hockey Joe. "This is the best you've ever played."

"I can do more, let me come up bit on the point," offered Dan, the new guy.

It turned out Dan was a good defenseman. He angled himself into every play he could from the position Big Steve has assigned him to, never going more than twenty feet from my right side. Big Steve nodded his permission, too tired or angry to come up with a different strategy.

I was relieved that smashing our opponents into walls didn't get brought up as an option. I wanted to do this straight up, honorable, no matter how much it was killing us.

During our not so fake injury timeout, our opponents brought in a fresh goalie. I was so drenched from the stifling heat; I could wring out my shirt. My eyes stung from the sweat. I loved it. I loved every moment of it.

Dan ignited our offense, taking a drop pass from Big Steve which he drilled into the top corner of the net. But the next time he tried it, it turned into a three-on-one breakaway that left me flailing at air when the third pass found an open net. Once again, they held on to the lead. One of our opponent's favored plays was to charge forward, drop a pass back to the point, and then head for the net either screening me or hoping to pick up a rebound. It worked more than once because as I said, these guys were good. They managed to curve that ball around me with unnatural accuracy and I just couldn't get out there quick enough. Hockey Joe could only cover one guy at a time and no one in their right mind was going to stand in front of a blazing slap shot in their gym shorts.

Hockey Joe however, did exactly that. As the shooter drilled the ball toward our net, he ran directly into the line of fire. The sound of the slap shot ricocheting off his bare shin bone brought a collective gasp from the entire gym. Caught completely off guard, the shooter faltered as Hockey Joe picked up the rebound and headed towards their net. A quick head fake left the new goalie standing there looking foolish as Joe politely deposited the ball behind him.

Even a guard yelled out, "Are you "friggin' kidding me?"

A few shots later Big Steve, in an effort not to be out done, slid directly in front of a shot. To witness a six-foot-six man slid-ing across the floor in a deliberate attempt to block a shot was in a word inspiring. Un-fucking believable. That was it. On the next shot on net, I held onto the ball until everyone gathered around.

"I will not let a single shot by me," I vowed. "On my life, nothing catches twine for the rest of the game. Go to the net. Take it to them. Don't worry about me."

Losing with honor was one thing. But winning with honor would be spectacular.

Dave the Fisherman reached out bare-handed and caught a slap shot mid-flight, tossing it ahead to young Dan who barreled in alone for his second goal. Even Dan took a shot off his right ear when he dove behind me helping seal my promise of no goals for the remainder of the game.

Our opponents were simply unprepared to make that level of physical sacrifice. Their polished persona fell away as we piled on goal after goal, blocked shot after blocked shot. Big Steve took a slap shot to the thigh and simply flipped the ball back to the shooter.

"Try again," he nodded, which he did, striking Steve square-ly in the shin, drawing blood.

I looked around me at the battlefield intensity of our team trying to slow time down so I could take every second in. Never again in my life time would I be a part of something like this.

When the guard shouted time, we simply walked off the floor. No arm-raised cheers. No celebratory high-fives. It was as if we were saying "What did you expect? This is who we are." And therein lay the contradiction. Just when I thought I understood the mind of an inmate, I was confounded. We could have beat the Boston Bruins on that night. Well, maybe not, but we would have had them on the run.

"Kind of makes you wonder, doesn't it, Baxter? Different time, different place. Who knows..." said the guard handing me my glasses.

"I'm just getting started, Sarge," I smiled.

"You're going to be all right, Baxter."

"Ya, everyone keeps saying that."

Back on the block, we had our movie ending. A slow-motion walk down the flats, the four of us, battered, bruised, bleeding, basking in the afterglow of an impossible victory. Straight out of "The Right Stuff". At least that's the way I'll always remember it.

The following days brought the real Stanley Cup Finals and, wouldn't you know it, our beloved Boston Bruins, coming from behind taking game seven in Vancouver. The victory set off a late-night celebration that rocked Walpole to its foundation. When the final buzzer sounded, the applause from hundreds of inmates locked in their cells echoed thru the night for what must have been miles.

I jumped up and down pounding my screened window screaming, "Nicholai! Nicholai!" as if he could somehow hear me in Los Angeles. I knew he would be watching. I just wanted someone to share it with, to share anything with. As I was yelling out the window, spotlights from the guard towers swung wildly across the yard, not because someone was trying to escape, but because the lonely night guards on tower duty had no one to share the moment with either. I started to cry.

I was both happy and sad. Everything at once fell out of me. I couldn't stop it. Every moment of the last few years came tumbling out of my hidden corners. I had never felt more human. In that moment, my empty cell filled with every event of the last few years. I could feel Doc, and then Alex and Nicholai. I sat with them and I cried. I felt so much loss and so much hope all tangled up together, and then it was over. I was made new. I had crossed some hidden barrier and the choice was mine: the safety of what I know, or the place beyond the wall without footprints. The choice was clear. It was time to embrace whatever came next.

The following day Jenny returned. I thought she would be long gone after our last uncomfortable visit. She made it quite clear we were never to discuss Doc's past again or she would not return. I quickly agreed. There was something different about her now, or maybe I was seeing things differently, either way, there was a dynamic change. She told me that Doc had asked her to watch out for me and that she would continue to do this for as long as she could to make my life here a little easier. Doc had asked me to make the same promise to take care of her. At the time, it seemed like the desperate plea of a dying friend.

For now, that promise would remain intact. As I looked at this woman sitting across from me, hands folded in her lap, trying hard to keep her tears at bay, I think we both knew this was the beginning of something new, scary, uncertain, bizarre, but new.

New was good.

THE THIN LINE

Prison was full of guys with hair-trigger tempers, armed with an eye-for-an-eye mentality, and cursed by shortsightedness. It didn't take me that long to understand how this perfect storm of challenges landed them in Walpole. There were a few who were more refined in both their emotional restraint and their criminal behavior incarcerated here due to an unfortunate miscalculation. It was the rare inmate who understood exactly where they went wrong and took responsibility for their poor choices and the often-devastating outcomes. Bruce, my next-door neighbor, was the latter.

Bruce was in his late sixties and basically kept to himself. When I first moved onto A-1, it took several weeks before he decided I was worth even saying good morning to. Over time, our conversations expanded to the occasional "alright."

The "alright" comment was one of my favorite prison rituals. Pronounced "ah-rite," it was not used as a response to a greeting. It was more of a formalized response employed anytime someone made eye contact with you. It was both the" query and the response," kind of like "Aloha." If you were on good terms with someone, the "ah-rite" would be accompanied by the short fist tap, right fist only though. Some prison protocols remained a mystery to me.

Bruce knew that I had experience regarding health-related issues from being a first responder, so he viewed me as someone with something to offer. He was a mild hypochondriac with an impressive collection of medical journals accumulated over the last 30 years. I asked him what he was researching.

"The only way I am leaving this place is in a body bag. I just want to know what I'm going to die from."

This was depressing, but I admired his resolve.

When he slammed down several large copies of *The American College of Physician's Complete Home Medical Guide* on my desk and invited me to give him my assessment, I took it as a compliment.

"You've done a great deal of highlighting," I said.
"I think you've narrowed down your demise to just about everything short of Dengue Fever."

The self-diagnosis sections of these books helped the reader connect the dots of their symptoms to any fatal illness imaginable. In Bruce's case however, he was justified in his fears. Prison can take a toll on your health. Having been here for half his life, Bruce had become the prison's jack-of-all-trades. You'd find him everywhere, changing lightbulbs, painting doors, unclogging drains, or buffing floors, anything to keep himself busy. Inevitably, he would find his way to the kitchen and never failed to come back to his cell without something to eat: chocolate chip cookies, chicken breasts wrapped in cellophane, pizza from the staff kitchen, blueberry muffins, or my favorite, fresh fruit. I would be sitting on my bunk writing in my journal or trying to solve some elaborate checkmate -in- two chess scenario when an orange would land on my bunk, expertly thrown there through the small opening in my door. The air vent near the ceiling indirectly connected our cells, allowing me to hear him reveling in delight as he unloaded the night's haul onto his bunk to feast while watching some World War II movie in black and white. Bruce did his best to be happy despite his circumstances. He had accepted his lot in life, and at this point as he edged in on 70, simply wanted to be prepared for how his journey would end. I spent several weeks explaining each and every highlighted passage to him.

After a few of these sit-downs together, Bruce began to tell me stories about his life.

"I was a professional house mover; I could move anything."

He described step-by-step the blocking systems, the hydraulic lifts, the truck suspensions and load bearing capabilities, jacking techniques, the precision required in measuring angles and support points.

"You got to be up on power lines and bridges. Got to know how to navigate them with big loads."

Bruce obviously took great pride in his profession. His current job seemed to be navigating the precarious load on his body and immune system: Hepatitis C, diabetes, chronic kidney disease, high blood pressure, diverticulitis, and MRSA. He was certain his cornucopia of symptoms added up to a cancer diagnosis, or maybe some rare blood disorder.

"I think I show signs of bi-polar disorder and schizophrenia too."

Bruce was an overachiever. I think my expert opinion only added kindling to his funeral pyre. I couldn't with any confidence rule out any of these conditions.

Bruce knew where he would die. He also knew few people would care. His cell would be unceremoniously cleaned out, his stuff packed away for the allotted sixty days when it would then be donated, destroyed, or stolen, not necessarily in that order. The state would reluctantly conduct a simple funeral which more than likely no one would attend and that would be that for Bruce.

One day after returning from work, I saw Bruce sitting at the table outside his room mumbling under his breath.

"What's got you going today, Bruce?" I asked.

"These fuckin' kids. All they do is complain. Their girlfriends don't visit enough. Their families don't send enough money. There's not enough microwaves, not enough showers."

His eyes grew wild as he ramped up over the complaints for more TV stations, less count times.

"Shut the fuck up! It's prison!" he banged his fist on the table.

Everyone was looking as his rant continued. Bruce didn't miss a beat.

"Don't sit outside my cell and complain about your pathetic lives or how you got smoked in court."

"Tell em' how you really feel," I said.

He laughed "I'm just venting, Kenny. You know how it is. No one's got any respect around here anymore."

"What did you watch last night, Bruce?" I asked hoping to distract him from his outburst.

He looked at me, and in the calmest voice said, "I shot them both."

"In fifteen years of marriage, I never asked for nothing. You want a divorce; I can't stop you. All I ask is that you treat me with respect. Just wait until it's done before you shack up with someone. That's all I asked."

Bruce went on to describe how he came home from work and found his wife doing some guy in their bed.

"I shot them both. that's what I did, there's nothing to complain about now. She made a choice. I made a choice. You want a chocolate chip cookie, Ken?"

I was never sure why Bruce chose this particular moment to reveal this bit of information.

Bruce committed his crime in America where the punishment for spousal elimination bought you a life sentence. Doc used to muse that we didn't learn as kids how to deal with our feelings. "We spend more time teaching children to tie their shoes then to deal with their emotions."

"Can't teach what you don't understand," I would say.

Humans excel at creating personal dramas to justify the level of difficulty they believe their lives warrant. So, they feel important, alive. Amplify this tendency with illegal or prescription drugs and alcohol and you have the recipe that created my neighbor Bruce. There are endless Bruces out there. They live next door to you; they are related to you. These individuals are not aberrations, they are your friends, your co-workers. We like to pretend they are other people.

Often, they are us.

THE THINNER LINE

I don't remember why I went to the house that day.

I was building a post and beam on a stunning ten-acre lot overlooking the Quabin Region in Barre, Massachusetts, that I never did get to live in. As I turned into the driveway, I was greeted by a huge white sailboat blocking my way. Nicholai told me he went sailing with one of his mom's new boyfriends, and as much as this betrayal stung, I knew this was inevitable. After all, my wife of fifteen years was attractive and a free-agent. In fact, her latest boyfriend was someone I had gone to school with. I could only imagine the pillow-talk conversation that led to him storing his boat in what was still my driveway, at least until her divorce lawyer had his way. As I skidded to a dusty stop, I imagined him telling his friends how much effort he put into maneuvering that monstrosity down those narrow country roads far away from any sailable body of water just for the sheer pleasure of gloating that he had won my wife's affections.

As I got out of my truck, I caught sight of another vehicle parked off to the side of the house, yet another invasion of my territory.

I tasted acid in my mouth and a familiar feeling came over me. It was just like when I was ten years old and smashed Davy Johnson in the head with a minnow bucket. I was tired of fishing and wanted to let my half of the minnows go, and he tried to stop me. I swung the bucket and hit him squarely on his head. It was never spoken about again. After all, boys were boys.

I pushed the front door open and heard murmuring voices coming from the upstairs bedroom. I grabbed the first object available and started up the stairs. To think I came here to tell Joy that I was ready to grow up and be an adult. To be a better father to our boys. My feet didn't touch the steps. I emerged into the bedroom, where I had made love to my wife underneath the skylights I installed so we could look at the stars together and talk about the future. An uncontrollable rage flashed thru my synapses.

There was nobody there. Nobody hiding in the bathroom or

cowering at the back of the closet. Just a table radio playing. The sun was shining down on to the bed. I was shocked back to reality, squinting from the glaring reflection off the forty-one-inch blade of my ivory-handled Katana Sword. It fit perfectly in my hand, an extension of my arm. This deadly instrument had been leaning against the wood stove. No one was here, but I could feel their energy, like some radio-active half-life emanating from the bed. Without thinking, without the benefit of Aristotle and Socrates to talk me down, I flipped the sword over in a reverse attack position and with the greatest of ease I jumped and landed on the bed, driving the sword through both futon mattresses, bed frame, and two inches into the carpeted floor. I bowed a reverent goodbye to my razor-sharp companion, turned and walked out of the house.

Dazed, I made my way towards my truck, pausing momentarily by the sailboat to contemplate whether I should puncture a couple of holes into the hull. I started to l laugh at myself as I realized there was no honor in that. As I drove away a car was coming in the opposite direction and even though it was far away, I could tell it was Joy. She saw me too and slowed her car, rolling down the side window. I hit the gas and never acknowledged her. My petulance was read loud and clear. I was done. I was done with everything. I was done trying. I was done pretending. This marked the exact moment of my downward spiral, the day I gave up on life. I continued down the road, turned left, and then left again. It didn't matter anymore. Eventually, I reached the water. All roads led to the reservoir out here. It dominated the landscape and demanded your awe. But on that day, I saw nothing. I got out of my truck, dropped to my knees, and cried uncontrollably. Would I have killed them? Call it temporary insanity, call it a crime of passion. But yes, had they been there, it would have been over in seconds, for him anyway. How much vengeance would I have been capable of channeling? To what depth would my rage have blinded me? I would never know. The moment came and was gone.

It was weeks before I could bring myself to talk to Joy and when I did, it was with angry words chosen to inflict maximum pain. That was another benefit of knowing someone so well. You knew exactly how to hurt them. My words hit so close to their target that she picked up a large jar of quarters, throwing the jar with all her might at the back of my head. I recognized the sound of shifting change in the jar and was able to spin quick enough to shatter the jar with my forearm. Quarters sprayed everywhere like metallic confetti. My arm was sore to the touch for weeks.

Sometime later when calmer minds prevailed, I asked her whether she realized that she could easily have killed me.

"I knew you could block it," was her sole defense, and we never spoke of it again.

Bruce placed his gun on the kitchen table, called the police, and sat patiently. I left my sword deep in our marital bed and drove away. A thin line at best separated the two of us.

THE WAY BACK HOME

The last time I was awoken at 4:30 in the morning by the sound of a cell door opening, it was Doc leaving and that didn't work out so well. When *my* door opened, I was unprepared for the adrenaline rush that instantly flooded my brain with a multitude of possibilities.

"Baxter, you're going to court."

"Why?"

"Don't know. Get moving."

I couldn't for the life of me think of a reason why I would be going to court. I exited my cell. I noticed Reggie coming out of his on the third tier. He was a street-hardened middle weight boxer from Worcester who had a shot at a serious career but was derailed by a hair trigger temper. I was annoyed that he had chosen the exact same outfit I was wearing for his own court appearance. Gray pullovers with the large letters D.O.C written on the back.

Reggie ran a store on the block. A store was an unauthorized place you could buy food items. Technically, stores were illegal, but like most things in prison, there was always a way around.

Doc used to say that going to the store was not only financially stupid, but a lost opportunity to practice my will power. Since I had the bad habit of devouring all of my canteen within two days, I found myself at Reggie's doorstep more often than I cared to admit.

Reggie also played left field for our softball team. We had endless discussions about him hitting the cut-off man instead of trying to throw every runner out at home plate from two hundred and eighty feet away. It's not that he couldn't, he had a cannon for an arm, but much like his life, he had terrible aim and a poor choice of direction.

"We're going for our *Revise and Revoke*," mumbled Reggie half asleep.

To a new inmate, *Revise and Revoke* were golden words dangled at the end of a stick promising the proverbial last straw of hope that the miscarriage of justice would be set right and their freedom restored. In reality, *Revise and Revoke* was nothing more than a courtroom charade to chalk up billable hours for lawyers and allow judges the facade of genuine consideration of the rights of the poorly represented.

I hadn't been out in the world since I arrived here sixteen months ago.

The prospect of a van ride filled me with excitement. My anticipation was quickly dashed when I climbed into the cage-like vehicle that allowed for very little movement or line of sight beyond the metal mesh that surrounded me. My stomach flipped at every sharp turn that flung Reggie and me in tandem from one side of the van to the other. Our shackles made it impossible to brace ourselves. I was reminded of family trips and being packed away like luggage in the way back of the family station wagon holding my queasy stomach and fearing my father's punishment if I vomited.

Ed the Lawyer had set me straight nearly two years earlier. This was not a new trial. This was merely a procedure to ensure that all facets of our sentencing were within legal guidelines.

Reggie was in on an eight -year bid for a probation violation on a charge that was dropped.

"How is that even possible?" I asked.

"My prosecutor was a jerk. He kept managing to push off the hearing to make the original charge stick. It's the same guy that put you in here for seven years," Reggie said laughing. "It's why we're here at the same time. You didn't know that?"

"No," I said, now concerned.

"He's here trying to get you a longer sentence."

Now, I had no illusion of going home on this day, but if I remembered correctly, this prosecutor didn't like me very much.

"He doesn't like anyone," said Reggie. "None of his colleagues like him either."

I did remember that. After you went to court a few times, and especially if you arrived early, you got to see the lawyers and prosecutors hanging out together laughing, joking, trying to impress each other. Everyone except our prosecutor who was shunned by the others. Once the Judge came in it was much like professional wrestling where both sides went to their prospective corners and came out swinging at the sound of the gavel, feigning disdain for each other. If my life wasn't on the line, I might have actually found it amusing. But this particular prosecutor stuck with me. He was so angry.

After being deposited in a holding cell, Reggie was taken before the three-judge panel. I sat patiently waiting my turn. My mind drifted to my original trial. My court appointed lawyer Vinny had little or no experience, or so it seemed, in any aspect of criminal law other than what he might have learned on TV.

As Vinny approached the bench to begin his opening statement, his feet started moving on their own, slowly at first. His left foot would go left and the right would follow, then the left would go forward and the right would follow. The right would go right, the left would then reciprocate until he was back where he started. The process would repeat faster each time until he was literally doing the fox trot. The jurors were the first to notice. Their faces contorted as it became apparent that he couldn't stop himself. I was hoping he just had to go to the bathroom, but I soon realized that he was having a bout of extreme anxiety and it was getting worse. The prosecutor fiddled with his neck tie as this was clearly not normal and tried to look away, but he couldn't. No one could. It was in a word: mesmerizing.

The bailiff that was standing behind me leaned over apologetically, and said, "You're going to prison."

I knew I was going to prison. That was the plan. But this? This was embarrassing. As far as the jurors knew, I hired this guy. He was a reflection of me. Even the judge leaned out over from his perch for a better view. I could hear the benches behind me squeaking as civilians jockeyed for better position. Vinny spun on his heels and headed back toward me. I wanted to hide under the table because instinctively, I knew what was coming, and then he said it. "I get a little nervous."

"Are you kidding me? That's right out of the movie. That's exactly what the lawyer said in the movie." The Judge slammed his gavel because you're not supposed to speak out loud. "You know what I'm talking about," I said louder, pointing right at him. "That was right out of *My Cousin Vinny,*" I almost thought the judge was going to answer me, because he did know. I saw it in his eyes.

The judge pounded his gavel again as the jury had begun talking among themselves. They hadn't heard a single word he said. An early recess was called and that was all the relevance those days would ever have. I never gave them much thought beyond that one paradoxical moment.

Sitting in the holding cell, the comedy of that court room faded. I began to wonder why I had found all of that so funny. As a writer, I was learning about what lies beneath the story I was telling, to dig deeper into what I was truly avoiding, what was too painful to face. The reality of the unknown was frightening to me. The prosecutor, though small in stature, seemed largely driven by anger, an anger made worse by my nervous smile. Looking back, it must have infuriated him.

Nietzsche said: Beware of those where the tendency to punish is strong. The court room on that day seemed thick with the power of the dark side. On several occasions, I had to hold back the desire to yell out, "I'll take the plea deal."

I focused all my thoughts on Alex. Remember why you're here, I told myself. Remember the punishment you deserve. Alex is dead because of you. Think of your son's face, hear his voice, tear yourself from the fabric of your life for his sake. Humor was my crutch, a foil to help me stay the course. When humor fell short, I began to hum the melody to a song, a song about my cousin Vinny. The lyrics came into focus: *"I loved a movie called my cousin Vinny, made me want to marry Marisa Tomei. How can you blame me she's just so damn pretty and I... well I'm just a guy that can't say good bye."*

"Mr. Baxter, Mr. Baxter," came a voice from the slot in the door.

"What?" I said, caught off guard by the intrusion.

It was him. Again. Vinny, the fox trotting, lawyer from my trial.

"What the hell?" I said, "What are you doing here?"

"It's your *Revise and Revoke* hearing. I'm here to represent you."

"Represent me?" I panicked. The vision of him laying out an ineffective defense horrified me.

"How are you doing?" he asked stepping away from the door. "You look very fit."

"I don't need your help." I exclaimed.

Vinny took an additional step back, correctly sensing the hostility in my voice. I could read his mind as if it were an open comic book. I was becoming more like The Hulk than Bruce Banner.

In the court room, Vinny shuffled through papers nervously. He eyed my wrist bracelets making sure they were securely in place. I watched the prosecutor. The same prosecutor from my original trial. He seemed even shorter, and frailer as if the world had taken its toll on him. I believe he was wearing the same suit. I nodded politely to the three judges that were seated a little too high up off the floor than appeared necessary. All of this seemed so different than I remembered. This time I was not intimidated. I was empowered. I realized how far I had moved forward. I wouldn't trade places with anyone in this court room for all the honey buns on A block.

However, my new perspective was short lived. The prosecutor was screaming something about my sentence being too short. I needed to act. I needed to take matters into my own hands.

"Your Honors," I said. "I want to go home."

Vinny turned to me, "I don't think they're letting you go home today."

"I mean Walpole. I want to go back to Walpole and finish my sentence."

I could handle that. The courtroom was where the real danger lied. Much to the dismay of the prosecutor, my wish was instantly granted. I was never so happy to be shackled and tossed around in the back of the transport van as it brought me closer to home and the comfort of my cell locked away from Vinny and the vindictive prosecutor. My sentence intact, I slept deeply.

MY FIRST PRISON

One day, the attic door was opened and I was thrust inside. The door slammed behind me and I couldn't open it no matter how hard I tried. I told myself it wasn't real. I screamed and no one came. I ran my hands along the walls in a frantic search for the light switch. I flicked it on and off a thousand times without receiving the light I so desperately desired. Would light even help? I crumbled to the floor, pressed against the door at the bottom of the stairs, sobbing uncontrollably.

Our attic in the three-decker on Shirley Street where I lived was accessible from our back porch. The door did not lock and the stairs that led up to this forbidden world would normally be irresistible to an explorer such as myself. I was shown it once, the dusty stairs that led up. All I saw were the tip of those boots at the top of the stairs and was told I was never, ever, to go up there. The rest of the monster was cloaked in darkness. I was informed that he stood guard night and day over the treasures of the attic and he would not hesitate to defend its entry against anyone, especially a child. He was neither ghost nor beast, simply Boot -Man. The door was slammed shut; no locks required. The mere mention of Boot Man would start me crying much to the delight of my family. They seemed almost proud of this soulless creature that lived but inches above our heads.

"Shouldn't we call the police?" I would ask.

"No policemen in their right mind would go up there," would be the response followed by a sinister laugh. Even my mother joined in. Convinced, I imagined, that it was all for my own good. Anytime I got out of line or complained, "We'll feed you to Boot Man" was all that was needed to be said. At night I could hear him walking the floors above me, laughing. Even the monsters of my closet were afraid of the Boot Man.

After a time, my eyes started to adjust, one by one the steps came into view, and there he was, Boot Man. The boots started down the stairs. Chips of paint lodged underneath my finger nails as I clawed at the door of my prison.

I closed my eyes not wanting to see what was coming next. He was behind me. The stairs creaked under his weight. His breath fanned the back of my neck, and then it happened. He did not attack me or claw at me. He went in me. Every ounce of evil and pain became me. I sensed his thoughts. I saw his clenched fist. I heard his rage. and I was consumed by his horror, and then it ended.

Was any of this true? I don't know anymore. Real or imagined, I thought of monsters or ghosts as an imprint left on this world if they did exist at all. The electrical signature left behind, all very explainable, all non- threatening. However, as a four-year-old, I was pushed too far, exposed too soon to an unresolved horror, and it opened a door to something.

Boot Man was as real to me as any memory in my life. I will never understand why someone threw me in with him that day. What level of evil is required to do such a thing to a four-year-old? Some things are simply unexplainable.

You would think that if an imprint of someone's existence would be left anywhere surely prison cells would be high on the list. Think of Walpole and its long history of Boot Men. The occupants, and the crimes that put them here.

The notorious past of Stanley Ray Bond, a bank robber who would perish here. Tom Manning, the United Freedom Front leader responsible for bombings of United States military bases finally jailed after killing a police officer. Albert DeSalvo better known as The Boston Strangler paced his existence away in one of these cells. Richard Colvin Reid, the shoe bomber. Joseph

Druce, a common criminal who became famous for murdering his fellow inmate. The infamous and disgraced priest, Father John Geoghan, who molested half of Boston's children before finally being caught. Tony Costa, who killed three Cape Cod women and met a bloody and violent end to his own life at the hands of his fellow inmates. John Salvii, the Planned Parenthood murderer in Brookline, Massachusetts also had his life ended by a suspicious suicide. The list was endless. Many a criminal would argue over their deservability to make this list. In fact, many of my current breakfast companions who would meet their end in here one way or another, were far more interesting to me than these famous occupants of the past.

The Craig's List Killer, aka Philip Markof, was responsible in most inmates' minds not for the girl who he lured to her death, but for the fact that because of him we were no longer allowed to have garbage bags in our cells. Philip figured out how to take his life correctly after two failed attempts. Brandishing a sharp object of his making he slashed his legs and ankles wrapping them in garbage bags to contain the flow of blood long enough to bleed out. He followed this with cutting his neck and swallowing toilet paper (to avoid being resuscitated) and finally pulled the covers up over his head, which he had wrapped in yet another bag to suffocate himself. The body contains about five liters or one and a half gallons of blood which would have otherwise been noticed during rounds. Our only concern was not for a tortured life gone astray, or for the victim or her family but for the new memo sent out that inmates were not allowed to have multiple wastepaper bags in their cells. Not that we required them, but no one liked something taken away from them for any reason, justified or not. So many of the rules in prison were implemented after an incident altered current policy regarding everything from clothing to visits to what you could or could not have in your cell. You name it, sooner or later someone would screw it up for the rest of us. It was in our nature. Accept it and move on. Still, even I was surprised at my own compassion level, (in this case lack thereof) towards such an end. Empathy was the first to go, I guess.

On a late afternoon visit to the library Doc had suggested I sit across from Clarke Rockefeller aka Christian Karl Gerhardtsteiter, Chris Crow, Chris Smith. This world class con man who fooled everyone from the Hollywood elite to the Art expert and investment broker worlds of New York was sitting hunched behind a book. Rockefeller had been arrested and charged with kidnapping his daughter after his current wife discovered she had been conned by him for years. Captured and revealed, he sat beaten and broken before me. His facade laid bare, it was like looking into the eyes of a frightened child, confused and vulnerable. He recoiled in his chair.

"What do you want?" he said.

"I require nothing," was my only response. In that moment, everything I needed to understand him was revealed. He was a small boy with an intelligent mind who wasn't willing to put in the work. I almost felt sorry for him. Rockefeller was on his way to California to face charges of murder. He was struggling to maintain the mask that had protected him for so long and his fight would soon be over.

Months later when I saw him on television in a court room during an interview and the con man was back on full display. Confident, intelligent, and annoyed that anyone would think anything different, but I knew. I had seen behind the curtain and had attained valuable lessons on understanding this strange creature. Sadly, in many ways the strange creature was me. As much as I would like to ignore it, I shared much of the same tendencies. Arrogance and short cuts were the tools of my youth. Had I changed? I would like to think so. I would like to believe a lot of things. In truth, I have met myself in prison on more occasions than I would like to acknowledge. With that in mind, and with Doc gone, I needed to keep myself busy.

Night jobs by myself in prison were the best, like painting the superintendent's office or the rooms on the other side of the trap that were forbidden to other inmates. I needed to be seen as different. Doc would say I needed to be seen as better, and he wouldn't be wrong.

I enjoyed the process of painting: the slow perfect motion of my roller, the sound of the paint covering the past, a new coat to make it all seem so clean and bright. If only life was that simple.

An uncertain future was the best gift you could ask for Doc would say. "Keeps you learning. Keeps you growing."

On nights when the rain fell on the heavy side this old building showed its age. Water cascaded down the walls in silence and puddles appeared. Buckets sat on desk tops or in corridors to catch the more significant leaks. Several days of rain would bring the unpleasant smell of the unit's human waste disposal systems into the periphery of your senses as it began to back up below us. Toilets bubbled under the strain and certain cells overflowed into the halls, adding to the overall negative attitude of the prison population. I loved the rain.

Late one night during a storm I stepped into the small room that used to house the electric chair at Walpole State Prison. Even prison officials had the common sense not to use this room for anything more than storage after forty some odd souls met their crispy end here. There were many a guard that would not step foot into this room late at night when the rain fell and thunder echoed in the distance. The guard I was with on that night was one of them.

"I'll be sitting out here," said Watson, a twenty-five-year vet. "Let me know when you're done."

I stepped inside and knelt down, placed my hand on the cold marble tiles and pressed my finger in to the holes where the chair was once bolted down. I pulled away quickly when I thought I felt an electrical current surge up from beneath the floor. I stood unfazed, roller in hand and faced the wall.

I fell into the meditative rhythm of painting. Time passed before the roller I was holding seemed not to require my hand to trace its journey up and down the wall. The feeling of someone grabbing my wrist was unmistakable. I became transfixed on the character that was standing next to me. Not an apparition or a shadowy figure mind you, but a person. A person not of this time. A small man with gray sunken cheeks and thinning hair, blue pants and a faded loose-fitting shirt, his left hand securely gripping my right wrist as he seemed to marvel at the opportunity to paint a wall. Together we finished in silence. As we bent down to obtain more paint, I saw the tips of his boots and a memory of Boot-Man had me gasp.

"Are you alright in there, Baxter?" asked Watson, and with that intrusion, my helper was gone.

Later in my cell I lay beneath the covers trying to understand my four-year-old self.

At my ancestral home on Shirley Street, I had the normal childhood indoctrination into the monster in the closet or the hand that reaches out from beneath the bed. Pulling the covers up tight around my chin too afraid of what would happen if I made a run for it.

Lying perfectly still in an attempt to breath as little as possible was my only defense. I had come to believe that it was a rite of passage to all children, a primal remembering of times spent huddled against the wind in an ancient forest where the dark meant death was within a breaths distance at any moment.

To my recollection the monsters of my bedroom had never actually done me any physical harm. The same could not be said for the monster sleeping next to my mom in the adjoining room.

The memory now restored completely, it was my father in a drunken rage who dragged me from the kitchen on Shirley Street onto the back porch and threw me into the attic. He laughed at my mother's pleas as I screamed and clawed at the door. A door held firmly in place by his large work boot.

So there I was, right back where I started, sheet pulled up under my chin, holding my breath, my body resembling a marble statue and off in the distance the footsteps of Boot Man were getting closer.

Stories get told around the campfire. Everyone can recall one or two such imprintable tales of horror that mark their life's journey into adulthood where you learned to pretend better that such things no longer bothered you. I forced myself to jump from my bed and face head on what I knew was just the guard doing his rounds as he approached my door. I tried to convince myself that this would somehow show how far I had come, because what was the alternative? That I was still the same child with the same fears that had gone unresolved over the years. Still driven by the same monsters seen or unseen. I believe that was the lesson here.

The world was designed to show you that at any time, your truth could be replaced by the possibility of a ghost from the past or a memory restored.

Use your intelligence, I told myself. Do not be used by it. That was arrogant. I was still in many ways as the others caged around me, ruled at some level by childhood things I thought I had locked away deep within my past. But as I was learning, nothing stayed buried forever.

WE COME WE GO

"Mason got lugged for inciting a riot. Sperzie punched out a guy in the kitchen."

"Are you sure?" asked Ron.

"Positive."

A few days earlier I was cutting through HSU, Sperzie was in the cage dressed in red, indicating he was bound for Ten Block and solitary. He told me he was tired of not knowing where he was going, picked out some loud mouth on the kitchen staff and buried him.

"Are you sure that was Spearzie?"

"Yep."

I had stopped to shake Spearzie's hand through the bars of the cage knowing full well it would prompt the lieutenant on-duty to scream at me. Prisoner-to-prisoner contact during an imminent transfer was a faux-pau of the highest order. Ron and I were just about the last two remaining from the original seventy-two A-1 residents and this would be one of our last walks around the track.

"Jog one, walk one," I said.

Ron chugged along beside me. He was trying to drop a few pounds (or forty) before he moved on to his next stop. Like the rest of us, he was unsure where his new home-away-from-home would be. The only thing he knew for certain was that it wouldn't be back to Missouri to the house he had shown me pictures of.

"Anthropopithecus?" asked Ron suddenly.

"One of the many possible stages connecting ape to man," I answered and we both laughed. This was Ron's favorite jogging pastime. He had become an avid reader thanks to Doc's influence and one of his main interests was anthropology, along with the Earth sciences, geology, and climatology.

"What kind of cloud is that?" I pointed upwards.

"Stratus," said Ron instantly. "Although gray, they do not necessarily mean rain. Now, if they were of the cumulonimbus variety, we might have wished we didn't come out."

"Oh my God," I groaned, "you sound like me."

Ron smiled. "Did you ever wonder what we would have become of us in here without Doc? I mean not that I understood half of what he said but, he had a way of getting the best out of anyone that wanted to learn something."

"Best memory of the three of us?" I said quickly

"A.V.P. Hands down," laughed Ron, "the look on that lady's face."

A.V.P. stood for Alternative to Violence Program. It was one of the few programs that earned good time and almost everyone took it. The course itself was two days long and like every program geared for rehabilitation was shallow with no attempt to breach any in-depth subject matter. Doc always made any class we took far more entertaining than it was intended to be by questioning the data and asking for statistics to back up the teacher's theories and methodologies. The female facilitator had broken us up into small groups. Our group consisted of Ron, Doc, two large Spanish dudes named Hector and Remy, and myself. Hector and Remy were from A-2 and were both on their second bid. They spent most of their time doing pull-ups in the yard and neither spoke English very well. Our assignment was to create and act out a scene in which we showed an alternative path through dialogue that would circumvent a typical violent outcome. We quickly devised our play and assigned roles. The premise was simple. Hector, Remy, and myself were gang members. Hector and Remy liked that. Doc was a convenient target. Ron played a passerby who witnessed the incident. We began theatrically roughing Doc up against one of the classroom walls, drowning out the facilitator's nervous reminder that no actual displays of violence were allowed. This came as a relief to Doc who was in the throes of his battle with cancer at the time. Remy and Hector got a couple of extra shots in on Doc (claiming they didn't understand English) and he crumbled to the floor. I pulled out an imaginary switch blade eliciting a panicked demand that no weapons real or imaginary could be portrayed in skits. Ron, standing back at a safe distance, tried to dissuade us from our assault.

"Do you believe that going to prison is really worth the few dollars this citizen might have in his pockets?" he dramatically implored.

"Please, consider what you are doing. The police are already on their way."

Our gang, moved by the wisdom of his plea, reluctantly dispersed, leaving Doc lying on the floor. I don't think this took much acting on Doc's part. Our teacher smiled, relieved that we actually seemed to grasp the crux of the assignment. Doc crawled to his feet and announced that we had another version we would like to share.

"Okay," she said apprehensively.

The second rendition was nearly the same except Doc played the part of the citizen whose job it was to dissuade the gang from beating up the defenseless victim now played by Ron. The absurdity instantly shown, considering Ron's size. Hector and Remy were not small by any means, but still we looked like children punching a professional wrestler's stomach for the entertainment of the crowd. Snickers started to rise up from the audience.

"Very funny," said the teacher in a stern voice as Doc made his entrance, clearly realizing she was losing control of the class. Ron held Hector and Remy at bay with two outstretched arms which left them flailing at air bringing the laughter to a crescendo. I stepped in with my imaginary switch blade. On cue, Ron slid down the wall to a seated position on the floor. We descended on top of him with a flurry of fake blows and kicks. Ron thrust his huge arm out a small opening which took on the appearance of a large black periscope emerging from a nuclear submarine and weakly yelled, "Help!"

Doc, hearing his desperate plea, came running forward.

"Do you need help?"   Through a barrage of swinging fists, Ron cried back, "Yes! Please help me!"

"I wasn't talking to you, black man," and with that, Doc leaped onto the pile.

It took a couple of seconds for Doc's punchline to sink in. Side-splitting laughter followed. We stood in a row and grandly bowed to the applause. As for our teacher, she sat there, her face frozen in shock, as if a meteor had just struck the baby carriage, she had only moments ago been pushing. The class never recovered.

Ron and I walked the track reliving this moment, both knowing we could retrieve this scene at will for years to come whenever we needed a laugh. That day showed a different side of Doc that most had never seen. He embraced the absurdity that prison served up on a daily basis, and learned to put aside the self-importance and arrogance that landed him here.

"It's so hard to come to grips that we'll never see him again," Ron said. He turned to me. "You've been a good friend, Ken."

"The honor has been mine, Ron." To have Ron in my life was an honor. Our walk around the track remembering A.V.P. turned out to be prophetic. It was the last time I ever saw him.

We come and we go.

LAST DAY

I awoke early just as I had on hundreds of mornings. I splashed water on my face, sat on the edge of my bunk and used my shirt to dry off. There was nothing else left. My room was empty. All my possessions were neatly packed in a single box marked "Baxter W95521." I straightened my posture and slowed down time with each measured breath. I was going to take this day in. The paper work was done. The evaluation complete. Walpole, my home, my school, the cement box that had been my adventure had served its purpose and I was ready for whatever came next.

I took a quick look out the window then closed my eyes. I would always be able to see that view with perfect clarity; it was etched in my mind for better or worse.

Most of the block was at work. I didn't know many of the new stragglers wandering the flats. I left a huge pile of canteen on my desk for anyone who wanted it. There was a policy against take out. During my time in property, I was the beneficiary of this rule, coming back to the blocks with bags of confiscated canteen from departing inmates. It wasn't fair. They had paid for the food and it wasn't like they got reimbursed. However, this made me very popular.

I had put in my request for Pondeville the minimum- security prison. I had seen many unsavory characters get shipped off there so I figured I had a decent chance. I did stay six months longer upon request helping the prison pass an institutional audit. Surely the board would take this into consideration, though I never got to meet them or plead my case. I was simply a photograph on a computer screen judged by two criteria, severity of crime, and length of sentence, and I didn't photograph well. Even more dehumanizing was the plausibility that there was no board, just an overworked clerk with an outrageous case file load assigning transfers by alphabetical order or one potato two potato. It's not like I had anything to worry about. Prison was prison. The rules were designed to eliminate the necessity to think: stop, move, sit, stand for count, stay behind the yellow line, strip naked and bend over. My one actual concern was they shut your phone account off when they inform you that you are leaving so you can't tell anyone. I did want to tell Jenny I was leaving in case she was sending one of the letters I now looked forward to. Nick only sent letters when I sent him one, so that was not a concern. Jenny had been sending wonderful articles and materials she thought would supplement my stalled education. She was also putting small stipends into my account to use for the phone and canteen. I assumed that Doc had left her instructions along those lines. I had grown accustomed to her voice and began to look forward to her visits. I had to remind myself that this surely had a shelf life. It was allowing me to care and that was a dangerous road.

The guard yelled into the day room that I had to go down stairs. He said nothing as he swung the gate open. I felt sad that I couldn't say goodbye to Maryanne, Penelope, Tommy, and the Rock. They had become my friends, and Property a place where I belonged for a short time. I hadn't realized that the Friday prior would be my last day at work or I would have said something profound or funny or stupid, but no one tells you anything, ever. "Nothing happens until it does." When I cut through H.S.U. I had no idea it would be the last time I yelled "ON THE GATE." If I had, I might have made it more memorable. I was hoping I might catch a sign of Ron since he worked in H.S.U. but no such luck. The Lieutenant didn't even look up as I walked down the stairs towards New Man's Land. I'm not sure why this bothered me. Well, that wasn't true. I knew exactly why. I wanted to feel relevant.

"Don't leave this place feeling sorry for yourself," I said under my breath, that would be an insult to everyone who invested time in me. My steps lightened. Suddenly, I felt like dancing and dancing was just what I did, down the rest of the steps into New Man's Land past the Sargent who sat at his desk shaking his head, past the holding cages where the rest of the miserable-faced transferees, right by the transport driver who stood holding the multiple shackling devices meant for me.

"Baxter, show the new guy where everything is. I'm backed up this morning."

"Everything, Sarge?" I asked.

"Don't be an asshole. The basics. We're on a schedule."

"Okay new guy." I didn't care what his actual name was. They come, they go, and I was leaving today. We started at the far end with the supply closets, the drop sinks, and as we walked by the cages, a young inmate called out. "Excuse me, sir?"

"Really, did you just call me sir?"

Kevin was twenty and fully shackled in his cage which meant he pissed someone off.

"Who'd you piss off?" I asked.

"I pushed someone."

"Who?"

"First guy who touched me. A cop I think."

"You shoved a C.O. Why?"

"Dunno."

"He doesn't know," I said to the new guy who was just taking all this in. "When did you do this?"

"Last night when I came in."

"You've been in here all night?"

"They said I'm going to Bridgewater or OC something."

"O.C.C.C" I said, "that's not great." I explained to him that Bridgewater and the O.C.C.C were mental facilities; they were both bad.

The suicide rate among staff and inmates alike were about the same there. Rumor had it that just recently a former Bridgewater superintendent killed himself after shooting his estranged wife, but I didn't think Kevin needed to hear that.

"Wait here," I said to new guy and headed in the Sarge's office.

"We're just letting him stew, Baxter." Said the sarge, anticipating my inquiry.

"I figured. You might want to stick him in OU," I said, turning around.

"Should I say you suggested that?" the sarge yelled after me.

Well, it was a good Idea, I said to myself.

"BAXTER!" A hard-cruel voice boomed across New man's land. Everyone else froze, but I smiled. Penelope stood hands on hips in the doorway of property.

"Not so fast. Where do you think you're going?" barked the cranky transport driver still holding my shackles.

"Fuck off, Baranger!" yelled Penelope. "You'll stand there all day if I tell you to." Get in here numbnuts," said Penelope, swinging her arm wildly, waving me into my former place of employment. New Guy followed suit, dragged along in the wake of my excitement. I felt bad as Penelope unleashed on him.

"Where the fuck do you think you're going, New Guy? You'll never step foot in here so back off." She yanked the massive steel door shut, leaving Baranger and New Guy standing side-by-side, the same stunned look on their faces.

Inside the atmosphere was much the same as it always was: very un-prison like. Penelope smiled.

"Don't think we're gonna miss you or anything."

"We could replace you with a bag of oatmeal," added the Rock.

It felt like I was leaving a fraternity.

"I'll miss you guys," I said with all the sincerity I could muster. "Thank you for the way you've treated me. I really appreciated it."

"Don't thank us too fast," said Tommy, coming out of Maryanne's office. "For whatever reason, classification sent you to Baystate. There was nothing anyone in here could do."

The dance drained from my legs. It was not like the opinion of four C. O's I worked alongside of for two years held any weight with the classification board, that would make too much sense.

"Bay State."   I couldn't hide my disappointment. W95521 was the reality of the day. I hoped this was a final practical joke.

"You'll be fine," said the Rock.

Penelope looked genuinely sad. "I'm sorry. I know you were thinking Pondeville."

"It's Ok. Where's Maryanne?" I was not about to start feeling sorry for myself in front of this group.

"She's having a moment," said Tommy.

Mary Anne was the emotional one, too attached to everyone and everything, apparently me included.

"Listen, fuck'em. Don't worry about it. You'll be fine." Tommy said.

I appreciated that, especially from Tommy who was the no nonsense C.O. of the bunch.

"What's this inmate doing in my Property Department," called Maryanne, as she came through the door, sporting her best impersonation of happiness. "I'm very sorry," she said quickly. "There's simply nothing we could do. I'm embarrassed."

"Don't be," I said.   "I'm just an inmate."

"Hardly," said Penelope who seemed about to say something else but was interrupted by a loud banging on the Property door. The muffled voice outside seemed desperate.

"C'mon you guys. I got a long day." It was Baranger, his face pressed up against the small thick glass panel of the steel door.

"Hold your horses," the Rock cracked the door open.

"I got twenty guys to move today."

"Let him go." said Maryanne, feigning a small smile. "My husband's over at Baystate. He knows you're coming. Good luck,

Kenny." She turned quickly and retreated to her office.

Penelope punched me in the arm and seemed again ready to speak, but nothing came out.

"Time to go, Baxter," said the Rock, bailing her out. Tommy stepped between myself and Baranger and looked me straight in the eyes. "In all the years I've been here, I've never done this." He reached to shake my hand.

I was stunned. Being the beneficiary of these small moments of civility, I felt like the Grinch who stole Christmas as my heart grew three sizes. This seemingly insignificant gesture of a handshake was the earmark of much of what Doc used to talk about. You'll recognize them when you see them, he would say. Moments born from genuine sincerity.

"It's been an honor," I grasped his hand firmly.

"For me too, Kenny. Now get out of here, you worthless criminal."

We all laughed, everyone except Baranger. He stood there looking confused.

The door slammed shut and that was that. I expected Baranger to put my wrist and ankle chains on extra tight as punishment for throwing his schedule off, but he didn't. He was almost apologetic.

"Seems like you've made quite the impression around here, Firefighter," was all he said.

Now I have to start again with a new place, new staff, and the biggest nightmare of them all: cellmates.

"What's Baystate like?" I asked.

"It's like prison," was the only response I received.

Arms pinned to my side; I began the awkward leg shackle shuffle that occurs when you're limited to about five inches of movement per step, anything more would have your ankle chains digging into your skin or worse land you flat on your face with no way to break your own fall. Like anything else, I would adapt.

THE RED QUEEN HYPOTHESIS

I sat shackled in the van, staring at the colossal thirty-foot wall constructed to protect the outside world from me. The gates reminded me of something out of King Arthur's time or from a scene from *Mad Max beyond Thunderdome*.

When I arrived at Walpole two years ago, these walls towered as an impediment to hope, a symbol of despair. Today, as the van readied to transport me to my next prison, it was less formidable and instead simply marked the borders of what had become my home. How strange that I would feel anything but glad to leave this place. This was progress I reminded myself. I'm moving on to greener pastures, but my mind wandered to all the people I had met here, everything I learned, the friends I had made. There were so many times when leaving these confines under any circumstances seemed like a dream, something so far away. Had Doc survived he would have been in a minimum by now.

Before I knew it, the doors were creaking open. The trap guards checked the van thoroughly for inmates hiding beneath the chassis or for an imposter behind the wheel disguised as a guard, and we were off.

I had the experience of leaving the prison for a couple of hours at my revise and revoke nightmare but that was early in the morning, strapped in a rolling metal box. This time was by day in a real van, and I wasn't coming back.

I felt a little dizzy as the van lurched forward. There were roads and trees, not just the tops, but entire trees. Cars. There were cars going past us with people in them. Behind us, the prison wall receded. I never imagined that wall could disappear behind anything. The van pulled up to a street light. It was red. Red meant stop. There was a father and son walking their dog. A dog. A sidewalk. A red light.

I had flashbacks of Alex and Nicholai being dragged down the street by Charlie, our unruly sheepdog. The boy looked up at me and tugged on his dad's coat and pointed. The dad politely lowered his son's arm. I hadn't expected to see houses in such close proximity to the prison; I guess I hadn't thought about it. Prisons had to go somewhere. The light changed green. Green meant go. The next left brought us into the parking lot of my new home. The ride didn't just seem like it took four minutes, it literally took four minutes. I looked around and saw inmates working. Inmates were outside the wall. Wait, there was no wall. There was a large fence with barbed wire on top, but no wall. I shuffled my way into a modern lobby. The metal detectors and decor were new, but the attitude and procedure were strikingly familiar. Strip down. Bend over. Do as your told. Fly right. Be respectful. Stand for count. Face front. Never be without your identification. Wait forever for anything else. Welcome to Baystate Medium Correctional Facility.

I required a new picture for my ID. The C.O. had to take mine three times because I wouldn't stop smiling.

"Are we going to have trouble with you?" said the intake Sargent.

"Why would you assume that?" I said, actually expecting a response.

"Move along," was all I got.

My sit down with the case worker (C.P.O.) was a little more cordial.

"Why was I sent here rather than Pondeville?" I asked politely

The C.P.O never bothered to look up so I answered my own question.

Severity of crime and length of sentence, and the standard response: bed availability and because we said so.

The C.P.O. laughed.

"I see you've studied the inner workings of the D.O.C".

"Indeed, I have. The unabridged version of compartmentalization and plausible deniability. Tell me, is there ever going be a time when I'll get judged by someone face-to-face instead of just a picture on a computer?"

"Not likely. Classification is, in your own words, purposely compartmentalized. This place is a lot nicer than Walpole though and you, of all people, will appreciate the Library."

"How do you know I can read? "I asked "Does it say I can read?"

"That and a few other things, Mr. Baxter." He closed the file.

"Interesting." I said "Do tell."

"Not my department. You'll be in the mods. Your belongings will follow you in a couple of days, give or take a week. Your assigned case worker will call on you in a few days. Assessment, discuss programs, and what's expected of you. Until then, settle in and enjoy."

How could I? I knew what was coming. A cellmate. The words of Carl the lifer came rushing back.
"I'd give up a pardon for a single cell."

The Mods resembled very cheap camp baracks. The doors were wooden and opened and closed like regular doors. There were no soilets. You got to leave your room in the middle of the night, except during count. The rooms were designed for three occupants. My first roommate was Jose', a Spanish guy in his late twenty's who worked in the kitchen. He didn't speak English. But motioned he had the bunk underneath me which left the single bunk on the other wall. I gestured to him as to who resided there. He shook his head and mumbled something which didn't sound much like a compliment. I walked to the dayroom. There I found the communal tv, pool and ping pong tables, and three phones. I Immediately thought of Jenny. She didn't know I was here.

"Kenny! Hey Kenny, over here." It was Dave the Fisherman.

I was relieved to see someone I knew, especially one of my former teammates. We talked about Hockey Joe going to Pondeville and Dave informed me that Ed the Lawyer was lugged to Norfolk Medium for helping inmates with legal problems. I explained how Big Steve got lugged for threatening staff over hepatitis medication and how they asked me to go help him pack as I was probably the only one, he wouldn't try to kill. Dave and I laughed over the absurdity of judging your friends by the level of likelihood that you would be killed by them. Dave introduced me as "the goalie I was telling you about" to Leo, a mafioasa from Fall River who asked what room I was in. Both he and Dave cringed when I told them.

"What?" I said, "Jose' seemed nice enough."

"Obviously you haven't met Pete yet." Said Dave.

"A complete and utter asshole," seconded Leo.

"Something to look forward to," I said.

"Pete's on his third bid. Doing an eight to twelve. B and E. Assault. Thinks he's brilliant."

"The toughest guy you've ever come across, just ask him."

"You guys are going to get along just fine," finished Leo. He and Dave both laughed.

Looking around the day room, I knew instantly that I would spend as little time here as possible. There were the requisite chess games, pool tables, and microwaves, but the crowd had a distinctly different air about them. They were louder, less respectful, child-like. There was a high school mentality, that never would have been allowed at Walpole. I felt as if I was a single-celled organism entering a new environment. Doc had taught me the biological term for this: The Red Queen Hypothesis. According to Evolutionary theory, when organisms were introduced into a new environment, they must fight for resources: It appeared I would have to begin again. I was the new organism. I must adapt or die.

As I stood gazing out the window of my new room, I opened myself up to the energy of this place and began the process of adjusting to my new world. Across the way stood the main building. Across the yard I noticed two picnic tables shaded by a tree. A tree that was located *inside* the fence. I could see its roots extending into the ground and immediately thought about climbing it. I wanted to run right outside and throw my arms around it. I started to imagine what the bark would feel like, when suddenly, the hair stood up on the back of my neck.

I felt "IT" coming from fifty feet away. In opening up my senses to the tree, I had let something else in, something vile and repulsive invading my cell membranes. The Red queen Hypothesis on full display. I knew something evil was coming, something abhorrent to existence, something that I was not going to be able to ignore. I turned and there in the doorway was "IT."

I immediately closed down my peri-personal receptors to the foreign particulate matter that stood in my doorway. There in all its repugnant glory was my new roommate "Pete," forever known to me as "IT."

"Yo, what's up dude. Let's get some things straight. I ain't no stranger to trouble. This is my third bid so youse respects that and we'll see wheres we stands. Capiche?"

"Well, I thinks wheres we stands," I said mocking him, "is in the room I was assigned to."

"Yo dude, you disrespecting me. You been here five minutes and you want to mess with me?"

"I don't want to mess with anyone, but I don't need your approval or permission for anything."

"We'll see about that. I ain't afraid of no one you gets that."

"Very commendable." I said, and hopped up on my bunk and laid back, eyes closed, hands crossed over my chest.

"You either think you're a tough guy or you don't know no better than to ever be turning your back on anyones in prison."

"Go for it." I said and relaxed into my bunk. My new foray into roommates was off and running. The bunk however was a revelation, it had a spring as did the mattress, no metal slab, no paper-thin mattress. Before I had more than a second to enjoy it, a loud voice boomed from the doorway.

"Settling right in, are we?"

"Hiya Captain," said It, sounding much more conciliatory.

"I was just telling this newby that youse don't get comfortable around here, but he don'ts listens."

"Worry about yourself, Jenson," said the Captain and returned his attention to me.

I hopped off the bed to greet my guest. I had forgotten Mary Anne's husband worked here.

"You don't have to get up. Mary Anne said you were coming so I thought I would check up on you."

"I appreciate that Captain. Truth be known I didn't think I was coming here."

"Don't worry about it. It's all just time. Take advantage of the Library. I'll check in on you from time to time to make sure you're not causing any trouble." Before leaving, the Captain threw a quick half-snarl toward It who stood there with his mouth half-open.

I hopped up on my bunk again. None of my stuff would be here for a few days, the library would not be opened till tomorrow, and my phone would take a week to be activated. I only had enough money in my account for a couple of phone calls so I wanted to let Nick know where I was. I wanted to call Jenny also, but it felt somehow inappropriate. With Thanksgiving approaching, she would be with her family. I imagined a call from an inmate would require some explaining; still it had been a while, almost a year since Doc died.

"So how do you knows the Captain?" came a much more subdued question from IT.

"I used to work for his wife."

"On the outside?"

"At Walpole."

"You were on the permanent workforce?" I suspected my elevated status had IT thinking he may have misjudged his new roommate.

"Yep."

"She introduced you to her husband? You a rat?"

"Yes. It's my life's ambition to gather information about people I don't give a shit about."

"I see you're going to be a problem." IT, stormed out of the room. I could hear him all the way up the hall. "My Roommates friends with the Captain. He thinks he's a tough guy."

"You straighten him out, Jenson," yelled somebody.

"I'm in high school," I said to no one.

I wandered down the hall to check out the showers. You could only use the showers during movement. I grabbed my miniature towel and off I went. One of the five separate showers with curtains was available. I hopped right in and prepared for my first real shower in two years. I let out a yell. The water was freezing. There was a chuckle from the next stall.

"Don't worry you'll get used to it."

"When is the best time to try to catch one with hot water?" I yelled back.

"Maybe next summer. Hot water heater went down about seven months ago and they said it might be till spring before they can replace it. Sometimes in the morning, if you're quick, its warm for a while. Not worth getting into a fight for it though."

"Thanks," I said and headed out of the bathroom where I

ran into Dave the Fisherman.

"I should have warned you about the showers. They take some getting used to. Sometimes they're warm in the morning, but it's not worth getting hemmed up over."

"So I heard."

The first night was quite comfortable on my upgraded mattress. My comfort was short-lived, undermined by the morning rush. Eighty guys were expected to share the facilities for teeth brushing, shaving, and the like. There was yelling and pushing and sure enough a fight broke out. No C.O.'s rushed in and it ended quickly on its own. As I headed down the hall, a voice caught my attention from behind. I spun around. I was staring up at the large grin of 'Max" who looked like he may have played for the Celtics at one time. I recognized his voice, it was from the day before in the shower.

"I told you showers in the morning were dangerous."

"Is it always like this?" I asked.

"Pretty much. It's actually worse at night in the rooms. Three to a room usually leads to something. Keep to yourself, you'll be okay."

During the next few nights, I was awakened several times by the sound of bodies slamming off walls, once right next door. It felt like they were going to come crashing through the wall.

The first chance I got; I made my way to the library. It was spectacular. Rows and rows of hard covered books alphabetized on oak shelves. Sections on Science, Non- fiction, and research; I was in heaven. Carpeted floors, large tables to work on and a quality seldom experienced in here, an air of quiet respect. I checked out several books and planned on spending the week writing and reading. Things, it seemed, might be looking up.

OUR HOLLYWOOD

I entered the visiting room at Baystate and looked around quickly like a small child entering a playground. There were large comfortable non plastic chairs in multiple colors. People sitting side by side. There were vending machines and then there was Jenny. She came through the door with a big smile looking so, well, looking beautiful.

Our short hug was a delirious blend of warmth and soft jasmine. The unexpected tingle of arousal shocked me. We both glanced uneasily toward the female guard sitting at the desk. We debated whether to sit down next to each other. Other people were doing it. This was a far cry from the no touch alignment of Walpole.

"This seems almost civil," said Jenny.

Usually our visits were half-conversations with rushed responses yelled over echoing arguments in multiple languages. We used to teeter on the edge of our seats straining to hear, and wincing at the inevitable command to "Sit back! Feet behind the yellow line!"

Now, I watched nervously as Jenny took a breath and relaxed. I felt like a teenager on my first date. The phone call on Thanksgiving had changed everything.

The morning of the call I had paced the floor of the day room, trying to get up the courage to dial her number. I was still nervous about calling her on a holiday when she was with her family. I wanted desperately to hear her voice and decided to risk the rejection of her not accepting my call. I held my breath. When she answered, the tone of her voice enveloped me.

"I was hoping you would call," she said.

My spirits soared for the first time in months. This marked a breakthrough in our relationship. She would be coming from now on to see me, not just mourning the loss of Doc.

Now, here, she sat beside me her eyes shone clear and blue. Then there was that smile, why did I not notice that before? Probably because it didn't exist up to that point. Most of the time at Walpole, I just wanted to hug her to take away some of her sadness. Now I just wanted to hug her because, well, because I just wanted to.

"I just put some money in your account," she continued, "so you can call your son more and so we can talk."

"Did Doc leave you some money?"

"No. It's always been me putting money in your account." I was stunned. I always assumed Doc had instructed her to do this. It never occurred to me that Jenny had been the source of the monthly deposits that started showing up after Doc died. Her generosity overwhelmed me. She quickly moved on and spoke in one long sentence, sounding a lot like me.

"How is the library? How long till you can go to a minimum? I don't think you should take a job while you're here? We should concentrate on the writing. Agreed?"

"We". She said "We."

I tried to rush past that before she could take it back. "I just signed out a course," I said "from the University of Illinois on astronomy and the chemical makeup of the universe."

"That's wonderful, but we are going to tailor your education to more practical matters from now on. Do you understand?"

"Is this a test?" I asked.

"Everything is a test." She exhaled for the first time and even that was attractive.

"We have all day, no need to cover twenty subjects in a half-an-hour."

I tried to pretend I was calm.

"Are all those people inmates? Which ones are the visitors?" She gestured toward a group of five men sitting across the room dressed in expensive suits and patent leather shoes.

"The second from the right is an inmate and don't point, they don't like that."

"They look like they are all in the Mafia."

"There's a rumor that several of the older gentleman here have ties to the Winter Hill Gang."

"That's Whitey Bulger's gang, right?" she said, her blue eyes widening.

"Yes, but you don't talk about it."

"Who's that?" Jenny pointed to Leo who was sitting with his wife and children.

"That's Leo. Let's just call him a business man. Intelligent, Angry, He's from Fall River and any conversation you have with him starts or ends with a story about either Lizzy Borden or a recitation of Theodore Roosevelt's speech called the "Man in the Arena" which he memorized. It's long and you are not allowed to leave once he starts. I've heard it three times already."

"Oh, look at that. That's so nice." Jenny watched an inmate at the end of the row. "He's playing cards with his grandmother. That's so sweet."

I didn't have the heart to tell her that he was a rapist, and that wasn't his grandmother. It was his wife. Before I had a chance to say anything, grandma leaned over and planted a long wet one on her presumed grandson and Jenny threw up little in her mouth.

She was like fresh snow on a beautiful New England morning just before the neighbor's dog pees on it.

"Oh my god that's disgusting," her face contorted in such a way I couldn't help but laugh out loud. "How? Why? Let's talk about something else, please. What do you think the mafia guys are talking about?" She said in a conspiratorial tone.

"Not what you think," I said. "The other day the mafia guy was holding court in the library and the topic was the origin of consciousness."

"One of your favorites!" said Jenny.

"Exactly. It was great. I got to spend hours with a group up to the task of discussing Julian Jaynes and the Bicameral mind, McGilchrist's *The Master and his Emissary*, Dawkin's The *God Delusion* as a little crossover argument."

"So, I was right. Doc trained you to memorize lines out of important books just so you could throw out some talking points and answer your own questions. Nice trick."

Not exactly the response I was looking for.

"If you are only memorizing things then you're not learning and doomed to forget them".

She was right. Lately I was frightened that I would fail to remember all the things Doc taught me. I told her that I was scared that all this effort and vast amounts of information would end up fading away into the dark recesses of my brain.

"Why do you think you never put your whole heart into anything?" asked Jenny suddenly.

"Well, that's a little presumptuous," I said.

But it was true. "I get lost, sometimes," I said quietly, not looking at her.

"Structure is good for you. I see that. It's a miracle you made it through high school. I suspect you never did a lick of homework or sat down long enough to read a book or write a paper. At least that's my professional assessment. Doc was good for you. He must have seen you as a challenge. I think the problem is that you need someone to help direct your energy, focus you. Someone to hold you accountable. That's my specialty. You have a case of ADHD, in short, you have a learning disability. But I can fix that."

"Just like that. You'll take over," I said.

"Just like that. Doc saw something in you and I'll pick up the baton. That is if you're up for it? "Tell me something you could write about in here," said Jenny, noticing my mind was drifting. "I'd like to hear what you find interesting."

I thought for a moment and said, "I was standing in the outside weight area the other day and it began to snow. It was so peaceful. Leo was talking some young kid's ear off on how to get around paying taxes and various ways to screw the government. There were two Spanish guys in their twenties talking about the litany of female conquests they would enjoy upon their release, a direct result of the incredible shape they were getting in. I found it interesting that neither seemed to have much of a plan beyond sexual conquests. Yet, they seemed very happy. They were kneeling on the ground holding a dumbbell in one hand while simultaneously grinding an object down on the cement, an action usually associated with making a shank. They were oblivious to any thing around them. Upon closer examination, I could see they were grinding down plastic dominoes. Though I couldn't imagine how these would qualify as weapons. They were not sharpening them. They were working them down as small and round as possible. One of them surveyed his handiwork and said, "Perfect. This is going to be awesome."

What their intentions were, I didn't have a clue, yet their happiness was undeniable. From over my shoulder came a voice.

"Trying to figure them out?"

I turned quickly, surprised that someone came up on me. I was completely unaware which was not a good state of mind to be in, especially in this place, but it was just the mafia guy from the library.

"The one sitting over there?" asked Jenny, pointing at the men sitting across from us.

"Yes, but don't point." I reached up and pulled down her arm. "Remember rule number one: don't say anything about someone that you wouldn't say to their face. If you're pointing at him then we're talking about him and that's not good for my health. But, yes him."

"What did he say?"

He said, "Kenny, you have to understand this is their Hollywood."

"Their Hollywood?" repeated Jenny.

"Yes. He explained that this was the coolest these guys were ever going to be. Right here. Right now."

"This is their Hollywood," he said. "Nothing will ever match this moment of delusion. Out here lifting weights in the snow. Feeling all tough and cool. Not a care in the world. They get fed. They hang out together. No responsibility. No concerns. This is it. It's never going to get any better."

"How did he know your name?" asked Jenny.

"Don't know."

"You make friends easy. That bothers me sometimes. I used to get jealous of you and Doc."

"Jealous? Why?"

"You guys got to spend every day talking, learning, laughing. No responsibilities as you just alluded to. He started to talk about you in his letters and I felt left out. I would drive all the way up here for a half-hour visit and he'd talk about you those last months. I was so happy he had a friend, but I felt like I missed out on getting to know him that way."

"Jealous of people in prison," I said, "Now there's a short story."

The next few hours were a blur of subjects from the game plan on how I would begin learning to write better, how I would discover my authentic voice. There was a great deal of discussion on focus. As our visit wound down, we couldn't believe the time had passed so quickly. We stood up and reached to give each other the brief prison goodbye hug, and I couldn't help myself. I pulled her into me with such force, she gave out a little cry. By the time the guard at the desk yelled "BAXTER" in response to what had been a paradigm shift of emotions that spread outward at the speed of light engulfing the entire visiting room, it was too late. I had pulled Jenny into my soul and resonated with every one of her billions of cells. In the same way I hummed to my body when I performed healing, I tuned my cells to her frequency. I learned every curve of her body, taking in every facet of her being, embracing everything she was. Her relative minor to my perfect fourth, culminating in one tantalizing moment.

It took several seconds for the visiting room to return to its awkward absurd energy. The guard stared at me with a menacing look on her face at my breach of protocol. There was supposed be a clear distinction between inmate and visitor. Two bodies were forbidden to be so firmly crushed together. One of them left. One of them stayed behind. That was the rule, but today, both of us left and both of us stayed and there was nothing they could do about it. It had been done; a bond created by the natural order of the universe because some things are just meant to be. Some elements are just meant to come together. Dare I say, some things may indeed be fated.

Half-dazed, Jenny bumped into the door jamb as she exited the room. I didn't recall the full body strip down in the holding cell but I'm pretty sure I had a more-than- healthy erection on display which I'm sure the C.O. did not appreciate, but I was unfazed. Embarrassment went out the window in prison and I had more important things to focus on now.

It's been said that when you come face to face with something that was meant to be, you just know it. I never put much stock in such statements as I follow the adage of "be very skeptical of things you want so badly to be true." I tried to temper my response when the librarian posted the start of the writing class "Pen New England" thumb tacked on the board just as I walked in. I passed off as coincidence the comment, "This is for you," as she smiled.

Sandy was a pretty girl by any standards, long blond hair and a look of education to match the wonderment of why this particular career choice. Who was I to complain? She could get any book I wanted on any subject I was investigating. She was in charge of the pristine compendium of happiness known as the library. It was a strange coincidence that just recently Jenny had mentioned during a phone conversation that the true endeavor of writing a book was about to start, and here was a writing class being made available.

"Is this for real, or just another mindless program for good time?" I asked.

"Oh no, it's real. The teachers are first rate, from Boston college I believe, and there is no good time. It's strictly volunteer; I told you this is for you."

"First things first," I said. "I have a homework assignment." I filled out the requisition forms for books on the endocrine system, the ancient Chinese Chakras, and articles on the second brain, the one in your stomach, the one that creates ninety percent of the body's Serotonin, the one that has as many neurons as the brain of a cat!

Although we both agreed that Intuition was untrustworthy without knowledge, Jenny insisted that Instinct could be a valuable tool if properly understood, and that it began with the understanding that it comes from a more ancient brain, the one located in your stomach. Jenny said the stomach creates the vast majority of the body's Serotonin, the neurotransmitter associated with pleasure, memory, learning, sleep cycles and the possible culprit in the battle with depression, anxiety, self-confidence issues and mood swings. I was to write a paper on which came first, The Chinese Chakras or the endocrine system. Jenny, as it turned out, was harder on me than Doc.

PEN NEW ENGLAND

Weeks passed and the day I had been patiently waiting for was finally here, the start of the Pen New England writing course. I tried to reserve my enthusiasm, after all, how good could it be? It was prison.

I remembered my promise to Jenny to just take everything in stride, stay humble, listen, and write honestly. Her voice on the phone was filled with the same excitement that I had been experiencing, but was stressing a much more reasonable approach. Both Leo and Blane were also taking the class. There were more inmates signed up than they were prepared for.

"I'm not getting stuck in a room with amateur writers," said one seasoned vet.

"Or some second-rate teacher either," added another.

As it turned out, I need not have worried about being arrogant, there were plenty of people willing to fill that role for me. Some inmates had been taking this class for years. With the increase in participants, we were broken up into two rooms. The first ten minutes were spent listening to a few of the long timers complain that they should be in the other room, and were reminded by the teacher, a young woman, that this was a voluntary class and they could leave if they wanted to. I liked her right away.

Miranda was young, yet had a look of an accomplished writer, she spun a pen in her fingers as if it were an extension of her very being. Our first lesson was to look at several pictures, we were to choose one and write a short story describing the adventure in what you saw. We were given ten minutes to complete the task, which instantly threw me. I like to take notes, try ideas out, sleep on it, ask for other people's opinions, genuinely procrastinate, do several rewrites then lose interest and go onto to something new. With two minutes remaining, I chose a picture of cardboard boxes and wrote a short prose on leaving the safety of your own box and exploring the world around you, which I was mildly pleased with. There were some notable writings by some of the long timers, nothing spectacular, but impressive.

When someone asked Miranda to read hers, I was dumbstruck. It was clear, inventive, surprisingly in depth for ten minutes, and I thought nothing short of brilliant. I could not have been happier. I was going to read every handout and listen with the eagerness of a student whose life depended on it. This was indeed made for me, cliches aside, I was all in. I could see the light at the end of the tunnel. I would shoot from the hip and beat swords into plow shares (whatever that means.) Suffice it to say, I was excited. I had one paw in the chicken coop, and it was time to get to work. You can't learn to swim without getting into the water.

ABOUT TIME

Writing became an obsession. It seemed to come so naturally, maybe because I was so open to being taught, maybe because Doc taught me how to learn. The reasons seemed unimportant. Writing class was like being on a giant treasure hunt, where every bit of knowledge was devoured and the next clue nourishing, intoxicating even. The English language seemed to become food, that when prepared and served correctly was so satisfying: Find your voice, show, don't tell, when to add details; When to be succinct, coy, aloof, direct. The art of surprise, the art of straight forward, naked honesty. I had never felt so comfortable with an art form. I had never thought of writing as an art. Music, as much as I loved it, was always a struggle. I will continue to pursue it, I couldn't think of a life without it, but since prison had for the most part removed it from my life, I had to learn to adapt. I originally thought that writing could help fill the void, but it was doing something else, it was, dare I say, healing me.

In our last phone conversation, Jenny had asked, without the slightest equivocation, what I had done to her. Was there an actual attempt to achieve an intentional altered state of some kind with the Cellular Melding Hug I gave her at the end of our last visit?

I was at a point in my life where making up stories to make me look better were not required, especially with Jenny. But something had changed and she knew it instantly.

"Just because our relationship has changed does not mean you get to withhold your true thoughts. In fact, it means I demand more from you and on deeper levels." She was right, of course.

"You have thirty seconds remaining on your phone call." I always dreaded that loud voice signaling the end of my coveted connection. It was a continual reminder of where I was and how little control I had over any event.

"Oh, you are so lucky," she said quickly. I'll be there in a week, this Isn't...

"Over," I assumed would have been the next word.

It started to snow lightly as I hung up the cold receiver and it made me think of winters at Walpole. I used an outside phone only once there talking to Nick, who could barely hear me. There were several phones in the yard, but they didn't last long, they would succumb to the elements or more often the beating they took as an angry inmate smashed it to pieces after not hearing the words he wanted to hear. I adapted quickly to not needing to hear the reassurance in someone's voice. A voice from the outside saying that everything was going to be OK. I recalled the years on the fire department when I worked the night shift, everyone would take turns on one of two available lines to call home to say goodnight to their kids or to say I love you to their wives. Funny how the fire department prepared me for so much of what I had to get used to in prison. Sleeping in strange places, not knowing if I'd make it home. Difference was in here you kept to yourself and tried to avoid those you didn't like or that meant to do you harm. On the fire department at any moment a person I didn't trust or respect could have my life in their hands.

Lately I had been dwelling on the past and worse thinking about the future all too much. This was because of the double-edged sword called Jenny. Her last letter had small indications of what appeared to be flirting. Subtle comments about sounds she would make while sipping her Darjeeling tea that could make a grown man blush, relaxing in her coffee shop in the sleepy town of Lemont Pa. where her office was located. Not that I didn't enjoy it, to the contrary, but it left me uneasy. There was no future for us, we both knew that. I was in State prison, and was a convicted felon, how would she explain that to her friends? How, come to think of it did she explain Doc? Yes, she had said she would oversee the process of writing a book but what about that? What happens when I started talking about Doc and the reality of how he really ended up in prison? The truth seemed much harsher once it appeared in print. How do I write about myself? There were moments in my life I was not ready to share, there were moments in prison where my conduct would send Jenny running.

COFFEE WAR

Larry was a common crook of the small-time variety, back at Walpole in for his third bid. Sitting on my bunk, I watched him just outside my cell, as he stared down the flats waiting for the guard to turn and shut the gate after the last call for movement. His plan was to slip unnoticed into my room and abscond with some coffee to fill the empty cup in his hand. When he spotted me, his face was priceless. I said nothing at all. I just watched him try to recover.

"I thought you were going out to the yard," he said quickly.

"And you thought you'd just help yourself to some coffee." I wasn't even mad. It would have almost been funny if it wasn't one of the biggest violations in all of prison. To be known as a cell thief was the worst thing you could be labeled as. It was his reaction that upset me.

"I wasn't takin nothin. Don't be calling me no cell thief."

"I didn't call you anything, yet." I said getting to my feet. Larry wasn't a tough guy, he would fight if he had to, we all knew the rules. I even took his tone of voice in stride, "C'mon you got caught. Just admit it. You even said it; you thought I would be in the yard."

"I didn't say that."

"You work in the plate shop, you make more money than I

do, so why do you have to sneak around and steal coffee?"

"You tell anyone I was trying to steal anything and it'll be the end of you."

I just wanted him to stop talking, I don't even know how it happened. I caught his coffee cup before it hit the floor, if there had been coffee in it not a drop would have been spilt. I sat him on my bunk as he clutched his throat gasping for air. The quick open hand strike to the throat was not meant to kill at that level of impact, which I assumed up to that point was of the right proportion. It was just meant to shut him up. Several long seconds passed wondering how I would explain the dead inmate on my bunk, the one with the crushed larynx. The one that would cost me my freedom. I quickly grabbed my coffee bag, which I always left on the desk in plain view, which now in hindsight might encourage exactly this chain of events. I dumped a rather generous portion of coffee into the cup I was still holding in my hand, "Here, take this," I said helping him to his feet, and gently pushing him towards the door. "Please ask next time," I said. He turned, still trying to form words. I wonder what Jenny would think of that side of me.

Your Truth

Jenny knew right away that something had changed in me the second she saw me. After a short formal hug, which I originally had planned to be a little longer, she held my hand.

"What happened?" she said, genuinely concerned "Is everything alright?"

"We need to talk," I tried not to sound too dramatic. I could see her face change to one of soft sadness as her shoulders sank and her eyes drifted to the floor.

"You're wonderful," I said quickly, realizing this was the last person on the planet I wanted to offend. I quickly explained my thought process of the last few days and told her the Walpole story of the coffee thief and my desire to eliminate my current roommate from existence.

"You make me think about the future, so forgive me if this is inappropriate, understand that I am not immune to wanting to have someone in my life that I could count on, but being in prison makes me grab at straws."

She let me go on for a while before saying that she also had been having similar thoughts about what we were doing and the fact that she could not bring herself to tell anyone about me was weighing heavy on her mind. This stung a little but at least she was being honest. It was as nice a "break up" as you could ever have asked for, at least the most grown up one for me.

"I won't apologize for becoming attached to you, or trying to become your friend," I said

"We're already friends," she said with a warm smile. "That's the best thing about us. If we were on the outside, we may have started a relationship out of our grief over Doc and it would already have ended in a disaster. This is more like a Victorian Courtship where we aren't allowed to engage beyond a certain point and I must admit, I was struggling with my feelings thinking I was attaching myself to you over my loss and that wasn't fair to you. So, I have come to a decision."

I was hoping at least our visit would last a little longer but Jenny usually got right to the point. "We will work this out in time together, Ok?"

"Yes," I said quickly.

"Good. Now let's get you something to eat and you can tell me all about the writing class."

The next several hours flew by as we discussed authors and writing styles. I asked her if she knew Dostoyevsky wrote *"The Gambler"* in a month to pay off his own gambling debts, and that he had spent several years in prison himself. I was astonished to find that she had never read *Crime and Punishment*.

"Some of us don't have the luxury to sit around and read every great novel," she snapped back. She commented on how lucky I was having all this time available to pursue an education. And followed with, "I think your book could be converted to a screen play very easily." She knew a lot about movies as it turned out, her first degree was in film from Penn State, and she had spent years in New York and Los Angeles, pursuing a career in the film industry until she decided that the lifestyle wasn't for her. She moved to Seattle, got job in a health food store and pursued a degree in alternative medicine. There was so much more to this girl. Maybe she was right, on the outside our paths were not likely to have crossed, and if they did, it would have been short lived. Caught up in the world of the chameleon, trying to impress each other by pretending we were someone else.

Sitting there during that long visit was effortless. We never seemed to run out of things to talk about. She still couldn't bring herself to look at the 30-year-old rapist and his 80-year-old wife and made us sit so her back was to them. "How are you going to write about Doc?" she asked quickly.

I paused thoughtfully, not to look as if I was hesitating.

"COUNT TIME" yelled the C.O, from the desk. Saved by the bell.

"All inmates stand against the wall ID.'s visible."

Jenny had never witnessed Count time. At Walpole visits were short and everyone was locked in when count time came around. But here with our long visits you were forced to stand against the wall as someone with a clip board checked each I.D. slowly and carefully while our guests looked on uncomfortably. I admit it was embarrassing to some extent, as it once again reminds you who you are and the level you exist at. When I looked over at Jenny she was smiling almost as if she was proud, which was a strange response. When I sat down, she said "You look so cute, everyone else is leaning against the wall or slouching, head down, hands tucked into the front of their pants, but you stand up perfectly straight like you're in the military or something".

I hadn't realized it before, but some things die hard. "It's from the Fire Department sometimes I stand at attention sometimes at parade rest. On occasion I will salute. Other inmates don't like it, but I miss saluting, I don't know why."

"Do you miss the Fire Department?" she said.

"I miss some of the people, not the job, I am ecstatic to be out of that city."

"You can't go back there again; I simply won't allow it," she said.

"Someday, I will write about it, a 48-hour special perhaps. The strange Negative energy of Worcester." As soon as I said it, I knew it was wrong. Jen had never seen the 48-hour special on Doc apparently; he made her promise never to watch it.

She let it go, but it did return us to the conversation about what I would be writing about when it came to him.

"If you're talking about his crimes, or more specific, what I'll write about them, that's difficult."

There were topics of certain events in Doc's life that were never talked about and I accepted that. Jenny avoided the subject entirely, because like me, she did not know him during the time in his life when he was caught up in the middle of some pretty horrible circumstances. The taking of a life, whether premeditated, or an act of passion was a difficult subject to breach. We had spent the greater part of a year with Jenny grieving trying to wring every drop of insight out of my conversations with Doc that she somehow felt excluded from. Yet, we did not tread into the forbidden areas of his truth. She was horrified when I told her how many times someone like PJ would just blurt out what seemed to be the most inappropriate comments.

In many ways it was the simplicity of prison that cut through the bullshit and made life much clearer. Face your truth and get on with it.

Looking back, it was not very difficult to see which parts of the Three Reasons I allowed to reign free over my decision- making process. Plato aside, there were some whose crimes were so unacceptable that denial was the only option. Doc would just shrug off most comments, but, on occasion, just under the surface I would detect an anger or a shift in control, which was quickly corrected. Probably, only I would notice these subtle blips on the radar, after all he trained me to observe such things, and he knew it. On many occasions you could see him contemplating whether we should just sit down and get it over with, especially towards the end.

"And did he?" asked Jenny, sounding curious.

"He didn't have to. Remember, I knew he had cancer by just placing my hand on his shoulder. What would be the point of making him relive the worst moment of his life? You didn't require such acts from him, you were the last one to see him alive, and didn't need some bed side confession." Jen's eyes began to tear up, and I so badly wanted to change the subject, a subject that she herself had made a stipulation not be raised at her visits.

"Did he ever say anything?" she asked very softly, almost as if she was surprised the words were coming out of her mouth.

I knew better then to hesitate when asked a direct question by this woman, so I said quickly "He said enough."

"So, you know about the civil suit?" said Jenny "And how it all fell apart and why he was charged with perjury?" She didn't wait for a response, she just continued. "It's that compartmentalization you were talking about, everything kept in its own box. Appearance was paramount, family kept at a distance. And the money, funny how that does in so many people. Losing all that money in the civil suit was devastating to him. It was the thought of being without all the money that led him to pursue the stupidity. And, it was stupid. Someone that smart, you think he would have come up with a better plan than two friends suddenly remembering seeing someone near his girlfriends' car the night she was murdered. Someone who's description of course was the exact opposite of Doc. Like ten years ago by and out of the blue someone just remembers that night and comes forward. Even a dimwitted detective would have little trouble tearing this story apart. What was he thinking?"

Apparently, Jen knew a lot more about the details of Docs pre prison life than I did.

"It was the thought of leaving his kids without anything. They would need to go to good schools, and that was in jeopardy. Did he ever share any of that with you?" Jen asked.

"I walked into his room to check up on him one day near the end. He had become so weak that he was barely able to stand on his own. He had fallen asleep with the pictures of his three girls pressed against his chest, you could tell he had been crying. It's an image I will always reflect on. It's a reminder of the desperation and helplessness that prison can bring out in you. It was Doc at his most vulnerable."

"Somehow you forget it's not so clear-cut on the outside either," Jenny added in a somber tone. "So that's what you'll write about," she said, bringing the topic around.

"I can only write about my own experience; I don't know if I can portray to anyone what Doc taught me. This is definitely a 'You had to be here' Experience."

"Anything else?" prodded Jenny.

It was a very short conversation and I remembered it very well. I can still see the look on his face. We were moving him down to the flats, because he could no longer manage the stairs up to the third tier. We both knew this meant that his stay at Walpole was fast coming to an end. In the D.O.C.s eyes the semi- Permanent work force was for those who could work and those days were over for Doc. Soon he would be moved, in the middle of the night, to either the Shattuck or perhaps Shirley Medium and that would be that. We were standing in his cell and all he wanted to talk about was my future. Right to the end, my well-being.

"You can't lose focus. I can't stress this enough," said Doc. "Use your Pause, become Plato. Implement your own imperative, and never stop looking for the patterns." He stopped mid-sentence.

The silence that followed was stifling. You seldom saw Doc hesitate, or be at a loss for words, yet the far-away look on his face was new, and it spoke volumes. Facing his own mortality, I imagined, would account for such a prolonged silence, so I simply stood motionless holding the box filled with the contents of what was left of his life.

"I did this to myself," he said finally, his gaze never leaving the blank gray wall he had been staring through. "This cancer, its self-manifested as punishment perhaps for not seeing the world as it could be. Maybe more, it's funny don't you think, people have no problem agreeing that the human mind can inflict disease upon itself, but they struggle with the possibility that it can also heal itself. You've never asked," he said suddenly turning towards me. "You've never asked about any of it, and I thank you for that."

"It's not for me to ask," I said.

"You're the best friend I've ever had," said Doc, "who would have thought any of this was possible in such a setting, but here we are." Again, the blank stare returned as he faced the wall again. "So much has happened and so much has changed, and I suppose that is the real punishment. To understand what it truly means to be alive, the connections we so easily avoid or misread, and to have it all taken away like this just when you come to understand it all. But you, you have a chance to take this forward, you get to apply all of this someday out there. You get to make a difference. I envy you. You talk about the bleakness of your future, yet I think even you know it won't turn out that way. What I wouldn't give to be a part of the possibilities you will create. Who knows, maybe you'll let me tag along."

"If anyone can find away, it'll be you," I said trying to keep the conversation normal. Sometimes I think that's exactly what Doc planned all along. To hitch a ride, in some fashion, or at least have his theory's move forward in me. I humbly reserve a place for anyone who might think walking in my footsteps is something they would want to do. I would consider it an honor. Plato was here, my son Alex was here, so why couldn't Doc come along.

"What you don't ask about was a long time ago," said Doc, looking suddenly composed and resolute. He began in almost a story teller fashion. "There was this guy," and as quickly as the story began, it ended. The expression on his face replaced by that blank sullen look he had been wearing earlier. The dead air seemed to suffocate us both. When he finally turned back in my direction, he looked me directly in the eye and with the most sincere, honest face I had ever seen from him, said in a tone of finality, "But I won't do that to you."

That moment which both of us gave a small nod towards each other was over, just like that. Back to the reality of living, or in Doc's case, dying.

"At any point, would you like me to address any of this?" said Jenny, looking rather annoyed. "Wow, you're going to be a lot of work; were you always like this?"

"Yes", I said, "But without the focus or the proper education. Perhaps the understanding of the true meaning of consequence, and compassion. I think I originally misinterpreted compassion, and possibly respect, and consideration for that matter for what anyone else has to go through, or say; but other than that, yes."

"Again, wow. Let's get you something to eat first. I worry so much about the effects the food in here is having on you. It may take years to fix."

This seemed a little odd to me, that Jenny would not instantly acknowledge what I had just told her. This was a rather significant realization about the man we both so admired after all. Maybe she was processing it all. When we returned to our seats, she launched into impressive detail on how the body functions as a whole.

"Most illnesses are a result of the body's natural 'state' being out of line, out of tune if you will with your normal state of being. The symptoms that people want treated are the surface result of a body crying out. It was the shoes by the way, that's when I knew. It was the shoes."

I said nothing, I didn't dare. There was a short pause, like she was choosing her words carefully, and she went on to explain in great detail the murder scene. Doc's girlfriends' body in the back seat on the floor, covered in a blanket. Her car was parked at the far end of the lot, and then there were the shoes. Placed neatly side by side on the floor in the front, placed there with purpose, with thought.

"No one else would do that," she said. "I never figured out why no one ever brought that up, but no one would do that unless they cared, unless they felt guilty, and that's when I knew. It was the shoes."

All I could do was reach over and place my hand on hers, there was nothing to say. Her eyes watered slightly, and I felt hollow. She continued in a far-off voice, "I don't have a complete explanation yet for why people do what they do. Maybe a life led in attempt to maintain perfect control is too much and you snap for an instant. I only know that it could be any of us under the correct circumstances, or under the worst circumstances, but I believe in you," she said looking directly at me. "I believe that what you are experiencing in here will lead to something extraordinary."

I could not help but believe that she was over estimating me. I did believe a place of isolation was exactly the setting that offers the best chance of growth and clarity. Tucked away from the distractions and temptations of the outside world I could thrive. But most don't, for the simple reason, they can't sustain the process.

It's as if they live in a vast ocean, and never learned to swim. You can only tread water so long, eventually you grab the first thing that floats by, and cling to it in desperation and out of fear. I've watched too many people drift away from shore caught in a current that has its own destination, irrespective of its passengers. I've been there, but my crime was worse. You see, I found many wonderful floatation devices in my lifetime and happily took them wherever they went. The thing was, I knew how to swim. Again, I felt like a coward. From this impossible situation though a small light can shine. A Philosophy can be born in the silence of time, that can benefit anyone, the convicted and the confused alike. Those that are in prison, on both sides of the wall.

"We will work all this out," she said, squeezing my arm. "I will take you home to Pennsylvania, and we will work all this out," and with that Jenny buried her face in my shoulder and drifted away.

I remembered all she had done to get Doc out of prison to spend one day out of this horrible place to die with some dignity. A day that never came.

As our visit came to an end, my mind was exhausted. All the insights I had gained into the world of this woman and her realization of Doc's own truth. This girl who claimed to be taking me home to Pennsylvania. In my confusion instead of hugging Jenny good bye, I gently kissed her forehead, and by what I still maintain as a wonderful mistake our lips touched briefly on the way by, which had her turning and smiling as she went out the door. I swear the female guard at the door had a small grin that quickly disappeared when I caught her eye, as if she had been thinking, It's about time, Baxter.

3.9 SECONDS

Tuesday was my favorite day, it meant writing class. I sat in anticipation as Juan, the youngest member of our group, prepared to share his latest story. His voice was soft yet confident as he described a scene where his girlfriend confronted him with her feelings about him going to prison. His writing was revealing as he detailed the depth of his girlfriend's despair. He put us right in the moment. We connected instantly to the reactions of a loved one dealing with incarceration. He described her vulnerability and tears with vivid sentences that leapt off the page, so unexpected from a young writer. He made us all proud. Miranda complimented him on his openness as we nodded in agreement.

"Any comments?" asked Miranda.

"I can relate," came one voice.

"You put me right there, man," nodded the guy next to me.

"I need more," I said.

The room fell silent. Miranda nodded at me to continue.

"I love what you wrote," I started, "but it's incomplete. I feel for your girlfriend, but not once did I hear a single word about you, about how you feel about her or about coming to prison. Nothing."

Juan looked down at his papers and I wondered if I should go on. He had talent. I could see that.

"It's a good story, but there's nothing to make me care about you. If you can write about how you felt, then you'll have me. Go a little deeper. Show me who you are."

Juan had been listening intently. He looked me in the eyes. "I'm not sure I can do that."

"Why?"

"Cause that's scary?"

"Good, then write about that."

"That's what I'm talking about. That's why I come here," clapped a veteran writer sitting in the corner.

Inside I felt a surge of pride. I was confident my analysis was on target. I felt like I was becoming a writer.

"Good work, everyone," said Miranda. "Now get out your notebooks. Write a letter to a family member or friend. You have five minutes. Begin."

I would have preferred longer, but I dove right in. I finished signing my letter just as Miranda called time.

"Ken, please read yours for the class."

I hadn't thought about reading this out loud, but after the

advice I just doled out to Juan, it seemed appropriate. My throat tightened as I began.

> *Hi Alex,*
>
> *Sorry I haven't written sooner. Life moves so fast. Like a road with black ice on a Sunday morning in New England it can catch you by surprise. I read the last letter you wrote again, and I did the math for you.*
>
> *I still have a couple of questions. You made some great points. Your writing is insightful. You really captured my attention with the scope and depth of your emotions, but I think you put too many of the worlds' problems on your shoulders. Why do you feel a need to do that?*
>
> *I agree with your Mom. As much as a conduit as you are for the world's problems, you're not responsible for everyone else's feelings. That's too much for anyone to handle.*
>
> *Anyway, 3.9 seconds. That's how long you fell for.*
>
> *Like I said. I did the math. I didn't know what else to do.*
>
> *I miss you Al. I'll write again soon.*
>
> *Love,*
> *Dad*

When I got to the end, I suddenly wanted to be anywhere else. I kept my head down hoping Miranda would move on. She repeated my last few words.

"I didn't know what else to do. Very evocative," she said quietly. "I was not expecting that. How old was your son?"

I couldn't answer. Sorrow seized my words. From across the room a sarcastic voice said, "Awe, poor baby," in a tone meant to ridicule.

You'd think I'd be used to this by now. No personal tragedy left un- kicked. Nothing was sacred in here, not even the death of my son. Instantly, everything seemed wrong. I wanted to lash out. I wanted to climb the fence and run. My fist clenched as I stood up and walked out, the door slamming behind me.

Walking through the yard the confines of prison began to close in around me and I felt suffocated. I thought I'd been dealing with the loss of Alex. This was the perfect opportunity to demonstrate my new mindset with a "pause," but it wasn't going to happen. Not today.

Entering my room, I had the overwhelming need to wash this whole place from my body. I flung open my locker door, slamming it against the wall which woke up "It," who was trying to nap, exhausted from an entire day of being an asshole. I grabbed my towel and soap and I reached for a new razor. My hand froze mid-motion. There, hanging off it, was a big piece of skin the exact shape and dimensions that result from shaving one's head. I have a full head of hair. My attention turned towards 'It', who sat on the edge of his bed mumbling under his breath. The waning day's sunlight light reflected off his shiny scalp.

The next few moments unraveled quickly, like the spring from an old pocket watch breaking free from its casing. Deferring to Occam's Razor (no pun intended), the odds that the culprit was anyone other than the low-life thief with the IQ of a shrubbery sitting in front of me were miniscule. I witnessed all that I thought I'd become spin wildly out of control as I covered the ground between us in milliseconds.

"You used my razor."

"It" scrambled to his feet, "I didn't take shit."

"Don't fucking lie to me." I shoved "It" into the wall.

"You want to take this into the bathroom," he tried to recover.

"No problem." I pushed my face right up to his. "But understand this. I will do everything in my power to leave you staring up at a ceiling from a hospital bed for the rest of your life. I will take great care not to kill you, but to cripple you."

I knocked him backwards onto his bunk and hurled open the door. Stomping down the hall, I threw the hepatitis-laced razor into a garbage can, purposely ignoring the onlookers.

From behind, "It" yelled after me.

"What the fuck is your problem? I got a concerned look from the guard at the desk who was talking hurriedly into a phone. I suspect he was calling for the Move Team in case a full out brawl ensued. I didn't expect "It" would follow me. In some ways, I almost felt sorry for him. He didn't know any other way. His whole life was spent stealing, conniving, all the while knowing he was a piece of shit. Today was no different. His only real upset was that he got caught. He'd be smarter next time. My real problem wasn't "It," it was me. I had too many years left on my sentence to be falling apart now. This place sucked.

I gripped the sides of the sink with both hands controlling my breathing. I saw my reflection in the full-size mirror. I had not seen myself for a long time. The mirrors at Walpole were a doll-sized plastic approximation offering a funhouse version of your face. I stared into the mirror and saw Alex's reflection intermingled with mine. Mine angry. His disappointed.

Suddenly, I was in San Francisco at Alex's service. That morning too restless to sleep, I wandered in the pre-dawn light through Golden Gate Park and came upon a bench overlooking the bay with a direct view of the bridge floating in the fog. I was compelled to walk out across to where my son made his last conscious choice. We knew where he jumped from. It was captured on film by a camera permanently mounted and constantly recording people's last desperate acts. I walked up to the railing and peered over. I saw him jump and heard him scream as he fell plummeting towards the base of the cement pylon below. The horrific impact ended my boy's life. I was undone. If Nicholai and my nephew Brian were not waiting for me back on the bluff, I would have considered jumping myself.

Standing in prison looking at the reflection of my son's eyes within my own, I heard the scream again, but this time the voice was mine.

Act Three

THE LITERAL WARRIOR

THE DOMINO EFFECT

It was on a Tuesday. I remembered because I had just dropped my laundry off with a bag of chili, when there was a knock on my door. I recognized Maurice as the laundry guy's roommate, also as one of the young Spanish kids who was scraping dominoes on the cement outside the weight area that day. "This is their Hollywood," I thought, that classic line that described so many people in here. This is the coolest they will ever be.

In Walpole I had spoken about my aversion towards paying for or having to bribe certain individuals to simply do their jobs, in particular laundry. I cared little about how I looked in gray prison clothes or gray t-shirts at Walpole, but in Baystate, I had new white thermals and a nice dress shirt along with dungarees that I rather enjoyed wearing to visits. When my new white thermals disappeared, or were replaced by older worn out versions I became somewhat annoyed.

After confronting the laundry guy about this obvious scam, he pretended not to speak English, which left me with a few options. Considering my promise to Jenny that I try not to antagonize too many more people, the art of the deal seemed like the way to go. Negotiating a bribe also seemed to give my new friend a much better grasp of the English language. For a small fee which usually consisted of some form of food item my laundry became cleaner and newer by the week. This pleased Jenny to no end who seemed to have her own issues with cleanliness, and she added a stipend to my account for just such briberies, as she appreciated the clean attire I now showed up at visits in.

Maurice didn't look that cool standing in my doorway, in fact he was in a fair amount of distress. He was sweating profusely and looking a wee bit nauseous. "You gotta help me poppy, can I come in?"

It was with some caution and a touch of curiosity that I motioned him inside.

"My roomie says you used to be a Doctor or something, you got to help me."

"I didn't used to be a doctor." I started to say, but Maurice wasn't listening.

"I gotta show you this." Maurice reached for his pants.

"Whoa, oyai, they'll be none of that."

I can't even begin to list the reasons why someone pulling their pants down in my room screamed of wrong on so many levels. Maurice could tell instantly that his intentions were not being shown in the bare bottom light that he had hoped.

He pleaded "Please, Poppy, I don't want to get lugged, I don't know what to do."

"Jesus, Ok, hold on to your pants." I glanced down the hall before I closed the door, my mind clearly running through all the scenarios in which this could go sideways so fast.

"Ok," I said "What's up?" hoping that wasn't a metaphor for what I was about to see. My limited medical training had made me very calm in the face of an emergency, and calmness was what was required as Mo dropped his pants to knee level exposing his bloody swollen penis to my stoic gaze.

"Well, that's quite an infection you have there, Maurice. Want to explain what happened?"

I couldn't help it, I had to know. There and then the mystery of the dominoes was solved, and I couldn't stop looking. I didn't care who told him to do this. I heard the rumors; I just didn't believe them. You took a razor blade and sliced a thin gash across the head of your penis and slid in the smooth ground down triangular pieces of dominoe under the skin. Why?

"Because the girls love it," said Maurice, wincing.

"Of course, they do, what was I thinking?" Mo didn't seem to appreciate my bed side manner. "Ok then, well that explains the infection, no surprise there. You have to go to the H.S.U. You need to kill that infection, cause I'm pretty sure the girls aren't gonna love that. And I certainly don't have the correct solution to address this."

Maurice was pleading now. "No, No hospital. I can't, you don't understand you have to help me."

I did have an Idea; I just didn't want to be part of it. But here was a young Spanish kid in my room with his infected penis hanging out. "So, Ok Maurice, up with the pants, here's what you do, and you're not going to like it. You clean the floors around here right. Go to work this afternoon and ask the desk Sargent for floor stripper, they'll give you a small amount, right?"

"Ya, I guess," said Maurice, starting to sense that this might not be all that much fun.

"Why floor stripper, Poppy?"

"They're not going to give you alcohol, so floor stripper it is. Go into your mop closet and pour all of it slowly and directly on the infection, and you might want to put a rag in your mouth."

"A rag," said Mo, his voice cracking with realization.

"Cause it's going to burn like a son of a bitch. Can you do that? Cause if you can't then you had better run to the HSU."

"Ok, Poppy, if you say so, I'll do it."

Now I'm not saying I've grown that unsympathetic, but after a while you lose patience with this sort of self-destructive nature or at least you grow impervious to its effects. I was well into a book and a wonderful section on Descartes seven years of cellular regeneration when I heard a muffled scream off in the distance. This was followed by a quick round by the C.O.s and a room check to identify the source of the disturbance. My door opened slightly and a voice asked. "You alive in here, Baxter?"

"Far as I can tell," I replied, without looking up from my book.

Several days later I returned from a run to find an assortment of food stores piled on my bed. Coincidentally, all the items required to make Eric, my new roommate's famous spicy crab cakes. When questioned Eric said "I might have mentioned to Maurice what we might both enjoy, do you mind?" said Eric, scooping up all the items. "We're gonna eat well tonight. Don't know what you did, don't want to know, but my stomach thanks you."

Couple of days later I saw Maurice walking to chow and asked how he was doing.

"The mamas are going to love me Doc, I owe you one, did you get the food?"

"I did, and Eric and I both thank you."

"No problem, you're the best Poppy!"

In some small way you had to admire Maurice's conviction, it is a quality that few outsiders could appreciate. The procedure he carried out on himself took a certain amount of dedication. I'm not saying the reasoning was sound, but the follow through was quite impressive. It brings up the same question over and over, how do you harness this energy? It's still about remaining relevant, forcing all of this to mean something, so how does Maurice learn to use this commitment for a better purpose, How, do I for that matter?

The Domino effect as I will now call it had me questioning myself to a troubling extent. What were my convictions? Had I really addressed them? I felt different, but what did I really believe in? Granted, I would probably not be grinding down dominoes anytime soon. For the most part I stayed in the moment and immersed myself in study, but just below the surface lied a churning desire to accomplish, to be recognized, and most of all someday, to be loved.

Our last visit had ended with the slightest hint of a kiss, the brush of lips so quick it could not be counted as legitimate. We both knew that this would progress in some fashion, a more undeniable step forward, towards the cliché of a prison romance. I had many years in front of me, and she was free to come and go. Two entirely different worlds meeting as virtual particles in the space between where matter is formed. We will either unite and form a permanent bond, at least as permanent as humans are capable of, or we would annihilate each other like anti particles from different dimensions, either way it seemed inevitable. Evolution would not wait any longer.

Jenny was coming for two days of visits this time which meant fourteen hours. We were still the only ones that would sit for the entire allotted time, which seemed to horrify other inmates.

"What could you possibly have to talk about for that long?" asked Eric. "There's no way I could talk to my wife for seven hours; I don't even talk to my girlfriend for that long!"

Still, even for us, there were some obstacles to overcome like sitting for that length of time especially considering she drove seven hours to get here. Another was going to the bathroom. She could go if required, but it was met with extreme suspicion, not to mention an escort. I, on the other hand would have to be strip searched just for requesting a bathroom break, and considering the vending machines were the glimmering beacon whose bright lights and low hum drew inmates like moths to the flame, visits meant a full bladder. I was usually busting at the seams by the end of a visit. We, both knew there was time before the "Kiss" was going to happen, but the anticipation was palpable. The first day was filled with stealthy strokes of the forearm and extra-long gazes of silence. I believe I even growled at one moment like a cat stalking its prey. The chairs were comfortable, just sitting on something that wasn't plastic or metal was a treat for me. Jenny got reprimanded for leaning back too far in a suggestive pose. For the first few hours we talked about writing, and she critiqued the stories I sent, always harping on my lack of proficiency when it came to punctuation.

"You have to put a comma after a Non-restrictive clause."

"A non-restrictive what?"

"Before and after a non-restrictive clause," she went on. I began to wonder if this girl ever had sex. And that was always the next topic, she obsessed over the details and time lines of any relationship I ever had in my entire life. She wanted every detail and pointed out inconsistencies to any degree, her memory appeared to be flawless. She had a better understanding of the order in which my life played out than I did. In truth there was much of my life that I struggled to place in the correct chronological order and some periods were actually missing. As far as she was concerned, all ex-wives or girlfriends must have death certificates or marriage licenses to prove they were out of the picture. Apparently, Doc had told her I was a rock and roll whore with a propensity for the lime light. Well, ok, so that's somewhat accurate, but still I wanted to make a good impression, and she was making it difficult. To distract her I told her about Maurice and the dominoes which stopped her in her tracks. In fact, it seemed to horrify her, which was my plan, except it also put a damper on any meaningful romantic gesture at the end of our visit. Seven hours just flew by. I couldn't help but make the analogy between my Walpole days and one of my first written stories called Seven Minutes. Once again Einstein's Kappa effect was on full display as time being relevant to the experience at hand. Fortunately, neither one of us would be deterred from the desire to test the waters of compatibility. For me anyway, kissing is the most essential part of a physical relationship. Many other aspects could be worked on but the Kiss was Essential, and I feared quite justifiably, I was out of practice. Our embrace at the beginning of the following day's visit was an indication that our pursuit of intimacy was still on the forefront of both our intentions. The greeting hug was border line inappropriate as there was not a photon of visible light that could be detected between any part of our bodies. Cheek to cheek toe to toe, pelvis to, well you get the picture. The stern warning from the girl at the desk drew the eyes of everyone in the visiting room as this breach of protocol harkened a sharp "Baxter" in an accusatory tone.

"God," said Jen. "What's with the puritanical attitude? It's like we're at a junior high dance and the chaperones are there to make sure we're the right distance apart. What in the world is their problem?"

We were both blushing when we sat down. Jen had a full list of subject matter to get us through the day, which she seemed to be able to pull out of thin air. As wonderful as the thought of a possible next stage of this Victorian romance was, her topic choices were right on when it came to my current mindset. I had told her about my reservations towards gaining any true insight out of all the studying I had been doing. My feelings of resentment that had been creeping in, even my admiration of Maurice, the domino guy, no matter how misguided. She listened carefully.

"Most college students," she began, "start to trail off a little at some point in their sophomore year and focus on just getting through it. I will not allow you to just get through this because that's what you're asking, right? You want permission to make time go by, to get out of here quicker, believe me I am right there with you, but it's not realistic. It's just a plateau that you have to break through."

I listened as she began to dissect my entire way of being. "You have a touch of A.D.H.D. We have discussed that. You have an active imagination and it gets tempting to allow your mind to drift off to somewhere better, somewhere rich in distraction. You're a dreamer. People with highly creative minds find it more difficult to focus on the subject matter at hand, and you always want it to take you to someplace magical. Your type tends not to be the best student from an academic standpoint. People with your brain patterns tend to procrastinate, and procrastination is an addiction. It is a release to a place with no worries, nothing to solve. It's a bad habit to get into, it can create resentment."

"Bitterness and resentment are energy." I said, "And sometimes running in circles on a muddy track doesn't do it."

"Yes, I see that. I'm pretty sure that self-doubt and self-pity is not the way to retrain your brain though." She was direct and blunt and most assuredly correct.

Next on her list was a hearing I had coming up. They would be asking why I had refused to take the good time by attending any programs and also why I had refused a job here, and quite frankly they were not going to like my answers.

"I'm tired of hearing that an Arsonist can't go to minimum security, and I'm tired of not telling exactly what happened to me. Everything I wouldn't divulge to the judge or the D.A. What's the point of Doc's 'No lie on the Soul' if I don't adhere to it?" Jen paused and reached for my hand.

"I have real reservations of you telling a room full of unsympathetic prison staff the truth behind why you came to prison, and I am worried about the ramifications if you did."

"Me too, but I have to trust my intuition on this one."

"No. Trust your instincts, not your intuition," she said, "Trust your second brain."

Before we knew it, our visit was over and we had to say our good-bye's. I had a momentary twinge of hesitation as we stood up thinking this had been such a great visit, I didn't want to ruin it by being overly aggressive. I could sense she had her own plan in mind and maybe I should let her guide the exit. I don't know what happened, but as we looked at each other, it was clear that we were both thinking the same thing and I guess I took this as a green light. But before I knew it, we were somehow thrown into the middle of a movie kiss. The kind where the hero is about to be dragged off to his death or the scene where an unspoken love is in its last chance throes to reveal itself. Jenny was bent half way over at the waist caught in a French bear hug that would have small children turning away. I do know this was the loudest scream I ever heard that consisted of my name. The guard was furious, I quickly released my grip on Jen and headed for my seat against the wall like a subservient criminal. The large fellow who I sat down next to said with a chuckle, "what the hell dude?"

"Not sure," was all I could muster, as I was still a little surprised at myself. I watched Jen as she was struggled to walk in a straight line. She had to look around to locate the exit door from the visiting room. She would describe it later as jouncy and disarrayed. She said she tried to look back through the small thick glass panel in the door, but I was preoccupied. It takes a certain amount of time for certain parts of the body once aroused to return to their normal size. My embarrassment was over shadowed by one of the exit guards who rose from his desk in the procedure room to applaud my brazen assault, "Not bad, Old man" He said. The strip search guard was much less amused as he handed me back my underwear.

In the chow hall that night when I sat at my table the other inmates tapped their sporks in acknowledgment of my brazen Kiss; word traveled fast. Was nothing sacred in here, I thought. A week later I received a letter from Jen describing the kiss, and despite the fact that she inadvertently forgot to put my name on the envelope, it still got to me. On that same day I was told that I was to report to my case workers office at a specified time, which I did only to sit for about an hour waiting my chance to go in.

Every inmate that went in, came out none to happy which left me feeling a little anxious. When it was finally my turn, I sat across from three stoic faces. I imagined they would rather have been anywhere else then here doing reviews and recommendations for an entire day. Judging from the expressions of those that left before me the interactions were not that friendly. They spent several minutes thumbing through papers and reviewing notes. Carlos my case worker was at least civil.

"We have a few questions for you, Kenny, if you don't mind."

"Not at all," I no longer felt the anxiety that I was usually accustomed to when sitting before a review board. I wasn't going to be disrespectful, but I was also not going to hold anything back.

"Why did you refuse to go to the program down stairs? Didn't you want the good time?" asked one of the faces who never looked up. "And don't give me any bullshit about liking prison that you peddle."

I jumped right in. "Ohh, this place most assuredly sucks, but I thought that was the point. It's nothing more than a violent day care center for children. I would rather be back in Walpole. Prison in general though I actually do like, thank you very much; If you could just find a way to remove the criminal population from the place it would be great."

No one laughed.

"Have you ever done drugs?" said interviewer number One.

"Of course, I have, I'm a musician, it was required," still no reaction so I continued, "And when I decided not to do them, that was pretty much that. This program you offer is a format from the 70's that has long since proven ineffective. It's based on a theory of exposing weaknesses in individuals. I can get the book it's based on if you like. Its archaic and quite frankly, a little insulting."
There was some quick scribbling of pen to paper followed by, "Is work insulting to you too? You have turned down every job here, is that archaic also?"

"Well, if you've read anything about me, which I'm assuming you have, then you would know my work ethic is not a concern, but as for turning down mopping floors, I chose instead to utilize my time here learning to write and adding to my education. I have years left on my bid, and right now I'm going to take care of myself."

"Would you care to discuss your crime?"

"Sure, what would you like to hear?"

"You tell us."

"Ok I'll tell you what no one else sitting on your side of the table has heard. I'm ok with it."

And with that I began, it felt wonderful to describe my actions with such clarity. My son was no longer with us, the ex-girlfriend and her greed was barely a memory. I had come to accept almost all the aspects of my choices. I asked they respect my decision to educate myself in leu of some ridiculous program I could teach, and the dollar a day floor cleaning job that they thought would help assimilate me back into the collective. I explained that my new girlfriend (Wow, I just called Jenny my girlfriend) had decided a path through this together and she would see that I did not require the income for the time being. And then came the question that is asked of every convicted criminal,

"Do you feel remorse for your crime?"

That's the dangerous one. I never hesitated. "Not in the least. I went out of my way to make sure no one was injured. And everyone got exactly what they wanted."

"Well, the D.A said a firefighter was injured."

"Total Bullshit," I replied, "the prosecutor had no case and a huge axe to grind, no pun intended," which brought a chuckle from the sergeant who had sat stone faced throughout.

"No axe to grind I like that."

"They found some rookie who I never met nor ever heard of, and some two years removed from the fire claimed he was injured. The D.A made it sound like I was lying in the bushes across the street shooting firefighters with a sniper rifle as they came out the front door."

"Why didn't you take the plea deal?" asked Carlos.

"Because I did it," and there it was. "It's not about a greedy ex-girlfriend and a son I can't bring back. The bottom line was the culpability lies with me. What was the point of any of this if I didn't come to prison? Somedays I still wonder what any of this is still for." My voice trailed off into my own remorse. There was total silence.

Finally, Carlos said "Thanks, Kenny, that will be enough." The remaining members of the board were no longer looking down at their papers, and the sergeant even nodded in my direction almost to say, "Sorry."

As I left the room I felt as light as a feather, sure I probably sealed my fate, that much I was aware of but there it was. Now everyone knew and what would be the difference. Nothing, I was part of the system now. As I was closing the door to leave, I heard one of the panel members say "Jesus Christ, have you ever heard anything like that?"

I barely settled into my bunk to feast on Erik's meal of the day when I was called to the front desk.

"What the hell did you do?" said Eric, "Get yourself lugged."

As I approached the desk, Carlos was standing talking to the desk sergeant and motioned me into his office.

"I'm going to see if I can get you out of here and moved to Pondeville is that ok with you?"

I wasn't sure why, but I didn't argue, and said quickly, "Sure, thank you very much, Sir."

"My name is Carlos," he said and reached to shake my hand.

"Hell of a story, Kenny, hell of a story."

I hardly slept a wink that night in anticipation of what might someday be a move to the next step. I couldn't wait to call Jenny when the phones came on, but I never got a chance. There was a knock on the door and some young C.O. said, "Come on, Baxter, down to the cage with you, you're going to Pondeville."

"What, well ok let me pack up quick."

"No, no time for that your roommate will do that for you." At least it was going to be Eric. Never more was the nature of the D.O.C. on display. Everything takes forever until it doesn't. One minute I'm waiting for the phones to come on, the next I'm sitting in the cage out front waiting for the transport driver. I was a little concerned about my belongings and at least Eric was an inmate of some means, meaning my meager possessions were of no use to him. But still what would have been the harm of letting me pack up my own stuff? As it turned out, I could have walked to Pondeville faster. I sat in the cage for six hours with Max, who barley spoke a word. He just snarled and stared into space. I began to realize that I wouldn't get the chance to complete the writing course or thank the people involved for how much they influenced me, but that's just the prison way. Change comes slow until it doesn't. Several inmates strolled by and looked confused as they were among the many that said I could never could go to a minimum.

I began to wonder why I was so excited in the first place. Progress that's why. This would be the final stage of my journey. I couldn't help but think that Jenny was somehow prophetic. She focused me again and reminded me that my future was un-see-able. It is created in the moment by the small details of my pro-longed and consistent effort. No matter how slow or cloudy your path may appear to be, it's the small steps of the everyday that seem inconsequential or insignificant that are the key to every-thing. Stay the course and the dominos will fall.

If Mind and Body are aligned, you have the power of the universe behind you.
When we learn to enter a state of "Being" our mind and body become one
and all the gears are set in motion to have change become a permanent state...
"That is Evolution" Stephen Pinker M.I.T.

EVOLUTION

In Walpole, I used to imagine what the woods looked like from the other side of the west wall. I used the meditation tricks that Doc taught me to place myself at the base of a tree. I felt the au-tumn leaves crumble in my hands and imagined the sound of birds or even a squirrel at my feet foraging for acorns, unaware that I was there. I failed to do justice to the techniques Doc had me painstakingly rehearse over and over again until I mastered them. Doc got great pleasure out of me describing a bare foot walk to the top of the dunes in Wellfleet on Cape Cod. Feeling the tall marsh grass brushing against the palms of my hand, the sun-baked sand between each toe. Small white clouds clumped above my head as they met the off shore breeze. Delicate terns whistled sharp warnings if I trespassed too close to their nests. The sound of the waves, the taste of salt on my lips. The awe-inspiring sight of the North Atlantic and the sense of freedom that comes with...

"Baxter, you coming or would you like to spend the rest of the day in the cage?"

That was the folly of road-tripping my imagination. I never

knew when I would unceremoniously reach the end of my leash and be yanked back into reality. But today was an exception. Today, I would get to see what lay beyond the wall. Pondeville, my final destination before I entered the outside world. There were times when I questioned who I was beneath the stories I told about myself. Who I was without the titles and labels I had acquired; Firefighter, musician, father, husband, even convicted felon and arsonist? Now, I marveled at what I could become; philosopher, author, student, teacher, but alas, first things first.

My trip from Baystate to Pondeville was much the same as my trip from Walpole to Baystate. In fact, it was exactly the same. I had a momentary twinge of anxiety as the van approached the front gate pocketed into the unremitting gray wall.

"Miss this place, Baxter?" teased the guard as he slowed the van down just enough to make me think this promise of a new horizon was all a hoax. I laughed uncomfortably as he continued down an access road adjacent to the old west wall. The wall I had spent two years roaming beyond in my mind. As It turned out, what lay just out of sight was simply more criminals.

Pondeville as it turned out was but a few hundred feet beyond what I had spent years imagining was endless wilderness kept pristine just for me.

I performed the leg-shackle- shuffle up the front stairs of my new home. I looked around, shocked by what I didn't see. There was no wall. There was no fence. Just woods as far as my eye could see. There appeared to be people wandering in all directions. The building and grounds looked more like a retreat center than a prison.

I walked through the front doors unimpeded. There was no trap. No metal detector. In fact, there were no correctional officers. The place seemed to be run entirely by case workers all dressed in gray. Not a single blue uniform anywhere. Painted in cheery script on the wall above the front desk were a collection of encouraging affirmations: confidence, integrity, honor, perseverance. Jenny would later refer to this place as a demented YMCA you couldn't leave. Maybe that was the point. Perhaps it was meant to be disarming. It just seemed there were too many ways that this could go wrong. Max, my traveling companion and I both looked at each other and couldn't help but smile. It was a trick, right? A van pulled up in front and a half dozen inmates jumped out and headed up the stairs unaccompanied by, well, anyone. As I turned, I caught sight of Hockey Joe who strolled down the corridor and appeared to be walking a bouncy yellow Labrador retriever.

"Baxter!" he yelled out. "Welcome to Pondeville."

It was almost as if he were happy to see me. It was true the rumors I had heard about the service dog program. Maybe I would do that. I liked dogs.

"Hey, short stop," I turned to see Mello sauntering towards me.

"Baxter, don't talk to anyone until you see me. You'll be playing for us."

"Firefighter! You made it. What took you so long?" came a familiar voice from behind. It was Ed, the lawyer from my Walpole East Wing days. Everyone one looked so different. Not happy so much but civil and almost carefree. It was like some Stepford house I thought. They'd all been replaced, brainwashed, or something worse.

I was temporarily assigned to a room in the work release dorm with no roommate. The inmates here were quieter and better neighbors. They had real jobs outside of prison and left very early in the morning.

I was informed that breakfast started at five thirty. There was no official chow call. If you missed it, you missed it. Mello told me they had pancakes and coffee.

I settled into the bottom bunk. No roommate meant I had first dibs. Here I was in the prime bottom bunk looking out a window that actually had a screen that went up and down. Up. Down. I was fascinated by the pleasure this simple action ignited in me, and tried it several times.

My window looked out over the front entrance and the parking lot where people came and went at will. Cars pulled up, people got out, guards and visitors alike, doors opening and closing, engines starting. I had not heard these simple sounds of humans-in-transit in a long time. My window opened out to a small shingled roof which dropped onto a well-manicured mulch bed planted with flowers. A bird feeder hung in a Japanese maple. Amazing. Nestled in the branches of the tree was a pair of sparrows busily building their new home. I was instantly torn between the duality of my thought process. On one hand, I was lost in nature's peaceful simplicity. The nuances of a scene from some distant world that in the past, I would not truly have appreciated. On the other hand, I couldn't shake this feeling that I could just crawl out the window, slip off the roof and drop down onto the soft ground below and run into the woods. I wouldn't, though would I? I couldn't decide if it was because I knew better or that I had been trained like a dog with a shock collar whose paws skid to a stop at his boundary line, anticipating the electronic shock even when he no longer wore the device.

Suddenly I felt guilty, as if my mind was being read and the guards would storm through the door at any minute. This feeling intensified as I ventured into the hall. "Baxter to Property!" Muddled the loud speaker. This building was much nicer I thought as I approached a railing that overlooked the front desk.

"Excuse me. Did someone just call my name?" I asked respectfully.

The man in gray looked up from his computer.

"Is your name Baxter?"

"Yes," I replied my voice rising at the end as if I was happy to just get that simple question right.

"Then go to Property."

"Do I come down this way?" I gestured towards a large stairway that led down to the entrance area.

"No. You never use that staircase. It's not for you."

Instantly I felt better. This was a tone I was familiar with. Translation: Don't ever come down these stairs you piece-of-shit criminal.

"Down the back staircase, through the day room and down the corridor," he barked "First right end of the hall. Knock on the door."

The building was small. The rooms I passed resembled more of a college dorm style. The day room was smaller. Small tables and rows of windows that looked out over vast wooded areas. An inmate was accessing a vending machine with his own card, that was new. The closed chow hall was on my right and again the downsized theme continued, forged by the diminished population of less than two hundred. There was only one more corridor to try. As I passed by one of the bathrooms, steam emerged, which translated into hot showers. At the end of the hall Max stood against a wall. He appeared to be waiting for something, as I approached, he said, "I knocked but nobody answered." The door said Property. He seemed relieved to see me as if he was also suffering from the same culture shock.

"Yo, this place is crazy."

"Yo, totally," I responded. I was developing a new appreciation for this often-used phrase. I knocked on the door politely and was answered by a muffled angry voice.

"Wait your turn."

"That's what happened to me," said Max. The door opened and an inmate came out carrying a TV.

"Lewis" came the angry voice which apparently was Max's last name as he stepped through the half-opened door. Max emerged with the same box he came in with. My box was filed with just the essentials; toothbrush, soap, a change of underwear and such what, along with the most important item, my coffee cup. Not that I had coffee. I knew the rest of my belongings would be a week or so out, if they came at all. I was assigned a mattress which I had to sign for and promise full financial responsibility for if anything happened to it. I asked the tall stoic faced gentleman, who had me sign for it, if I could leave my box here while I dragged my mattress up the stairs.

"I don't give a shit what you do, I'm not going to be responsible for it."

So, with that I began the awkward attempt to carry and drag both my mattress and the box down the corridor towards my room when Mello appeared.

"Let me give you a hand, where's your room?"

"455," I said, "and thanks."

"Why'd they put you up in work release? They won't let you stay there."

I was thinking about the last time I saw "Mello" and it was back at Walpole and we were studying for his GED, which as it turned out he received. "Good for you," I said "what's this place like?"

"Lame, petty bullshit."

As we deposited my new mattress which was indeed an upgrade from the past few years, Mello tossed a bag of artificial imitation freeze-dried coffee on the desk and said, "Consider this a signing bonus, first game is Saturday."

I took a complete walk through of the remaining corridors which took all of about 2 min. The library was a disappointment. A shoe box of books might best describe it. A rack of out dated magazines and rows and rows of, for whatever reason, the same copy of a Spanish bible. Visions of The Baystate library danced in my head as I thumbed thru the section of Harry Potter, and Nick Savage detective novels. You never know what you have till it's gone. The reason given for the pretense of a library was that this was a work release facility, and reading was not the priority.

I looked thru the half-drawn shades into the visiting room which appeared quite nice. Comfortable, spacious, there were even tables to sit at if you chose. My mind quickly jumped to thoughts of my first visit from Jen, which had become the punctuated Oasis of my bid. I wondered if Nick would consider coming here. The last time I saw him was Walpole. Wow had it been that long? Walpole's visiting room was enough to end anyone's desire to visit someone in prison. Out behind the main building was a structure, possibly a gym, and/or classroom. I was sure that an alarm would sound if I opened the door, as it would identify me as a threat.

Out front was a parking lot, out back a gym and it was all encompassed by woods. The newness was overwhelming. A smallish man was observing me, and as it turned out, he was the current superintendent. "What are you thinking?" he asked as he must have noticed the perplexed look on my face. For some reason, I babbled some nonsense about pondering a scientific theory on quantum gravity. He didn't call me on it but he knew I was lying which completely caught me off guard. Why would I say that? Why would I lie about something so innocuous? I prided myself on not lying. The door swung opened and Hockey Joe appeared, "Wanna see the gym, Baxter?" he said holding the door open.

The gym was more than adequate, in fact it was one of the highlights of this place. I hesitated, staying inside, because there were no guards. It must be closed I thought as I continued along what appeared to be a walking path. There were signs in the woods marking them as "out of bounds." Some sort of honor system I thought, how bizarre. It seemed like an invitation to a child not to eat the bowl of candy placed in front of him. The path led all the way down to a huge field that encompassed an actual baseball diamond, backstop and everything. The walking path seemed to go all the way around its edges. It looked too far from the prison to be allowed without an escort.

My feet refused to go any farther. I simply could not get them to move. This must be the field we play on; Mello said the first game was on Saturday. Maybe it was off limits till the weekend, what day was it? I truly didn't know. Too much input for one day, I thought as I reversed my direction. Back in my room I closed the door and was comforted by the small tight enclosure of a prison cell, that seemed so much more familiar.

I sat on the bed and began the slow counting style of breathing that went along with the ritual that had become second nature to me now. The years spent rehearsing the healing process that Doc and Rupert had instilled in me.

The move from one prison to another in a single day can be unnerving to say the least. This day care center approach to re-habilitation combined with open fields and freedoms not experienced in many years was startling, and I was caught unprepared. My level of Institutionalization was astonishing, and a brief period of refocusing was required. This would be the last facility I would be kept at, albeit I would be here longer than Walpole and Baystate combined. Still, this is where I would re-enter the world from, and I must admit a level of panic set in. What would this mean for Jen and me, or my relationship with Nicholai. Had I come to any understanding with any of the truths I wanted to experience with Alex, or my Philosophy's. My place in the world would eventually get a whole lot bigger, and I was in a phrase "freaking out."

It was with a clear purpose that I sat on my bunk and relaxed into the familiarity of my small cell to seek refuge in the world of focused meditation. My breathing was mathematical. Doc had offered many alternatives based on tried and true Buddhist practices or long-standing yoga techniques, but as I have said, this must be personal, and it must ring true to my nature.

Different tones vibrate different parts of my body, and were the basis behind what Rupert and I defined as meditational sounding. The yoga practice of the Ooohhhmmm, or, oh mani pad mi ohm. Repeating a phrase that was primal to the beginning of its philosophy, tied you with the past in some way. Of course, it bothered Doc when I could not find resonance with any of these sounds which led to the somewhat unique practice of reciting "Pi."

Doc would have been proud of the fact that I was now approaching 1500 digits. A number that had Nicholai questioning my sanity, as it was his job to keep sending me more digits to satisfy my quest. The concentration required to hold such a number in place, was enough for me to block out the world.

Vivid dreams, which are actually rare are so realistic and clear that they get stored in the brain the same way as actual memories. Some of the vivid dreams I have had in my life are as realistic and permanent as any so-called real-life experiences. The procedure involves learning how to be aware you are dreaming and alter the outcome. Over the years I had become quite adept at this, to the point that I preferred spending my time in this altered state. Any fantasy could be lived out, any fear overcome, creating a permanent memory that I can recall on demand.

While sitting on my bunk I could breathe a short recitation of Pi and feel the breeze on my face, the taste of salt in the air. Somewhere between the brushing of marsh grass on my palms and the feel of warm sand between my toes my meditation would turn vivid. At will I could converse with Doc, walk alongside the beautiful, opinionated, woman with red hair. Mostly, I would spend hours sitting with Al, watching sets of waves crash against the shoreline.

The memories are permanent, stored chemically or electrically as Doc had described. I sensed that it was just the first step to what he had labeled as evolving within your lifetime. I also sensed there would come a time I would have to choose between these two realities.

AN UNFAMILIAR ROAD

"Embracing every day," had worked for me up till now, so I would continue to apply it in everything I did. I would play shortstop in softball, utilize the entire boundaries of the prison which allowed a half mile of running along the edge of the woods. Embrace every opportunity offered.

My first job at Pondeville sent me back to Baystate, the prison I had just left. Only this time I worked on the outside of the fence cutting the grass. It was strange seeing inmates I had just left weeks earlier, walking the damp, wet path that I used to trudge around. They looked so miserable. Mowing the lawn out by the street seemed bizarre as civilians drove by in their cars leading normal lives. You could just jump into a car and drive away. Tony, one of the guys I worked with, was an angry drug dealer that spent most of his spare time in the weight room. He was none too pleased at my constant requests that he show me the ropes. His growling and one-word answers were always met with a smile and a thank you.

Our Boss wasn't a bad guy, I grew up with true meanness, this guy was just doing his job. Our bag lunch consisted of slimed baloney on stale bread with a small milk which I never drank. I don't drink milk, never have, never will. I chose the fury of my father trying to impose his will over the consumption of this beverage. I will always wonder if that was a battle I should have taken up. Tony was the beneficiary of this childhood distain along with staff food that the boss would sneak us for a job well done.

Tony eventually lightened up. He told me about his youth, his family, his son, his motor bike accidents, one of which ground one of his fingers to the bone. He shared his hopes and dreams and the regrets of walking sleepily downstairs after hearing what sounded like a break in, only to point his gun at police officers carrying out the drug raid that would land him in State prison. By the time I moved on to my next opportunity, we had become friends.

I had to go through a probation period to be cleared for the real work adventures so when my time came, I was thrilled to be assigned to the 3 dollar a day D.C.R. jobs. D.C.R. stood for the Department of Conservation and Recreation.

The building we worked out of was in Roxbury, a suburb at the south edge of Boston. Just the thought of a van ride up old route 1 nick- named the Auto mile, for all of the car dealerships was an exciting prospect to say the least. I got to wear an orange shirt that said STAFF on the back. Apparently, the letters D.O.C. would be too frightening to the public. Eight large and scary clockwork orange shirted criminals carrying shovels and rakes all coming at you at once must have been a much more reassuring sight. I still question the logic of the D.O.C. Eight large excitable inmates also did not fit so well into a prison van, which led to a hierarchy of seniority when it came to seat selection.

But, still, Boston! My favorite city. The Red Sox, the Bruins, the North End, Faneuil Hall, Beacon hill. The House of Blues, the Esplanade on the Charles; what great memories I had of these places. Nicholai went to school here at The Berklee School of Music, and although I never thought I'd be visiting here as a convicted felon, I would get a chance to experience the outside world through a new set of eyes with a new philosophy.

As we pulled out onto route one we drove by Gillette stadium, home of the New England Patriots, and for some reason I had a flashback to the famous snowplow game against the Miami Dolphins, where during a time out in a blinding snow storm a work release inmate drove onto the field and cleared a spot for kicker John Smith's game winning field goal. It's my turn now, I thought. This was going to be great.

It was like a ride in a time machine taking me back to sights and sounds I no longer belonged to. As we passed the car dealerships, everyone yelled out what car they would own or steal once they got out. All of this should have been amusing, but it wasn't. Something felt drastically wrong, so wrong I was beginning to feel sick. Car lots and stores, food markets and retail outlets, one after another all screaming at me. Signs and more signs, blinking and flashing, enticing and prodding us to buy. Two for one, buy one get one free. One year of free interest, Lay away, free delivery.

Super-sized and win a prize. There were signs for lawyers and doctors, travel agencies and eyewear, furniture, gardening, gravel and building supplies. Ted's Diner and Flo's chicken, Bill's Burgers and Jakes bakery. Best pizza in the south end, largest supplier of home goods.

I had to close my eyes, what was happening to me? And then I knew, Doc happened to me. We had talked about this. I understood the world now and why I didn't want to be a part of it because I knew. None of this was sustainable, none of this was real. Doc was right, people feed off each other to survive, buying and selling each other things we didn't need, there was no other way. The economy driven world I had left behind was still functioning despite its doomed future, why had I thought it would be any other way. I could hear Doc's words as if I were sitting in his cell. "Out there," he would say, gesturing to the land beyond the wall, "You are simply fuel for the economic engine. There are very few companies or municipalities that have your well-being as their priority. They are certainly not run by Philosopher Kings. They don't even have their own well-being at the core of their actions. How scary is that? We live in a time when the economy is god, Consumerism must continue.

I saw it now for the first time. To paraphrase a bad 70's Sci Fi movie, "The spice must flow." Spending and buying whatever the product might be is the only point. Your personal well-being is not. I saw the consequences, the economic impact on our nation if people started consuming only what they needed. It would be Catastrophic. Why had I not seen this before, out there you are under a lot of pressure to do your part to keep the American dream alive, to be compliant.

I had to close my eyes. I needed to be anywhere else but in that van.

Pi was my savior, 3.14 159 265 358 the mantra that had set my mind at ease. The process that allowed me to access a part of my brain where the neurons fired and synapses led the way to a place reserved for knowledge. The gate way to another world. Defined as the numerical value of the ratio of the circumference of a circle to its diameter, Pi was so much more to me. It was the gateway to stillness meditation, and vivid dream states and now hopefully the escape of this nightmare trapped in a van with eight loud consumer inmates. I had never tried to do this anywhere but the quiet of my cell. Was it possible amid all this noise and chaos? I would try. Shut out the world and go deeper,979 323 864 2643 3832. To me Pi was the proof that there was no center to the circle. Proof that you could travel inward forever down past the confusion, step out of time, create a place for more, deeper and deeper still. To the depths of the deepest cave, to sit with Plato, for I was invited.795 0288 419 716 939 937 51058, the access code to an elite club, and there written on the wall the words of Aristotle: We are what we repeatedly do, Excellence is not a virtue but a habit.

One swallow does not a spring make, nor does one fine day;
Fifteen hundred digits later we arrived.

The inside of the D.C.R. building was as dirty a place as I could imagine, the highlight being the small condemned area we sat in while waiting for the words "move out" from our driver which would be more appropriate if we were actually well -trained soldiers instead of a group of uninspired chain gangers already asking when lunch was.

We started our journey thru the Southwest corridor park of Boston, armed with rakes and edgers and the simple instruction of start here. This particular park ran over four miles in length so I imagined it would take some time to edge every flower or mulch bed by hand, so off I went. It was wonderful. Mindless work that would take forever, what a great idea! What could go wrong?

It wasn't until I heard my name yelled in the distance by the guard running toward me that maybe I had been in my own world for a while. When I looked up, I was completely alone.

"What in the world are you doing, we're leaving, look at you," he added. "Did you leave any dirt on the ground?"

The other inmates weren't happy with me either. It seemed working hard was frowned upon. The ride back was much more comfortable as I got the only single seat near the front of the van. Apparently, no one wanted to sit next to me.

Entering the lobby at Pondeville, we lined up at the front desk waiting for our chance to be stripped searched. The desk Sargent did a double take when he saw my appearance, and smiled. The shower was warm and satisfying as I washed the day from body. Physically, I was sore. Mentally, I was confused and worried, "How will I find my way in this new world?" I thought, and felt an unfamiliar happiness that I had years left to figure it out.

THE TALK CONTINUES

I walk to the Lonely thru a crack in my patience when you step out from behind a tree.
It's funny I say that you only appear when I'm tired of life and struggling to breathe.
So today I will listen but you'll have to walk with me
'Cause I can't be caught standing in the cold talking to a tree.

I met Sam the Crow on a warm weekend cutting down brush around the ball field. I had heard him muttering to himself on a nearby branch, so I began to mimic his tones and he seemed to respond. In a very short time, the conversation grew as we began to trust each other with our secrets. He told me that he had lost his mate, that she had stopped moving one day, and how lonely he was now. I told him that I had lost my way and that this was a prison. He didn't comprehend the idea behind incarceration and suggested that I simply fly away. We were from different worlds yet, we completely understood each other and a friendship was born.

Sam would swoop down and land on the edge of my wheelbarrow in search of the hard to get to berries from the thick brush I would deposit there for him. He began to recognize me from a distance and could pick me out from a hundred yards away as he would appear seemingly from nowhere when I emerged from the tool shed or out the back door by the weight room. Some days he could barely contain himself with his rapid-fire cawing that became almost unintelligible. I would have to slow him down. "You went where? And saw what? You argued with an eagle and flew how high, pretty impressive for an old bird." He reacted the same way that I did about being called old and reminded me that I was losing a step on the base paths.

One particularly hot weekend Sam sat on a branch unbeknownst to me and listened as I argued with myself. Finally, he could take no more and asked who I thought I was conversing with. After pointing out that it was rude to eavesdrop, I said,

"I do that a lot. God seems to look for days when I'm feeling a little down to appear and argue his case for believing."

"Believing in what?" said Sam.

"That He exists",

"That who exists?"

"God."

"Who's God?"

"OK where to begin?"

In the next hour or so I took Sam through the history of religion and the premise that there is someone that watches over each and every one of us. Sam thought for a while, cocked his head and said,

"And you get what if you believe?"

"You get the promise of an afterlife in heaven I guess."

"You guess?" said Sam seemingly annoyed now," And this heaven place has anyone ever seen this?"

"Well, that's the belief part of it."

"The Belief part well how convenient, you know only a human being would think that all of this, his wings spreading wide, is not enough, that you somehow need more, that having to endure such a gift needs a promise of more. Top of the food chain my ass," he said as he flew away in a flutter of indignation.

An hour went by before I heard the satisfying munching of a full-grown crow feasting on the berries, I left him in his wheelbarrow, when I looked over Sam said, his mouth still full of his afternoon snack,

"That's how you talk to your son Alex, isn't it? Pretending there's a God. You think that if there's a God then somehow your son still exists."

"I don't think anything," I said, "but I do like thinking he can hear me."

"Then why the middle man, why can't something of Alex

still exist on his own. And speaking of this do other humans have this same crazy thought processes as well?"

"Oh, you have no idea," I said laughing now, "You wouldn't believe the extent that some people go to."

"Well, I don't care at the moment what other people do, I am only concerned with my friend, do you have this type of honest conversation with other people?"

"No," I said without hesitation, "When it comes to talking about things I struggle with, I prefer to talk to you. You don't judge."

"Of course, I don't judge, you're my friend, you need to move on from this. It occupies too much of your day, it's not an insult to your son to live your life you know. You do realize, that right? My silence hung in the air. "You don't. Oh, my, you're still punishing yourself. You're still stuck in a promise."

HEARTBREAK HILL

Jenny made me realize that I needed to make a decision on how I was going to choose to exist in this world. A new Ontology beyond the pages of my journal, a blue print to move forward. Jenny and Sam the crow should meet, they have so much in common. They both kept pushing me toward the future, reminding me to stay engaged with forward thinking. How could I move forward when I wasn't sure I wanted to? Ultimately, I needed to learn to face my truth and the choices it offered. Unfortunately, I still resided in a violent arena of distrust and condemnation disguised as a rehabilitation center. And finding opportunities to grow were getting harder.

I resisted change, when it came to Alex. I was firmly anchored to the past. In many respects, Alex did what I had thought of doing. Was suicide the ultimate tearing myself free I wondered or one step too far? I must choose. Alex was right of course; humanity is in the wrong lane. We missed the exit. We seem trapped by so many things that feel out of our control, yet grasping this knowledge and pointing out the error of our ways is not a victory. Besides, I didn't want an answer.

I didn't want a solution on how to deal with the loss of my son moving forward.

A simple answer would seem to trivialize his death. I needed the complications of the heart and to feel the misery in hopes of justifying or immortalizing this tragedy into an epic event, almost like the tragedy that overtook Worcester after the big fire or as Doc would put it, "Just another of my own dramas that have little to do with a choice my son made." Yet if it is broken down in that fashion, then what was it all for? In truth, that is up to me to decide.

Some people would say I deserve a second chance, others would say I should rot in prison. Most won't give it a second thought; they have their own dramas to support.

My dilemma seemed more about what other people thought of me than what I can do to make something out of the rest of my life. A life with a past. A past that includes Alex and a future that, for now, includes work, the harder the better.

The D.C.R. crews offered hours of mindless work and unique ways to see the city of Boston through a different lens. Countless events on the Boston common, Beacon hill from the shores of the Charles at the head of the regatta rowing races. The fourth of July Fireworks on the Esplanade was probably my favorite. One year we were watching the fireworks and listening to Jennifer Hudson sing. The night had called for rain, but it had held off so far. I used to attend such celebrations as either a firefighter or part of the on-stage entertainment. On this night, I was the clean-up crew. The fireworks were about half way through when the skies opened up. They took on the look of a water color painting left out in the rain. It was a torrential soaking that seemed to hold it self-back for as long as it could off out of respect of this historic day, but once the dam broke there was no stopping the deluge. The rain was so sudden and so completely drenching that people just ran in any direction seeking shelter, leaving behind, well everything:

blankets, food, chairs, backpacks and even a baby stroller (It was empty, I checked). There was literally no grass visible for 3 square acres, just piles of soaking wet trash, and we weren't going home until the entire park, and its surrounding bridges, on both sides of the river were clean. In my mind, it was the perfect analogy for life. As overwhelming as this disaster movie looked, you simply dealt with it one item at time.

We began jamming picnic blankets and half eaten pizza (some of which the new guys devoured) into 50-gallon bags, which would then be carried to the dump trucks parked along the paths, with their drivers and other parks department workers all tucked away quite nicely in the warm dry cabs. One item at a time, one bag at time. Just like life. Our reward when we finished? We got to load the thousands of folding chairs scattered around the Hatch shell stage and stack them into trailers. We arrived at four in the afternoon and returned to Pondeville at six in the morning, at least the ride back was quiet.

I used to tell myself that I did these chores with a smile, to the best of my ability to show Alex that any moment, no matter the circumstance, could be turned into a triumph of the spirit, yet I have come to learn that I would do it anyway. It is who I had become. If I chose to credit Alex for this breakthrough, so be it. I knew that was all part of my drama, my story.   When watching fireworks on the fourth of July or picking up trash in the aftermath of a downpour gives you the same feeling of satisfaction, you are on the right path, no matter where your destination. The destination is not the point, it's the moments along the way, good and bad. They all can be revealing, fulfilling.

Months became seasons as Winters became Springs. One mulch bed at time became one shovel full of snow at a time. And the years marched on.

Some events were harder than others. The Boston Marathon at the top of the list. Not because we were the ones that placed the thousands of metal barriers along the route the night before and into the next day. Not from picking up all the discarded clothing: gloves, hats sweatshirts and what knot that are tossed willy nilly into the air by ten thousand runners within the first two miles of the starting line. Clothing we could only marvel at, as we stuffed them into those same garbage bags to be donated to the needy.

The real reason was because The Marathon weighed heavy on my emotions. I used to participate in it as a runner, three times to be precise. The same number of years I cleaned up after it. Just another reminder of where I was, and where I wasn't going.

I'd run over five thousand miles in prison yet it seemed so hollow compared to the energy and pride of the Boston Marathon. The same sacred event that was scarred by a pair of misguided terrorist bombers. We were there that day too! Doing our job trying to be part of something, and many inmates took this act of terrorism personally, as did I, perhaps even more than most. Why? Because I had the training to help as a first responder. I had the training to make a difference, a position that I threw away because I was not strong enough to move beyond my own shit, and this was a reminder of how far I had fallen when I gave up caring.

Now here I was, ducking in shame behind a tree, picking up discarded clothing because a runner recognized me. I realized in that humiliating moment that I still wanted to put one foot in front of the other and finish something, despite the uphill climb. How ironic, I thought, I've created my very own "Heartbreak Hill, the famed hill at the twenty-mile mark, that has been the nemesis of so many runners over the years. And therein lies the lesson.

Heartbreak hill is not a large hill, nor exceedingly steep either, watching from the sidelines, you might struggle to understand why runners seem to fall away at this point, some collapsing completely after completing this climb. Twenty miles in would suggest a number of reasons why your body would quit on you, but why the dramatic collapse? You're six miles out. You made it to Boston, there are no hills left, so why would you not be invigorated upon completing this final obstacle? The finish line is within your grasp, you can do this, you saw something thru to the end, where finishing was the reward. The answer lies in a culmination of factors. Like life, its seldom just one thing. The race starts in Hopkinton, a quaint, colonial town not surprisingly about twenty miles inland from Boston. You find your pace thru Ashland and Framingham.

April in New England is anything but predictable. You hope for a slightly overcast day with maybe even a slight drizzle if it's warm. Wellesley College is the first milestone of the race. The 13-mile mark for an average runner like myself leaves you questioning why you are doing this. 13.2 miles left, "Are you kidding me?" Doubt begins to set in and that's when you hear the sound of thousands of people cheering. I heard it two miles out, and it got louder and louder. It is for every runner that makes the commitment to attempt this lunacy and it lifts you up, your feet move faster, adrenaline rushes through your system. I can do this. As I passed the College, I couldn't help but smile. All of these people showing their support whether you're leading the race or holding up the rear. As you move on, you get to glance up at a huge tv screen showing the live coverage of the race, and as luck or fate would have it, I got to watch the winner crossing the finish line. 2 hours 7mins, that's impressive. How is that even possible? And then you realize you have 13.2 miles left of ever-increasing agony. It does put things in perspective. There are just certain individuals who are designed with elite talent and I am not one of them, but still, I must finish.

Newton and Brookline add to the weight and suffering now heaped upon you and just when it can't get any worse you arrive at the bottom of Heartbreak Hill. It's just a half mile you tell yourself, head down one step at time, before you know it, you see the top in front of you, except something is drastically wrong. Runners in front of you are staggering. One second, they are moving along smoothly, the next they are wobbling sideways, some collapse to the ground, where emergency workers rush to cover them with blankets that mark the end of their quest. Why? How? And then it happened to me.

I knew it was coming and still I stumbled and almost fell. Twenty miles of running through treelined side streets and towns, and suddenly upon cresting the hill overlooking the city of Boston, you run head long into the breeze off the Atlantic Ocean and it hits you like a virus; your body is no longer yours. It relents, it betrays, it tries to quit and this is where you discover who you are.

You can hear about it from others and read about it in books, but until you experience the barrier between mind and body, flesh and spirit, you do not know what it feels like or what you are made of. All the desire in the world sometimes is not enough, and many better than me have succumbed to the moment. Before I knew it, I was walking, looking for a place to sit down just for a minute, just a short rest, it's not like I have anything to prove I am not a real runner. That's a good place right there on that curbing next to the empty plastic bottles of water and spilled solo beer cups. I watched a woman in her sixties slowly jog by me "C'mon" she said, "you can do it."

"I'm coming," I said only half meaning it, the curbing beckoned.

"Not a chance," said a young slurred voice, "you come too far dude, let's go, I'll run with you." And he did, this drunken Boston University student named Dave walked at first, then jogged alongside me, spilling his beer every few steps, telling me that I was more important than the guy that won. "This is for you," he said "c'mon." And I did, slowly at first, then quicker than I'd run all day.

The last mile was the quickest of the marathon, and as I crossed the finish line it was with a combination of agony and elation that I could not forget and maybe never equal.

I would never have known any of this if I had not done it myself. The lesson. You must participate. You must strive to fail Spectacularly in Doc's own words, and more to the point, I realized, I did want to be part of something again. I didn't want to give up. I wanted to move forward. I wanted to try again. I wanted to stay in this world. I wanted to honor Alex. I wanted to re-engage with Nicholai. I wanted to marry Jenny. I wanted to Live.

SHE'S HERE

"She's here," Tony said.

"I saw her," I replied, trying not to seem like I was about to jump out the window and run across the parking lot to greet her.

Santiago came shuffling down the hall and joined us. We reached the railing just as Jenny was coming in the front door.

"Damn," said Santiago "look at your Mariposa."

Since my arrival at Pondeville, Jenny had begun to dress a little different. Her last visit she wore tight blue jeans, with a low-cut white top, and boots. Today she was in a red dress. The dress code was slightly relaxed here, but I had not imagined seeing her in a dress, let alone a tight-fitting red dress, with matching ruby shoes. Click my heels and call me Dorothy.

"Are they going to let her in?" said Tony.

"I hope so," was all I could get out.

"Shit, Donahue's at the front desk." Donahue, an 18-year veteran was new to Pondeville and took exception that I had a better relationship with the staff then he did. He made it clear that he could make things difficult for me.

Donahue made sure I was the last person with a visitor that day to get called down. I walked in as Jen was posing off in the corner of the visiting room underneath of one of the ceiling mirrors showing off her fancy new dress, with a twirl and a smile, and I must admit I may have been a little too enthusiastic in my greeting, because it took all of two minutes before I was called out to the front desk. Donahue had registered a complaint with the shift commander about inappropriate touching. As much as everyone knew that Donahue was an ass, he was in charge of the visiting room that day and that was that.

"Any more contact like that and we will ban her from visits, you get that, Baxter?"

"Yes," was all I dare say, this would be the first of many times he would try to get me lugged.

"I don't like that man," said Jenny, as I sat back down.

"Distrust all where the need for punishment is great," I said.

"Oh, I like that." said Jenny.

"Nietzsche," I replied, "We have to be careful with this one, he could really screw things up for me."

"Then," she said with a smile, "I'll be good, sort of," as she covertly rubbed her breast against my arm. "We have too much to talk about anyway so ignore him." That would be harder than we thought.

Donahue took his chair near the entrance of the sitting room and turned at an angle to suggest that he was only going to be monitoring us as opposed to Juan across the room who already had his hand slid into the back of his girlfriend's pants. Jenny, being Jenny, jumped right in. "I have been going over Prison policy. I think we should get married in prison at least a year in advance of your release."

"Why?"

"Your legal address will then be established in Pennsylvania. Any thoughts?"

Hearing her say it out loud made it real.

She didn't wait for my answer. "I've made up my mind. My instincts tell me this is right.
But first, I need to know if you will stand by me. Nobody has been allowed in my house for years, even Doc never saw my house. My own family is not allowed in my house. I need a place that's safe from outside contamination."

"Right," I nodded. I didn't know what else to do.

She continued. "I never thought I would consider a step like this, but I'm tired of going it alone. I need someone that won't judge me. Are you going to judge me?"

I was about to say "No," but never got the chance.

"My rules: No shoes in the house; No outside clothes in the house; No touching without washing: shower when you come in and before bed, nothing toxic in the house. All organic food, organic shampoo, fresh organic food for the cats, no soda: and no house guests. Ever. I have to know that you understand all of this before we move forward."

I sat up straight and took a long swig of my Coke.

"Thoughts," she said with a big smile.

I suddenly understood the red dress.

REALIZATION

After my visit with Jenny, I began to feel different about everything. I began to acknowledge my surroundings again. I removed the mechanism I had in place to filter out unwanted interactions. I had learned to implement this trick from having to be in such close contact with people like "IT" my first roommate at Baystate. Doc had taught me to open myself up to the intent process of others, through a form of intuitive meditation, which worked a little too well when it came to individuals like "IT." Time was also something I had learned to control, filter out, alter, or manipulate. Time is no different than air; they are both invisible tools to be absorbed and controlled. This reengagement with the world I was undertaking was a deliberate choice, I needed to prepare myself in the next year for emergence into 'society.'

Lowering my firewall had some unintentional consequences. I also had to rethink spending so much time in my dreams. As fulfilling as the vivid memories, I could create there, I discovered that they weren't all wonderful. A dream of Alex burned in a fire and dying in my arms now resides permanently along side long walks on beaches with a red- haired girl. There is a dark side to everything I was learning. Reengaging with the real world was proving equally difficult.

Normally the strip search at the end of visits much like the return from any work crew was just part of the curriculum. Donahue seemed to enjoy it a little too much. Even in those moments with the added humiliation of the look of superiority on Donahue's face I would take a pause and move on. I understood his need. However, Jenny did want me to engage more, so be it then.

"You could only hope to look this good naked at my age, Donahue," I said during a strip search, "so I don't blame you for staring."

"Don't be talking back to me, Baxter, I can make things very difficult for you," said Donahue, caught by surprise.

"If that helps fill whatever void is missing in your life, then I'm glad to help."

I'm not sure this is what Jenny had in mind. But there are plenty of Donahues in the real world so I had better start engaging with them. Exiting the bathroom, I headed to the front desk where the change of shift guards were gathering. Donahue headed straight into the shift commander's office.

"Ok," I said to the small gathering at the desk. "Mary is twenty-four. She is twice as old as Anne was when Mary was as old as Anne is now. How old is Anne? One of Einstein's favorites," I added.

As the night crew were scrambling for pencils. The shift commander came up behind me.

"Tonight's riddle I assume, Baxter?"

"Yup, you know how much the kids love them."

"Ya, well listen, as much as we all enjoy your company. There are those who would have you drawn and quartered if they had it their way."

"Understood," I responded.

"May I assume that you did not threaten Donahue in the bathroom?"

"I have no doubt that I threaten him, but no."

"Good, he just tried to have you lugged, said the shift commander as he pulled out his notebook. "So, I am suggesting for your own good you play nice. Now, who's Mary and how old is she?"

LAUNDRY, THE FINAL STAIN

At Pondeville you did your own laundry. Sometimes, the best you could hope for was to place your bag on a machine to be next. On occasion all three machines had four or so bags lined up from the night before, (a practice that was supposed to be against the rules) Many a disagreement at loud volumes erupted over the validity of this practice.

Entering the room there were several bags left on the machine so I did the courteous thing which was check the room number on the bag and see if the occupant was up yet.

When I returned, all the machines were already running, apparently two other inmates just decided that protocol didn't matter and were willing to take the chance that no one would call them on it. Burt, a short-tempered work release inmate opened all the machines and placed the wet laundry on the floor. Realizing that I was not one of the offenders, he offered me one of the now vacant machines, which I took. When the ensuing argument was about to come to blows a C.O. from the front desk yelled up that he would close down the laundry for the day if it continued. Three more inmates showed up. They were surprised to find out that I was somehow in the middle of this as I usually tried to avoid confrontation. Jenny did tell me to interact.

The laundry quandary continued as there were the three dryers that had to be procured next, well two actually, the third had been pummeled to death by an angry launderer a few days earlier. It was quite the beating, and the dryer was declared down for the count. Still three washing machines and two dryers meant a one man out musical dryers scenario as I stood waiting for the cycles to stop.

"Please be mine, please be mine," I said and presto it was. I quickly grabbed my entire load and headed for the dryer as the next two machines were but seconds behind me. As I opened the dryer door it was filled with wet clothes from the night before.

"Are you kidding me," I said panicking as the click of the second washer meant the next combatant was going to get the other dryer. I quickly opened the second dryer which was also filled with damp musty clothes.

"Fuck em," said Burt, "You're already in this."

I tore the wet load out and placed the contents on top of the dryer and threw my clothes in slamming the door with a loud thud and pressing full dry at lightning speed just as the third washer signaled its completion. Both participants scrambled to pull their cloths out first and I took advantage of the delay, grabbed the second wet load, and depositing that on top of its respective top, held the door open for Burt and clicked the dial to full in a display of teamwork I thought he might appreciate. That, and I wanted a partner against the two guys who were about to find their laundry violated; the enemy of my enemy don't you know. When the next yelling match began the C.O. ordered anyone without clothes in a machine out of the area.

These machines were the low water volume variety which most inmates took as a personal afront to their pursuit of clean laundry. As the wash cycle began most inmates would add a bottle full of water into the soap holder thus giving them the watery edge, they thought they deserved. it would matter very little if I tried to explain that extra water was not what these machines were designed to handle, so I held my tongue. But watching this idiot fill a bucket that had been placed under the water cooler just outside the door was too much for me to ignore. When I realized he was actually attempting to pour the entire five gallons into the machine (most of which was going on the floor) my pause disintegrated.

"What in god's name do you think you're doing?" I yelled, my voice getting louder with each word. "Do you actually think this machine is designed to handle that amount of water?"
Even Burt was caught off guard as he looked at me slightly shocked at my quick outburst, especially since we had just been warned.

"It's not going to hurt nothin, mind your own business," said laundry idiot.

"Really? This is my business. You break another machine and it effects everyone."

"It's just water. "

"It's just water," I snapped "Listen, Archimedes, do you know how much water weighs? No, of course you don't. It's 8.3 pounds a gallon...that's," I paused a moment, "that's 41.5 pounds. Do you think this machine can handle that amount of weight?"

Laundry boy stood frozen for a moment as if he was actually trying to compute something. And then said in the most disdainful tone he could muster, "that's the stupidest thing I evers heard, everyone knows water is measured in gallons not pounds, so there."

I had no reply, what could be said, as I looked toward the door, Carlson the C.O. was standing there looking at me. "Can't really argue with that logic, Baxter, keep it quiet." He said trying not to laugh as he turned and walked back down the stairs. My hands were still trembling as I turned to look at Burt who had been staring at me in amazement.

"What?" I said.

"Nothing," said Burt, throwing his hands up in surrender, then he smiled.

"Archimedes, I like that."

The weekly laundry ordeal out of the way, I could now focus on a long run, which I quite frankly needed. For me running is a slow and steady process which allowed for maximum engagement with my thoughts.

I believed in a literal sense, that somehow, I moved through this world at a different speed than others. My conception of time or my interaction with it was altered by my awareness of it. I used it, as opposed to it controlling me, after all, why not? Time does not take offense to my wanting to take reign over it. Time holds no grudges, it takes no offense towards those who place demands upon it, for in the end, it will only give so much of itself, irregardless of your arguments or beliefs.

On that day I ran toward thoughts. Thoughts of the past, visions of the future, Alex, Nicholai, Jenny, and the world outside. Twenty miles was the goal.

Some days it took a full two miles to completely loosen up. Like anything else in life, you have to push through the initial phases to get to the real work. Soft and slow, allowing my feet the chance to complain, the left hip, of the softball dislocation back in Walpole days, a stinging reminder of glorious pain.

Past the weight room, along the path besides the basketball court. The slight decline by the handball courts allowed me to throw my legs out just a hair to test the knee and heel that is still not sure if they are on board yet. "Hey, Poppy!" Santiago yelled out with the enthusiasm of a teenager. Santiago had become a bright spot in here for sure. He worked in the bakery in Dorchester making good money and was always eager to share his good fortune with a blueberry muffin or orange juice left on my bunk. Lately we were writing letters for housing so he could continue working when his bid was up. The legal hoops one had to navigate was daunting, but I happily trudged through it, for he was worth helping, and it felt good to be part of someone moving forward with such enthusiasm.

Tempered breathing led me past the front parking lot down toward the ball field where the worn grass path encircles the entirety of this field, all along the edge of the woods. The softer footing was a welcome addition to long runs. Sam let out a loud Caw as he realized I was out and about and followed along for a while skipping from branch to branch. He was going out for the afternoon with friends and asked if I could come. He couldn't fathom that for whatever reason I would choose running in circles all day. With a loud goodbye he was gone.

I would miss Sam, when I eventually left this place. I began to push these thoughts away, I was quick to remind myself this day's run was all about embracing the future, and accepting the past. In that moment, getting married, moving to Pennsylvania, and writing a book about fitting in as a convicted felon seemed harder than running twenty miles.

As I made my way along the outskirts of the ball field, I admired the preparation it took to ready it for that season's games. Malone, my boss, had come through with enough clay for the entire infield, which took all of two weeks to get just right. The grass was mowed to perfection, I used a large ride on mower for the outfield carving out a beautiful symmetrical arching pattern, before switching to a smaller hand model for the tight two -way cuts on the infield and along the foul lines knowing that no matter how defined I made them, there would still be endless arguments over the flight of a ball being called fair or foul.

My first couple of miles were relatively peaceful as I looked to settle in for the long haul. After ten miles I began to float. The pace was moderate and I barely noticed my feet touching the ground anymore; this is where my mind took over, and my thoughts went back to my last visit with Jenny. After laying out the rules of our new life, which were slightly overwhelming, we started on politics. She was horrified to find out I had never voted in a presidential election in my whole life. "You should be excited," said Jenny, "You will get to be a part of electing the first woman President; it will be historic."

It turns out Convicted Felons are allowed to vote in Pennsylvania which begged the question as to why you wouldn't be able to vote in the first place. Of all the rights I will be stripped of upon completing my sentence, not being allowed to vote seemed rather obtuse, if not downright ridiculous. If I was allowed to vote, what would come next, a claim of enlightenment?

Enlightenment in Jenny's experience was a double-edged sword. It was a transient moment for the most part, that many people experienced to differing degrees, but its commonality came from its own impermanence. She started this dissertation by reminding me that in the past I had confused Enlightenment with Non-attachment. I had arrogantly proclaimed my understanding of non-attachment to Jenny a year earlier telling her a story of confronting a yoga master with what I thought to be a misguided pursuit of nothingness.

Nothingness, as I had come to understand, was releasing yourself from the attachment to anything worldly, (this worldly as Nietzsche might say). That the goal of achieving nothingness while still of this world was a triumph of the mind. I proclaimed that we were animals living on a planet and that should be the point, that should be the experience. Jenny was kind in her refute by pointing out that Non-attachment came from experiencing everything of this world. The full range of emotions along with the physical pleasures of the body, while not attaching yourself to its outcome. "When you are attached to the past," she explained, "you cannot see the future."

With this one simple explanation came an anger. The realization that I had wasted two thousand dollars on a certification that was explained in thirty seconds in the visiting room of a prison. In conclusion, she went on, "Achieving a moment of enlightenment does not put you above others. It is not a badge of courage. Do not dabble in the human experience and claim knowledge that is not yours. So many people have experienced a brief moment of enlightenment and attempted to turn it into a career; doing so leads one down paths of seeing things that don't exist, making assumptions based on the need to have special abilities, in short, she concluded, "This is why I Don't Do Guru," I loved that. "This is why I don't do Guru" ;who is this girl I thought, and what did she see in me?

My run was in jeopardy from the very beginning; it started with a comment, as I ran past the basketball court, about why I don't play softball anymore. It's not that I don't play, it's just that my interests had moved on. There's also the mortality thing. I had come to realize that despite my hopes of transcending some new level of being, that I will probably begin to slow down, break down and eventually cease to exist. Most of our team had moved on to whatever lies beyond the confines of this place. Chicken Ditto, Mello, Tiny, G, K, Ed the lawyer, Sanchez and Flacco. Those that were still here had moved up to work release and were either too tired to come Saturday or simply needed a day off. Besides, getting injured was not a great idea once you had a real job, or at least as real as work release had to offer. The comments from the new kids on the block were relentless. "I heard he thinks he's the best that's ever played here," "now he just cuts the grass," "some people know when to retire, I guess."

I must admit that watching them warm up, they were pretty good, and they knew it. One of the more vocal gang members drilled a line drive out to right field where I was jogging at the time, and yelled out, "Hey, lawn boy, little help." Jen did tell me to interact.

There was no choosing up for sides. The new guys had their whole team set. We got who was left. Our second baseman was a Spanish ballplayer in his early sixties who I had seen around but never spoken too. He was quiet and competent. Our first base man much the same, an older guy who I talked baseball to in the library who said he used to play first in the old days and would revel in the chance to relive his glory days. Chipper handled the outfield, positioning his inexperienced teammates in the best place to at least keep the ball in front of them. The first inning was a little difficult to handle as we had to shuffle some positions around that were being handily exposed by our younger, more talented opponents. I had to put up with the constant banter of baserunners speaking of the end of an era, "sucks to be old," "gonna be a long day."

It was four to nothing before we got the first out, a double play started by our Spanish elder at second on a hot shot he flipped to me with a smooth toss, as I pivoted to first, I could see him smiling out of the corner of my eye and time slowed down, and I just knew. This was going to be one of those moments I would remember for a long time.

Rico, our Spanish interpreter, led off the bottom of the first with a well-placed ground ball between first and second, our pitcher popped out, and Chipper followed with one of his well-rehearsed line drives over the shortstop's head. As I walked to the plate the center fielder yelled out, "Move in, the old guy's up." Now slow pitch softball as we have talked about is not major league baseball, it's not that difficult. Proper swing plane, accelerated bat head speed through the ball with the proper torc applied on impact and control of your emotions. My emotions,I admit, were tweaked as I did have a slight ego. I saw the smirk appear on Chippers face when he heard the "old man" comment come from behind him. "Single brings in two," he yelled clapping his hands together, Translation, "drive the shit out of it and shut this guy up."

Now maybe the wind was blowing out or maybe there is a God, but something carried this ball farther then it had a right to go; I slowed, rounding first and watched in amazement as the ball landed in the woods on the fly. I have never, or will I ever, hit a ball that far again. I paused at second to admire the center fielder running into to woods before continuing on to home with the round off backflip landing on home plate which Chipper claimed he knew was coming. Don't judge me, its prison.

Toward the end of the game, the outcome still in question, our opponents self-appointed captain, an angry steroid user, came to the plate and drilled a ferocious shot up the middle which of course I dove at, because I dove at everything. As luck would have it, the ball ended up in my glove; I never saw it, I just felt it. Knowing this guy was fast, I was already back on my feet and firing to first which our first baseman scooped rather adeptly, (he talked about it for weeks) and the inning was over. When I came up to bat, the Captain, who I just robbed of a hit, was playing third, "C'mon, put it by me, I'm standing right here, you owe me," he yelled out.

"Ok." I said." Are you sure?"

"Yeah C'mon," said the captain hitting his glove with his fist as he shuffled his feet in a ready position.

"Alright, put it inside," I said to the pitcher who glanced over at his captain who nodded.

"Ya do what he says! C'mon, let's do this."

"Fine," said the pitcher as he lofted the ball to the inside of the plate as requested,

"It's not my face."

There was an audible "Whoaaaa" from his teammates as the ball ticked off his glove that he managed to almost get up in time, before it zipped by his left ear and down the left field line at about a hundred miles an hour. I must admit that I was somewhat relieved when the line drive did not come in contact with his face, but I began to wonder why I would do that in the first place? Because I could, should not be a viable response. But this was War after all, wasn't it? No, no it wasn't, and that was something to think about. I didn't know the first thing about war. I'd never been. Who knows, maybe I could have been a Navy Seal, yet I must never take credit for something I didn't do.

I had risked my life at fire scenes which was more than most, but still, this was a game wasn't it? I drill softballs at people's heads irregardless of the outcome because I can. That's exactly what gets the majority of inmates in trouble, they do things because they can without as much as a thought of the outcome, but it wasn't real life. Real life was returning, and I had to prepare myself. In many ways it seemed, I hadn't changed a bit.

A DIFFERENT TIME A DIFFERENT PLACE

"Kenny, do you see this narrow path here?"

I looked as O.G. pointed to a small strip of dirt worn down thru the grass, seeming to disappear into the bushes.

"This leads down to the water, why don't you walk down there and sit for a while, take your shoes off. I imagine it's been a while since you sat on beach."

"Really," I said, noticing his tone didn't seem to imply any deception.

"Ya, go ahead I'll come and get you; we have half an hour. "You won't swim away or anything, right?"

"Well, I can't promise, you know me."

I headed down the small path as if I were on some great adventure, an expedition into the unknown. The places we went and assignments we were given varied. Different schedules. Different crews. Eight guys accompanied by a rotating number of C.O.s all with their distinct personalities. Some cruel, some friendly. Out of all of them, O.G. was one of my favorites. He was from a place where driving vehicles was not common. He drove the van 40 miles per hour up route 93 into Boston with a death grip on the steering wheel, an entire van of inmates begging him to pull over and let them drive. As friendly and naive as O.G was, he didn't miss much. He knew who would work and who would spend their days trying to bum cigarettes. He brushed off with a smile the less then veiled attempts to insult his heritage or his sometimes-comical pronunciation of words. He was there thru it all, taking notes, watching. O.G survived the hard winters on the snow crews. He stood by as we cleared sidewalks in Dorchester, or storm drains in Brookline. One night we shoveled an entire bridge by hand in the historic city of Charlestown. Even I got tired. All part of the training I told myself as seasons began to blur together.

Of all the small parks and play grounds we maintained during the summer months one of the most beautiful might be the least known. It was an abandoned air field from the early twentieth century on the Squantum peninsula in Quincy. Far removed from the snowy nightmares of the dreaded shoveling crews, it was a mid 90-degree day in August and we were sent to this forgotten gem of a place that was now used as a walking park.

Hot weather brings out the worst in most inmates. Overall, summer time is far more dangerous in prison than winter. In cold times people tended to curl up with coats and hats, socks on their hands, wrapped in blankets and complained that the D.O.C. was deliberately freezing them to death. In the summer, much like heat waves in inner cities, crime and violence seemed to climb in direct proportion to the temperature. Walking on an abandoned airstrip, pulling weeds off plaques and maintaining the path from over growth was not very exciting work, throw in temperatures approaching 100 degrees and the enthusiasm of the average worker diminishes at inverse proportional rate to the rise of Mercury. After returning from such an excursion, I would be the one standing in the lobby of Pondeville soaked thru, scratched and bleeding from the forearms, courtesy of the close encounters with pricker bushes. Whoever was working the front desk would glance up and look away trying not to laugh at my appearance. O.G would start singing, "One of these things is not like the other."

The guards would draw straws to see who would get stuck looking through my dirt drenched clothing. It would be several hours before the showers were opened, so I would remain in this condition for quite some time.

On this particular day, I was taking my time and reading all the plaques that I came across in the park, I would never have come to a place like this if I was on the outside. What a shame, how many other opportunities were right in front of me that I didn't recognize, that I couldn't be bothered with. Amelia Earhart used this runway. I tried to picture what that must have looked like and wished I could scour through old photographs of that time period. The next marker commemorated Harriet Quimby, the first woman to receive an American pilot's license. I was astonished to read that she, along with her navigator, plummeted to their deaths in front of a large crowd here at an air show, falling from her monoplane and landing in the nearby Neponset River. Dumbfounded, I stared up at the sky trying to take in what that must have looked like from among that crowd that day in 1912. I had not heard O.G. coming up behind me.

"Is the sun getting to you, Baxter?"

"Not at all," was my quick reply.

I showed O.G the written accounts of this bit of aviation history and began instinctually to clear the area around the stone monument out of respect to a woman only moments earlier I had never heard of.

"You know you're the only one still working, right? Everyone else is sitting by the van in the shade complaining I'm trying to kill them."

"This is fascinating," I said moving to the next marker. "Thank you so much for taking me here."

"You're thanking me?" asked O.G, realizing that I wasn't being sarcastic.

The water's edge was no more than a few hundred feet off the runway, and although rocky and shallow it was the most wondrous sight these eyes had seen in years. I took my shoes off. When I put my feet in the water I was transported to another world. I was at peace, I was alone. I began to scan the harbor that led to the sea and imagined Amelia Earhart, and Harriet Quimby flying overhead. I took myself farther back in time to the arrival of the first ships to enter the hallowed waters off the great city of Boston, then to the revolutionary war; all this history happened right here, right where I sat.

Maybe it was the heat, or the fact that I had been so secluded the past few years, but this was an extraordinary experience. I knew most of the history of this place, I was born half an hour west of here yet it seemed to take on a new meaning, and it was overwhelming. I closed my eyes and began one of Docs meditations. Deep breaths take in my surroundings, I could hear the sound of the small waves lapping the shore line and focused on its rhythm. The serenity became amplified. The smell of the salt air, the wind playing in harmonic concord with the sound of the water hitting the rocks. Utter perfection.

When I didn't have to "imagine" the sound of the ocean or the smell of the sea I could go deeper, much deeper. I was the ocean, I was the breeze, I could fly with Amelia.

"What are you, the Dog whisper?" said O.G. stumbling over the rocks behind me. His voice startled me back.

"The Dog whisperer?" I was about to question, thinking that was a strange comment, when I noticed a dog sitting next to me, two in fact, one on each side. What appeared to be a Spaniel of some sorts was slowly trotting away down the shore line, startled by O.G.'s appearance, or from the whistle in the distance from his master; the other companion, a beautiful yellow lab, seemed content to sit at my side; apparently she had been partaking in the meditation.

"Wow, this is nice," said O.G. looking out over the harbor, "who are your friends?"

"Don't know, they just sat down, I guess. "

"You're a unique one, Baxter; sorry though, it's time to go."

I turned to say good bye to my beach mate when a nervous

voice came from the other direction, along the shore line.

"Oh, Milly there you are,I was so worried; I've been calling you and calling you,"

Milly turned to me as if to say, "Ya, I heard her,"

"She doesn't usually go to strangers," said the women whose tone had changed markedly. She was closer now and could easily make out my attire and that of my guards. To her credit she did try to hide her trepidation towards the unintentional encounter that Milly had put her in, mostly because Milly wouldn't move.

"Time to go," said O.G again, after all contact with civilians is punishable by death. I turned and knelt by Milly patting her perfectly groomed and manicured coat as she extended her paw, which I gratefully shook.

"Nice to meet you, Milly," I said rising and moving away. The look on the women's face was priceless as I glanced back.

"Did you like that man?" she asked the dog as if maybe I was someone, she was supposed to meet in a different life, or in a different time. In the days of early colonization perhaps, maybe she was the reincarnated soul of Harriet Quimby. I guess I'll never know. I'd like to think she was.

SOMETHING BORROWED

A clean pressed white shirt from Maurice. A life savers breath mint with blue flavor crystals from Leo. A beautiful day in June. A breathtaking girl.

She deserved so much more than the hum of vending machines in the visiting room of a prison on her wedding day.

Inmates peered through the blinds to catch a glimpse. They would be ignored. I would look no other place than into the eyes of the woman who was taking the biggest risk of all.

She was tearing herself from the fabric of her existence. She was charting a new course for both of us. A courageous journey into the unknown.

Jenny learned her vows. I read mine, quoting Plato and

Emanuel Kant. I still liked appearing smart. It had been three years since she said she would take me home. Jenny was a woman of her word. If she told you something, she would follow through to the best of her ability, her loyalty was unwavering. She beamed in a beautiful flowered dress. Her hands clasped, already missing the flowers taken from her by the guard.

There were only two others in the room acting as Minister and witness. Kathy and Gary lived on Cape Cod. Jenny stayed with them when she came to visit. Gary was a Homeopath, Kathy an author and actor. I had met them months earlier. They came to visit to verify my worthiness.

We had both talked about experiencing this day from the inside out. The rolling butterflies danced with anticipation from a day years in the making.

Not everyone one was as enthusiastic about our prison wedding as we were. It was met with skepticism by the few privy to its hastened pronouncement. Nicholai and my sister Jodie were less than enthusiastic with their muted congratulations. The rest of the outside world was kept at arm's length, with details doled out in the smallest portions as possible. Explaining Doc had been hard enough for Jenny. Even when he died, most of her friends imagined being a prominent doctor, that he passed quietly in a soft bed overlooking a sunset from the window of his lake house. Not the thin mattressed dorm room of a prison hospital.

Explaining me was another leap in judgment altogether. Jenny wanted people to meet me as her husband, allowing the story to unfold over time, giving me the chance to be seen without the burden of my past. Many years had come and gone from the time we first held hands. Clasped in the uncertainty of our Victorian Romance. Love the old fashion way when friendship and understanding of each other were the mainstays of a true courtship.

I smiled to myself at the progression of our budding love story that culminated with her sneaking wedding rings into visits. They varied in size adorned on every finger until the right ones were found. I would come to learn over time, in great detail, all the battles this woman fought to bring this day to fruition. The simple act of getting a marriage license, trying to convince the clerk that the insistent rule of both of us being present was not feasible as I was incarcerated. The clerk reluctantly relented only after the third visit. The endless forms to fill out and hoops to be jumped through, none worse than what the D.O.C. called its Home Plan.

In order for me to be allowed to leave prison I had to comply with a litany of paperwork and interrogations. Details of my intentions were compiled, collated and approved. A parole officer was sent to dig through every inch of Jen's home, like a cell block search. Intractable rules were then laid out. We were informed that entry could happen at any time. Jenny was forced to sign away her rights to privacy and civility. This process was enough to rattle the most compliant of citizens, but for Jenny it was a mountain never climbed before.

By choice, her house was set far off the road on eighteen acres of land in the deep Pennsylvania wood. Crippled by a severe case of O.C.D, no one had been allowed entry to her property for 15 years, not even her family. Her life's coping mechanisms were hard ones to understand. In her own words,"It was born of necessity and allowed me to stay in this world."

As far as bringing me home, she had been quite transparent about her intentions right from the beginning. Much like my need to send myself to prison, she also required a drastic change in her life to propel her toward a different future, one not so lonely, one with a partner, one with an intimate relationship. Jen had gone to great lengths to find the courage to make any of this possible. The first real battle with the parole officer took place in the garage which was lined in plastic.

Jenny stared out the door, her hands shaking as the parole officer made his way from his car to the front door. Several logs were placed in the drive way to ensure that he not drive up to the house. She got a good look at this total stranger sent to rummage through all her belongings.

The conversation was terse yet respectful as she demanded he cover his imposing shoes with surgical booties. After some protesting, he relented but not before he explained in no uncertain terms that he could come and go at all hours of the night, unannounced.

"Kick in the door if I want," he added for good measure.

Once inside he began to open cupboards at random, went through medicine cabinets, asked about alcohol and commented on the pile of boxes in the middle of the kitchen filled with new cooking utensils, glass wear, plates and cups.

"Wedding Presents?" he asked, trying to seem human.

"Yes," she replied, not wanting to lie.

Considering no one knew she was getting married or would be giving her a wedding shower, she gave herself one. Pots and pans were bought, drapes and bed coverings, coffee makers and a coffee mug adorned with the periodic table of elements was purchased. Real underwear and socks were stacked neatly in the closet marked 'Husband.'

She cleaned the house top to bottom as soon as he left. She would survive this encounter, this mammoth road block, this impediment to bringing her new prisoner husband home. She would change her stars. I would tear her from the fabric of her life, and free her from herself.

Back in the humble surroundings of the day room, vows were shared, promises were made and a great adventure was set in motion. The only problem being we were a year away from being alone together in a room. The short kiss that followed the pronouncement of man and wife led to the quick exit of my new bride, her back to the outside world and a celebration, me back to my cell. The only one to see me naked on my wedding night was the guard who performed my strip search at the end of the ceremony.

GOOD TIME

Sister Agnes stood before her unenthusiastic audience with an air of confidence. She was doing God's work after all. I would listen intently, for that was where I chose to be on that day. I didn't have to be saved. Like everyone else, I was there for the Good time.

With the exception of switching jobs, which I was unprepared to do, the opportunities for reducing my sentence with good time days were slim. There was a twelve-step program available, but this ended abruptly when I refused to turn myself over to a higher power. Taking responsibility for your own life was apparently frowned upon. I was therefore stuck with sister Agnes and finding repentance through God's Love, Oh Boy. Quiet reflection became my new goal in my quest for good time, which lasted all of 10 minutes.

Agnes began her sermon by asking us if we had ever heard of a man called Aaron Hernandez. Hernandez was the infamous member of the New England patriots that was being held on a murder charge just miles from the stadium he once played in, so "yes" we all knew him.

"By all accounts," said Sister Agnes, her arms raised to the Heavens, this man appeared to have led a dual life. On one hand he was a professional athlete, wealthy, respected, played in something called the Super Bowl."

"But if you can imagine," she went on, her eyes widening.

"At the same time he was involved in a separate life filled with unsavory characters, even drugs, all while plotting the murder of a friend. Have you ever?"

"Ever what?" Said Angel a large, bushy haired gentleman from the Dominican Republic, "Done drugs or plotted the murder of a friend?" a light chuckle rose from the sleepy Sunday morning contingency.

"Good Gracious, no," proclaimed Agnes but consider that there exists someone out there who appears to be living two separate lives. Lives that are diametrically opposed to one another. Can you imagine what that must be like?"

I couldn't resist myself and started a sermon of my own.

"I'm going to go out on a limb here, Sister, and speak for the rest of the class and say that right-left-brain chemistry aside we can all imagine that. I don't think I know anyone who doesn't have a dual life."

Angel thru his arm around my shoulder and bellowed, "Ya,

what he said."

Feeling like I had support, I continued.

"Do you really believe that people don't have secret lives. Don't you know it is our God given right to complicate our existence with dualities. Or are you so all consumed by the word of God that there is no room for anything else? How wonderfully naive."

Sister Agnes took a deep breath and sighed.

"Many of you may think me silly, old fashion, naive even," She shot a quick glance at me. I did not come to God without some reluctance. I have studied Philosophy; I am familiar with science and cognitive research. But I have come to think that the complications of secret lives are for the unimaginative and the frightened.

"Tell me, Sir," she said pausing at my chair. "Do you think Dual Ideologies and manipulative personalities benefit you," she did not wait for an answer. "I think it is counterproductive and shows a lack of character. Pick a path and stay on it, I say. Choose a direction you actually believe in."

"Belief is another word for subservience," I lashed out feeling I had somehow been set up and had to defend myself.

"Your defensive attitude betrays you," sister Agnes counter punched, "I am not trying to convert you. I am trying to set you up to fail. Do you have the courage to fail for something you believe in? Or would you rather allow the battle to continue in your head, trying to maintain your two selves. It must be an exhausting dichotomy. If I can teach one of you that, then I have done my job. You don't have to see the world the way I do. But you need to open your eyes."

Agnes refocused the class with questionnaires, a scale of 1-10 choices on how you feel about things like authority, or relationships. I swapped papers with Angel and we started conversing about life, kids, expectations and why all his answers were either a 1 or a 10.

"I know what I like and don't like," was his response.

Angel had two small children, yet had turned down Parole. "I refuse to go out there and allow anyone else to tell me what to do." Angel's plan was to stay in prison until his entire sentence was completed, as to avoid the oversight of probation or parole.

When I pressed him on this, he said, "You should talk, Professor; you can have any job you want in here and increase your good time to 10 days a month and yet you mow lawns. You just got married, yet you act as if you don't want to go home. How are we not the same?" Angel was right, of course. I didn't really want to stay in prison, but I was sticking with what I knew. In many ways I was a King in prison. It was easy, I could manipulate my surroundings to fit my needs. The outside world was the scary unknown this time. In truth I was scared to be the low man on the totem pole out there. Married to a woman with her own dragons to slay, uncertainty and failure could be lurking around any corner in a world I no longer fit in. I got prison. Of course, I was dragging my feet. Doc had taught me to embrace the uncomfortable. Sister Agnes had just challenged me to have the courage to choose a path and stay on it. Yet those same nagging questions still had me trapped in a cell of my own making. Had I learned enough? Had I changed enough? Was I ready? I believed people didn't change. I believed that the best I could hope for was to learn to Manage my Tendencies. I thought I had done that, so what was I avoiding? Strange how prison had become the safe way of being. Leaving would be the biggest challenge of all. A leap of faith into a world that I no longer recognized. I was just at the beginning, and I knew it.

NA NO WRI MO

Talia, our teacher was perfectly out of place. From her demure attire to her Southern Accent. The superintendent had said, "If you can get 4 other people to show up than we will bring in a teacher from NaNoWrimo (Write a novel in a month.)"

These were marching orders for me. While everyone else was working on a novel, I could continue on my own manuscript. I scoured the library, walked by cells, talked to anybody reading a book, and found four semi-reluctant authors to participate.

When Talia introduced herself, it was with a soft polite voice which dropped 2 octaves when she asked which one of us was Ken Baxter. I raised my hand.

"You will not be working on your existing book in here, Mr. Baxter. You will write an original piece like everyone else. 50,000 words in 30 days."

I had just moved to a new cell as my room in the work release wing was needed. I had to take a top bunk again. My new room-mate was Charlie, an Old timer who had a nervous habit of unconsciously tapping his ring on the metal post of the bunk. He even did it in his sleep. Except for this torture, he was quiet and respectful so we would compromise. I could leave the light on well into the night to write, and he could tap away to his heart's content.

Two thousand words a day every day for a month was difficult. I had a real job, which meant that my time was limited. Any available moment I would hop up on my bunk and pull out my note book and begin. Talia handed out paper after paper on topics ranging from plot, character development, creating a story line arc, and something called the hero's journey. Grammar, spelling, and punctuation quickly took a back seat as the complexity of this quest started to set in.

"Damnit," I exclaimed as I broke the tip off another pencil. Granted this one was but a nub, but they were valuable.

"Let me help," said Charlie crushing a disposable razor beneath his feet and removing the blade.

"I'll sharpen while you write," This went on for two days until Charlie showed up with a bundle of pens wrapped in an elastic band.

"Don't ask," He said with a smile, and I didn't. This moved the process along considerably. There would be no erasing, no starting over, just writing. Not having a computer with spell check and grammatical software led to some questionable sentence structures, but the story line began to unfold in front of me. Ideas just flowed; I couldn't wait to see what happened to my characters next. Wherever the scenario's led, I just wrote. It was if the story had a mind of its own. My existing manuscript was a memoir. Memoirs were factual and sometimes tedious. Fiction was liberating, and I, as it turned out, was learning to write.

To everyone's credit no one left the program. Talia not being unattractive did not hurt, yet I think everyone genuinely enjoyed the process. The level of heady literature that I prided myself in reading did not transfer to a writing class. In fact, Harry Potter novels became one of Talia's best teaching tools. (J.K. Rowling could write.) Talia had us study the opening, no wasted words no trivial facts.

Mr. Dursley was the director of a firm called Grunnings, which made drills. He was a big, beefy man with hardly any neck, although he did have a very large mustache. Mrs. Dursley was thin and blonde and had nearly twice the usual amount of neck, which came in very useful as she spent so much of her time craning over garden fences, spying on the neighbors. The Dursleys had a small son called Dudley and, in their opinion, there was no finer boy any-where.

These were eye opening learning moments that shined a spotlight on a whole new world of possibilities for me. In addition, Talia was an expert in dialogue writing. I credit her with showing me how to set my hands free. The art of writing without thinking. Not letting your need to write the perfect sentence get in the way of spontaneous creativity. She also reminded me that I still required oversight. I did better when someone kept me accountable. I had a substantial working knowledge of Plato's Three Reasons along with the Physiology, of how our brain functions. Yet left to my own devices I tended to procrastinate. I did much better when I am called to task by others. In other words, I still had a great deal of work to get to where I wanted to be. If not for Talia I would never have accomplished that proud moment of finishing over 60,000 words in thirty days. To be quite honest I don't have the talent to coast thru life or trust myself to stay on task. I never did. I wondered If Jenny was aware of this tendency. I wonder if she realized what she was getting herself into.

On the final day of class, we all laughed, high fived and read chosen portions of our books. It didn't matter if most were not complete novels, or barely short stories for that matter. Talia made everyone feel as if they had won a Pulitzer prize, or at least had won the right to write, what a gift. Just another in a long line of people that kept showing up at the right time. It was becoming harder and harder not to believe that some things just happen for a reason.

LETTERS FROM NICHOLAI

Nicholai turned and waved goodbye as he exited the visiting room. I sat silent, waiting my turn to be strip searched. The visit I had waited years for was over. I stayed in the moment as I had been taught, remembered to ask how his life was going. I tried to make all of this seem normal, knowing all too well the letdown that was coming. Still, as his car went by the window and down the road, my heart sank. We had been cordial and open. We said all the right things. He was happy to see me and I was proud to be dressed in actual clothes. I think we may have laughed.

It had been 4 years since I had last seen him. Dressed in Walpole grays was a sight that did not sit well with him. I had been trying to change that impression ever since. The many letters we exchanged over the years were my life line. A way to share and grow. To communicate about everyday things. His in the real world. Mine in a box. No surprise then, that it was hard to shake this unspoken feeling of embarrassment. Who could blame him? In my need to punish myself for his brother's death, I alienated him. I embarrassed him. I lost him. My punishment now seemed complete.

Nicholai's career was just taking off as I entered prison. Life in Hollywood was exciting and challenging. Gone were the days when he could call me at four in the morning for advice or just to talk. I hadn't thought of that. Apparently, I hadn't thought of a lot of things. When he won his first Grammy award for production engineering, I was beside myself with pride. A pride I could not fully share. It did not seem right to inject myself into his success when I couldn't accept Alex's choice. It was as if I didn't have the right to be proud. I understood Alex's decision but I was not proud of it. So, I was stuck in a no man's land of my own making. Nicholai now had a brother who took his own life, and a father who was in prison. In many ways we were both gone.

The letter writing had brought us closer. I reveled in any question Nicholai was willing to ask. My opportunity to show him how much I could learn in isolation. Letters entitled: The Prose to Randomology, The Legacy of Cartesian Duality, The Lateralization of Function, Ten-page diatribes on the effects of silence on the human brain. A question on why someone entering a room was humming the same song you were, turned into a Scholium on Left, Right brain hemispheres, the Evolution of birds and a thesis on which came first Music or Language. (Music by the way wins the day).

All of our words vanished once we came face to face. All my false bravado melted away, replaced by the sudden need for a hug from someone you witnessed being born. The awkward embrace between father and son whose only contact in 4 years was on the written page or a brief muffled phone call. The visual shock was noticeable on both our faces. Nicholai saw the chiseled frame of a seasoned inmate. I looked into the eyes of a man that was once a boy. A tall, lean, confident professional. A confidence which suggested he no longer needed me. I struggled to maintain eye contact as I could feel myself slipping into a place of regret. The smallest hint of doubt in myself could send me spiraling away.

"It's wonderful to see you," I said trying to rescue myself. "I wish we were golfing."

"Holden Hills," Nick replied, "That's the last time we played, Remember? First hole Par 4."

"You can't see the pin." I interjected.

"Which never stopped you from trying to drive the green," added Nick and we both laughed.

"As consistent as your slice anyway," I returned volley.

And just like that we were fine. The simple memory of a time less complicated changed everything. Nicholai relaxed and with it glimpses of the son I watched grow up returned. The laugh, the smile, the mannerisms that suggested that the boy I knew was still in there. That maybe there was a chance to reconnect in a normal fashion. We spoke of his career in Hollywood, and avoided the topic of what I might do when I got out. One thing was obvious we had both grown up. Granted, I was a little behind schedule. Better late than never as they say. We spoke of Alex, his mother, the technology I would have to adjust to and for a moment everything seemed almost normal. The years had changed the both of us, so any future relationship would have to be based on an entirely new set of criteria. A new understanding of who we both had become.

Back in my cell, I began reading through all the letters that Nicholai had sent to me. I had not recognized it at first, but the changes I just witnessed were there all the time, just in slow motion. The progression of both our lives over the last 4 plus years read like a time line of growth. The back and forth was open and honest. The topics varied from personal to philosophical. Uninterrupted pages of venting or ranting, but most importantly, connecting.

The questions, as answers were well thought out, worthy even. I wondered if I would miss that when I got out. There is little use for letter writing in the outside world.

There on my bunk sat four years of correspondence. Each covered with patterns of Pi and the secret to memorize them. Pi had taken a back seat to the responsibilities of a real job and portions of my numbered friends had begun to slip away with the exception of the first letter Nick sent with several hundred digits. This letter was worn thin as I held it dear. The folds in the creases were see-through like ancient scrolled papyrus. It brought into question Doc's theory of a place in my mind free of emotion that was only for learning. These numbers on this particular letter were seared in my mind not because of an isolated knowledge, but from a single emotion, Love.

I had read this letter dozens of times. Yet, sitting in my room, it was Nicholai's response to the first letter I wrote to him that caught my attention.

My letter was filled with apologies and regrets of a misplaced marriage, along with meanderings about drug addiction and the abstract art of parenting. I had thought that being a good father was simply not doing what my father did, and for the most part that worked. Nick's words were painful and comforting at the same time, and as I read them, I was embarrassed, yet pleased that I had come so far. And finally, that there was still time to re-write my ending.

> *Hey Dad,*
>
> *It was nice hearing from you. I don't think I've ever gotten a hand written letter from anyone before. It seems like your thoughts are clear, and being in jail has definitely given you time to reflect. It's always nice to hear you speak from your heart without any underlying influences or "he said, she said" drama. Your words when pure can be quite inspired. My favorite line (from your letter) "I feel like Joni Mitchell cause my perspective is truly well rounded now, up, down, loved lost, both sides complete."*
>
> *I've gone through most of my life trying to avoid any of the hard conversations with you, drug related that is. I'm very un-confrontational and have always been afraid to bring it up. And although your actions have been hurtful to other people you haven't really ever done anything to hurt me. You've always been good to me. However, I'll speak frankly now. I've seen addiction claim two members of my family. It's frustrating, heartbreaking and tragic. I've known since I was about 15 truly what was up and I've learned to weed through the clouded and tangled stories as best I could. There were many different Dads that could show up on any given day and as you put it in your letter, it's hard to admit or see that a substance is controlling you. I've tried my best just to stay out of any of the drama. I didn't pry or ask questions because maybe I didn't want to find out the truth. But as I mentioned before, you've never done anything to hurt me.*
>
> *You've always supported me and helped me through many tough times. I guess what I am getting at is that it's extremely refreshing to read some honest words. I really "Hope" someday your full potential will get the opportunity to shine through uninhibited. You spoke a lot about Mom in your letter and I guess it's true: It always comes back to the girl!*

It's always comes back to the girl, I loved that.

Father, husband, firefighter, musician, party boy. Nick was

right. Not even I knew which one would show up. Sister Agnes would have a comment about my multiple lives for sure. The problem was, that Was me. Which story was true today, which one did I tell yesterday was always right there to sift through? Wow, what a convoluted waste of energy. But there it was, in black and white, out of the mouth of babes, so to speak. One of my earlier credos used to be "never write anything down as it will be used against you." Now that seemed outdated to say the least. A narrow view to a life that no longer served a purpose. Now I wrote freely, for many reasons: first and foremost, I felt I had something to say. Although many nights I would find myself writing just for the sheer joy of crafting a story. And as much as I liked to reminisce or write in my journals, Nicholai had just given me reason to write to the future. A future where we might play golf again or share a musical stage together, perhaps in a way a true father and son should. A future where I could find, dare I admit it... Hope.

Tractor Ride with Alex

I was surprised to see Malone in the seat of the Ride- on mower when I came to work. I had finished all the cutting the day before. All my chores in fact were caught up. I thought my last day in Maintenance would be sort of a day off. Telling my Boss, I was moving on to bigger jobs with better good time was actually harder than I thought. Malone understood, and wished me luck.

"I had to start It with a screw driver," He said. "But it's good to go, there's miles of fire roads, just don't get lost and be back by the end of the day." Sensing my trepidation, he added "Go enjoy the day, you've earned it."

The ear-to-ear grin on my face said it all as I jumped on my old companion and raced off to parts unknown.

It was a glorious day, sunshine, blue sky, and the taste of freedom in the air. I had taken the next step, 10 days of good time, running the warehouse for Mass Cor. Then off site to a work release job in Wrentham building equipment and memorizing every item in their warehouse to make myself of value. Real money, real responsibility. Almost real life.

I felt a sense of freedom as I sped down the fire road behind the ball field. Being allowed to roam unsupervised for the day was an unexpected gift. To be trusted, even for a moment, filled me with the simplest form of pride, one I would never again in my life take for granted.

Pondeville sat behind the angry walls of Walpole. Somewhere to the north was rumored to be Baystate and its foreboding companion Norfolk where Rupert walked the halls.

The vast acreage of the Massachusetts correction system meant to encapsulate the incarcerated was a playground to me. The Oakes and the Maples of New England in the fall were the true Philosopher Kings of our Time, and I was but a humbled explorer.

I drove by ponds with picnic tables, saw a bald Eagle flying and fish jumping. Sam flew overhead, cawing about how much trouble I would get in. I came around a bend and drove right up to the perimeter of Bay State, my old stomping grounds, and turned on a dime when inmates walking the track started cheering me on, thinking I had made a break for it. As I headed down a steep incline, I picked up speed and, in that moment, I wanted for nothing. The simple pleasures of riding on a lawn mower on a sunny day was more than enough. I wished I could bottle this feeling. This was life. Pleasure from the smallest of things. I thought how wonderful it could have been to have shown this to Alex, and with just that thought he was there. My wide-eyed boy with this huge grin on his face was right there beside me on a lawn mower. He looked right at me and right through me at the same time as if to say, "I know." As if to say, "I get it." As if to say, "Its ok, Dad, I'm gone and its ok, I experience life through you now, so it's time to stop punishing yourself and get on with living."

I was so overwhelmed with the shock, the love and the sudden sense of forgiveness that I had to pull over by the pond and get off. A day that started as any other had gone from the mundane to the supernatural. I stumbled several feet and fell to my knees.

"I'm so sorry," I kept saying,"I'm so sorry. I'm sorry it took me this long to figure it out."

"Most never do, Dad," said Alex and with that he was gone. Yet, I was not alone. I was never alone; I would never be alone again. Of course, this is how it worked, it explained so much. We carry those we love with us. They experience life through us. And I am trusted to live the best I can for them. Responsibility is universal and timeless; how could it be any other way. Yet Al was gone, and a simple fact remained. Life was for the living. I might never stop blaming myself for Al. I might never stop reliving the ways I could have been better, or should have done more. It was time to pick up the pieces and move on.

The long walk back to the maintenance shop gave me time to collect my thoughts. I kind of remembered Malone telling me that the mower shuts down if you get off the seat, a safety feature in case you fell off, except I did not have a screw driver to restart it. The irony here was that life did not stop if you fell off, and it was time to get moving again.

It has been said that every lie owes a debt to the truth.

Parker McGowan

For most inmates the last few months before you go home are the most dangerous. I was to be no exception. One fight, one misstep, one anything could jeopardize it. I never felt more vulnerable than the months surrounding my parole hearing.

Jenny had gone to India of all places to harden herself against the prospect of me coming home. She subjected herself to hotel sheets being dried on the sidewalk. She stood aghast at the sight of body parts washing ashore after cremation ceremonies on the river Ganges. Dogs ran after one another, jaws clenched down on a femur bone, past piles of garbage left rotting in the sun for weeks. All this to prepare for me, I should have been flattered, except India was not where I wanted her to be when my surprise parole hearing popped up months early. My new roommate enjoyed telling me over and over I had no chance of going home early with the charges I had against me.

Parker McGowan was an ex -Hockey star from Summerville. Bigger than most, Parker came equipped with bullet wounds, scars from knives and a hair trigger temper, to go along with his hate of authority and anyone that wasn't a con's con, so in a word, Me. Five minutes of asking around and he knew everything he needed to know. I talked to the guards, I thought I was the best softball player in prison, and the kiss of death, I appeared to be enjoying myself.

He loved to taunt at loud volumes so all could hear about a variety of topics ranging from my supposed knowledge of the world, to the time line of my demise by his hand.

"You tell him, Parker," "Kill him in his sleep," "Show Em Who's boss." Even Donahue, the jealous guard, during count time would question why I was still alive.

"Haven't you taken him out yet, McGowan?" he would say almost pleading, which seemed unduly irresponsible to me. Although leery and concerned, I would remain unflinching. I would not speed up time. I would not live in fear. Every day, every personal attack was an opportunity to practice a Philosophy of Indifference.

On the day of my Parole hearing, before a full seven-member panel known as the death squad, I was nervous. The sessions were long and the first three inmates went down in flames. Leo was next, I lingered in the hallway to see if I could hear anything at the windows.

From within came the low theatrical sound of Leo reciting Teddy Roosevelt's 'The man in the arena' speech, the same one I'd been listening to since Baystate. Leo was consistent if anything. Although the more famous parts of this speech referenced Doc's advice to fail spectacularly. I do not believe Leo grasped the error of his ways. Reciting great speeches did not reveal anything to the parole board about him. Or maybe I was wrong. Maybe it revealed everything about him. Irregardless, Leo's hearing lasted all of three minutes. He was unreachable after that, fuming in his cell.

My hearing was much longer than I thought. It was cordial, almost light hearted. Someone actually asked me to recite Pi, and although highly inappropriate, asked about my friendship with Doc along with my overall opinion of the prison system in its current form.

When I emerged from the door by the front desk a small crowd had gathered consisting of mostly staff who were all curious as to why laughter was still emanating from within the chamber. Donahue stood silent, obviously disappointed in the outcome, for I was going home. The smattering of cons cons looked on in disgust from the balcony above. Clearly, I had made a deal, or was being rewarded for some unknown feat of betrayal, either way I was not one of them. They took solace in that.

News of my imminent release spread fast. Walking down the hall I could hear it from a distance.

"And he got the best work release job too, how'd he pull that off?"

"Same way he got early Parole," came another.

Parker simply brushed past me in disgust without a word. The vitriol that hung in the air was palpable.

After my hearing I kept more to myself than usual. When I wasn't working, I walked the track or wrote in my journal. I avoided conversations directed at me with one-word responses. No more riddles for the front desk staff, no chess games in the day room. At Jen's request, I stopped playing softball. No need to take a chance on an injury. I did my laundry on off hours and avoided the crowded times in the gym, I was a nomad. At night I would not bite at any barb thrown at me from my stoic roommate. I would read while he listened to science shows on tv, and wondered what his life could have been like had he not thrown away a hockey scholarship at a New Hampshire college for a life of drugs and crime.

Jen's final visit was the first moment of outward enthusiasm I showed in a month.

"So, this is real," said Jen, "Our next hug might actually be longer than 10 seconds."

"Much longer," I said in her ear as I pulled her even closer.

"Baxter," yelled Donahue, "You're not out of here yet." Even Donahue could not put a damper on our unbridled enthusiasm. As we sat down, we both exhaled deeply for this was real. Years of courtship and planning were reaching a climax and the talking segment of our courtship was about to become unsupervised.

"I noticed you're limping" said Jen.

"One final act of arrogance," I told her how Parker and his crew were watching a softball game and commented every time I jogged by that "the best softball player only plays when no one is watching."

"And you couldn't help yourself," said Jen.

"A player got injured so, without saying a word I took his place."

"And let me guess, you just had to show off."

"I wasn't awful," I said, smiling.

"So how did you hurt yourself?"

"Playing Football," I responded hoping she wouldn't question the sports change, but she did.

"Football, you call playing football living under the radar."

"I was walking back after the game and someone yelled, 'he only plays the safe sports,' and well, I was on a roll."

"And the injury?" asked Jen, now looking annoyed.

"Well, it was on a touchdown anyway; I don't know, something just snapped in my heel."

Limping back to my cell after the visit, I realized I had indeed incurred a real injury that seemed like it might hang on awhile, one that suggested I might be more vulnerable than I thought. I sat and went through my normal healing procedures, humming and vibrating my heel, yet to no avail. Every step was agonizing. If I had believed things happened for a reason, I would say this was a wakeup call. I am not impervious to injury or aging. Just then Parker McGowan walked in and seeing me eyes closed and humming, he laughed.

"You think your Philosophy Bullshit is going to save you."

"I don't think anything," I said, quite frankly I didn't have the energy to deal with him at the moment. "I'm just trying to remain unobtrusive," I said preparing to vacate the room.

"You're nothing but obtrusive," said Parker blocking my way. "So that's just another lie."

"Whatever you say," I said. Our shoulders bumped as I brushed past him and he erupted.

"You're a liar. You're a phony and a liar, cause everybody lies, you're no different."

"I don't," I said defiantly as I walked out.

Dozens of inmates appeared in their doors, this was the moment they had waited for. Parker seized the moment.

"Don't even think about coming back in this room, understand me!"

I just kept walking. I passed the bathrooms, the laundry room and paused at the railing overlooking the front desk. He was right of course, to some extent we all lie. Why would I think I was any different? And that was the crux of it all. Sure, Parker McGowan and I had our differences, but it was the similarities that I was annoyed by. Neither one of us thought this would be our life.

"Damnit," I said and turned and headed back to the room.

"You're right," I said walking into the room.

Parker leaped in anger from his bed. He had not expected me to return "What'd you say?" he yelled, taking a defensive stance.

"You're right, I'm a liar, and I apologize. I should not have claimed anything else," Parker stood stunned, his fist still clenched, his face softened,

"Just when I am completely satisfied with hating you, you come in here and apologize," he said shaking his head.

"Well, I shouldn't claim to be something I'm not, just wanted to acknowledge that; Thanx for calling me on it." I turned and exited, Parker McGowan said nothing.

Hours later I returned and placed a coke on the desk next to Parker's TV.

"Peace offering," I said to no response. I settled in to my bunk and listened to the sounds of prison at night. The subdued murmurs of soft conversation from surrounding rooms. Televisions and radios at reduced volumes. The work release wing was respectful. Everyone had to work in the morning. Parker McGowan was watching a science show on PBS, on the formation of the universe and he could tell I was listening and said, "You know about this stuff, don't you? "

Slightly hesitant, I said, "I do."

"They're talking about Suns forming, you know about

that?"

"Yes," I replied, still not sure where this was going.

"Well, I forget, what's the difference between Fusion and Fission?"

I answered cautiously. "Fusion is when nuclei, like the hydrogen in our sun combines to form helium. Fission is the splitting of nuclei." I kept my answers short knowing that this could be a trap of some sort, but this went on for a while. We discussed the limits of fusion in accordance with the size of the sun. Iron being the heaviest element, that can be obtained. The theories surrounding supernovas, and the heavy elements. The conspiracy theories surrounding cold fusion, the conjecture of things like the Oort cloud and how astonishingly far away it is thought to be. Suddenly from across the hall from another room a voice asked.

"How far are we from the center of our galaxy?"

"About two thirds the way out, or 26,000 light years from the center. I answered.

"And the center has a black hole?" The questioning continued.

"Yes," I responded, still not sure what was happening.

"But they don't know that for certain, right?"

"Well, not with a hundred percent certainty, no, but it's pretty definitive."

"What else don't they know for certain?" said Parker re-joining the conversation.

"Oh, a great deal," I said, suddenly excited by the prospect of real conversation. "I imagine more unknown than known, but theoretical physicists have been predicting things for years and a vast majority of their predictions have turned out to be true. "

"So that's why you like Philosophy and Science then, right?" asked Parker "You like the search for truth".

"Actually, no," I said "I was thinking about that today and thanks to you I have come to a new conclusion."

"Me?" said Parker, sounding genuinely surprised. It also occurred to me in that moment that there were no other sounds coming from the unit, no TV's, no radios, no small talk. Everyone was listening.

"As you so astutely pointed out, I am a liar. I spent a lot of time thinking about that today, And I have come to think that

Philosophy and Science should not be about the search for truth, it's too restricting. We live in a time where truth is relevant."

"Relevant to what?" came the voice from across the hall.

"Relevant to whatever you want to be true," I replied, "Philosophy and science I think, should not be restricted by what we need to be true. It should be about possibilities. It's the only way to move forward. The truth doesn't judge or need to be the goal. It's the pursuit that matters."

We went on for a while into the night discussing life on other planets, and the theories of alternate universes. When I suggested the thought of other Parker McGowan's running around it brought a chuckle from the new philosophers from across the hall. I thought it better than to share that I talked to other versions of myself all the time. A topic for another session perhaps. As we shut down for the night, Parker McGowan suggested I become a teacher when I left. Although my reply was, "not likely," I thought, Doc would be proud.

RESTITUTION

At first, I took no offense when I was woken at 4:30 am and told I was going to court. I was slightly ambivalent when the transport driver clamped on the leg shackles and secured my wrists to my side just a little too tightly. Protocol, l tried to tell myself.

"Where we off to, Sarge?" I didn't expect an answer.

"Find out when you get there, firefighter," came the reply.

The ride was long and with each mile my usual calm acceptance of the situation seemed to dissolve. I had earned my Parole, paid my debt, my release was arranged, Jen was coming and we would leave this place behind. What more could be required of me?

The shackles dug in hard and my limp was noticeable as I exited the van in the lower parking garage of the Worcester Superior Court House. I thought it was a Tuesday. I had learned to accept most of the circumstances created by prison: The not knowing, the never being told anything. But this day was different. This day

I was annoyed, concerned, nervous even. The building appeared the same. That same unsettled Worcester sensation. Same smell, same overall feeling of mediocrity, all sickly familiar.

I shuffled into the elevator of the courthouse. The memory of an aged, disgraced, out of shape firefighter, that stood here so many years ago, trying his best not to look too frightened, flashed in my mind. One of my bookend guards threw me a sideways glance as I laughed under my breath at my realization. I wouldn't trade my experience for the world.

"Put him in 5," said a Cop as we got off the elevator.

"But Rodriguez is in there, Lieutenant," said one of my chaperones.

"You heard me," came the reply. My shackles were removed and the steel door of the holding cell slammed behind me.

It was obvious that the cop threw me in here on purpose. But where was the animosity coming from, I thought as I laid back on the bench eyes closed and prepared for whatever was coming. Did he believe I would be frightened to death at the prospect of being locked in with a large angry inmate? Where did he think I'd been for the last five years? This couldn't be why I was here. Maybe the Idiot prosecutor had found some obscure unsolved crime to pin on me when he heard I got parole. Maybe I was supposed to stand before a judge and plead forgiveness.

Rodriquez paced back and forth looking menacing, mumbling in Spanish about the lack of respect sticking some old white dude in a cell with him.

"No mi culpa," I said which temporarily stopped him in his tracks.

An hour of no answers passed and I decided to engage my new cellmate. Though the language barrier was challenging, I ascertained that Rodriquez was here to plead to the murder of three people in Worcester. I had seen it on the news. He tried to ask me what I knew about trials. And I tried to explain that he was just here to be arraigned. He kept showing me how he made five people lay down on the ground and demonstrated shooting three.

"I let the other two live," he said. "I tell judge, that right? That I let two live."

I tried to show him that he should stop demonstrating to the judge with his hand in the shape of a gun how he only shot the first three.

"Oh, Poppy, you right, Gracious, Poppy."
I didn't have the heart to tell him he was getting life. The lieutenant who had me thrown in with Rodriquez came to the door and looked genuinely disappointed that I was not being killed.

"You don't remember me do you, Baxter?" came the condescending question.

"Not even in the slightest, Lieutenant," I said.

I turned back to Rodriquez. It was true. I couldn't pick that guy out of a line up, but he obviously had a problem with me. Most people I had worked with through the years, although I might recognize them, I would have a hard time recalling their names. Worcester seemed a life time ago. Anyone who had a problem with me from that epoch quite frankly needed to examine their own lives. This Lieutenant didn't know me, and he sure as hell didn't know the real story. The Lieut. walked away, unsatisfied, and was eventually replaced at the door slot by a young woman. "Hi, Kenny," she said, "I have something for you to sign."

"I am not signing anything," I said in a defiant voice.

"It's ok," she tried to continue in a reassuring tone.

"Ya, it's not ok," I said and turned away.

Undaunted, she continued. "Wow, you've changed," she said. She explained that her brother used to follow my band years earlier.

"Ok...And?" I said.

"They'll never let you go home until you sign an agreement for your restitution."

"My what?"

"Your restitution," she said "for the repayment of the insurance payout."

"I didn't get an insurance payout.".

"I know, but that's how it works."

"That's how what works? This is why I'm here?" My voice rose, "You're telling me I have to pay back the insurance money that my ex-girlfriend and her mother got? The same two people that made a half million dollars rebuilding the property. The same two who wanted the house burned down in the first place.

How much?" I said in a demanding voice.

She took a step away from the door.

"How much money?" I repeated.

"One Hundred and Forty-Nine Thousand," her words hung in the air just long enough for me to remember my Pause.

"One Hundred Forty-Nine Thousand," I snorted. "Why not? And, if I can't? Then let me guess, I can't go home right?"

"Yes. But it's only a hundred dollars a month, you can manage that?"

"A hundred dollars a month, I won't live that long."

"Exactly," she looked proud of herself.

"How is that possible?" I asked, now curious.

"Because I'm in charge of the department and I say what Is, or what Isn't, and if you sign here," she tapped her finger under my typed name. "Then you get back in the van and we process you out."

"Just like that?"

"Just like that," she said.

I liked the sister of some guy who followed our band much more after that.

She was right. In a matter of minutes, I was led down the corridor by a young court officer to the same elevator that led to the parking garage. The van drivers had a small conniption when they weren't notified that an unsecured prisoner was on his way down. The full body shackles were reattached for what would be hopefully the last time ever. The ride home to Pondeville was filled with conflicting thoughts. I pictured Rodriquez in the holding cell, with no idea his life was going to change so drastically. I thought of the bitter Lieutenant, and wondered how many more like him were out there. People living in the past with a need to see me punished for reasons I couldn't fathom. Then there was the restitution. 149,000 dollars. How was that fair? Would fairness be something I would ever experience again? The punishment would continue, it seemed, in all its forms for as long as I was still breathing. Suddenly, a conversation I had recently with a staff department head made so much more sense. Upon signing papers for my impending release, she said, "It's you, Kenny, that I worry about the most."

"Me? Why would I concern you?" I said, genuinely surprised at her statement.

"You'll probably end up on your feet. You're smart, capable, but what if things don't turn out well for you? You will be judged in a harsh way by some, so what are you capable of if things don't pan out? If life isn't fair by your standards?"

In hindsight now, she seemed to know what was coming. She seemed to have been warning me of what lay ahead. I was in my mid fifty's. I had my pension taken away, no form of income, few job prospects. Add the restitution and the fact that, as a convicted felon I had to pay for the right to be on parole for the next ten years. This would never be over. I would never be done paying. I would never be truly free!

I know what lies in the hearts of men, I have eaten breakfast with evil. I understand the feeling of living in a world gone wrong. Of feeling disenfranchised. I know what makes a person walk into a church or school room and pull the trigger. I have met them, I have spoken with them, yet I never thought I was them. I understood Rupert. I understood Doc. They were my friends. The world wasn't fair, it never has been. Then there is that familiar rumination, "Who am I, if not the stories and labels I placed upon myself?" I thought I was clear from that line of thinking and looking forward to being seen instead, as who I was focusing on becoming. I had not considered that many others may not want me to grow beyond the labels they required me to maintain.
This administrator knew that, she was being honest, but what was she really asking? Was she wondering if I would end my own life, or worse; would I fall under the category of someone who would take as many people with them as I could, to protest the injustice, to make a statement? Alex took his own life. Is his legacy to be, "At least he didn't take anyone with him?" Because I sure don't intent that to be me.

"Let's hope I'm better than that," I said to the administrator, "No, 'better' is not the word I'm looking for, let's hope I have 'empathy' enough for myself and for others. Let's hope I have learned enough inside these walls, because it's a fine line I am stepping over to reenter a world I don't believe in."

"Let's hope, Kenny," said the administrator, in a not so reassuring tone.

That conversation was still on my mind as my shackles were removed, I had to be customarily strip searched after my van ride and for the first time it bothered me. Suddenly everything seemed offensive. It occurred to me that the guard performing the search, although I considered him one of the good ones, was aware of my record. Like the administrator, had been through my files.

The details of my case had seemed unimportant at the time of my trial. I wanted to go to prison. Now I felt a need to explain myself, to explain everything. Now, I wanted to set the record straight. Now, I understood the meaning behind the administrator's questions.

What if fairness eluded me? My mind raced out of control to crazy subjects.

The surprising anger coursing through my veins in search of the fairness of it all had me questioning my own intentions, my own sense of righteousness. The sudden outrage of going through all of this, and in the minds of others, having it mean nothing.

Why had I thought it would be any different for me? There was an uphill battle coming that would make prison seem easy. My debt to society was not paid. It would never be paid. My deeper restitution would be applied at whatever level anyone deemed fit. There was no statute of limitations on cruelty. Suddenly Nietzsche seemed relevant, "Beware of those who are so eager to punish."

As I made my way up the stairs towards my room, the pain in my foot from the latest sports injury was excruciating. It felt like it was going to last. It felt like something I might not be able to heal. How ironic I thought, how mortal. How vulnerable I suddenly felt.

In the days to come, I took many walks trying to come to grips with what kind of life lay ahead for me. I tried to remind myself that all of this had a point.

I went on a work detail by request at Walpole to break up my anxiety and ended up spending the day talking to MaryAnne, my old boss from Property. She had moved out to a front office and was now in charge of Policy. Through the course of the day, Tommy, the Rock, the lieutenant and I talked golf. Others from so many years ago all came out to see how I was doing and to wish me luck on the outside. We spoke like we were friends, because in fact we were. It occurred to me in that moment, that there will always be people who will choose to give me a chance. They will appear as they always have, as long as I remained true to myself.

There will also always be those who believe I should continue to pay. But when it came down to it, the only true restitution I owed was to myself. There are no labels to define me. I could hear Docs words as if he was standing beside me. "Stay on point, Ken, remain even keeled. You chose this path; your adventure is just beginning."

PERFECT

I woke like any other day. I had not tossed and turned with nervous anticipation in the night. All was exactly as it should be.

My room was barren. Everything I accumulated over the past five years was donated back to the State to be loaned out to inmates, who could not afford a TV or running shoes size thirteen. All other perishable items I had left to Parker McGowan who was left speechless by the gesture. Besides, I couldn't take anything with me even if I wanted to. Jenny would not allow anything from prison to ever cross the thresh-hold of her home. Even my journal, all eight hundred hand written pages would remain in a sealed bin stored in the garage. If I wanted to refer to it, I could visit.

I walked to the day room in early morning silence, cradling the only thing I could not part with, my plastic coffee cup.

The day room was empty as it usually was that time of morning. I stared out across the   landscape that had become my constant visual companion and sipped the warm coffee. A smile crept across my face. I had done it. I had not simply survived prison, I had graduated from it. I had remade myself into an image I could stand to look at in the mirror and that was no small feat. I was a lot of work after all. Yet, I liked the person who I had become. I trusted the man I saw in my reflection and knew I could count on him to do the right thing. The world might not see beyond my press clippings, but there was little I could do about that. At times, I may be the brunt of the joke or wind up laughing at the absurdity of the world, either way I would still be standing. As far as I could tell, the universe liked me. It seemed to respond to my constant attempts to gain favor with its inner workings. I didn't know what the world had in store for me, I just knew I wanted to be in it.

In times of struggle, I would turn to song, to Pythagoras, to Plato. My life, after all was simply a performance. I would write my story. I didn't know if I was good enough to do the tale justice, I just knew I didn't want someone else writing the next chapter for me. I had been given the tools, by a list of perfectly timed teachers too long to recite. I had been given insight to build a Philosophy of my own. Not one in search of the truth of the world, but one of purpose, defined by giving everything I had to offer within the confines of my surroundings. Within the confines of a single moment. To make amazing the simple act of standing in prison for the last time, just sipping my morning coffee.

How this would translate to the outside world, I was about to find out. I felt my heart skip a beat with excitement as on cue, Sam the crow, flew out over the ball field and into the sun. I raised my cup.

"Perfect," I said aloud. "Simply perfect."

LOOKING FORWARD

I am writing this letter while seated in the passenger side of my minivan with none other than Ken Baxter himself at the wheel, en route from my home in State College, Pennsylvania to his home in Muncy, about an hour and a half away. His wife, Karen, is in the backseat, along with a pile of musical equipment that we'll need for our gig tonight at the Turkey Hill Brewery in Bloomsburg, not far from Ken and Karen's beautiful farm.

This all obviously requires a little explaining if you just finished Ken's first novel, The Philosophy of Arson. I can only imagine the questions that are running through your brain: Wait...what happened to Jenn? And who are Karen and Molly? Is Ken making music again?

You'll no doubt hear Ken's perspective on the answers to these questions (and many more!) in his second book, but he's asked me to give you my perspective here, in the form of this letter which is included in this second edition of The Philosophy of Arson.

The simplest place to start, as always, is at the beginning of my journey with Ken, which picks up where this book ends.

First, a little background about who I am. I am an Associate Teaching Professor at Penn State University in the Department of Human Development and Family Studies where I have taught since 1998. I met my husband, Rene, at the very end of 1997, when I first moved to State College and we both joined the same local band and began gigging regularly in and around Penn State. A few years later we got married, had 3 kids, and have made State College our home.

Ken moved to State College with Jenn in 2014, where he began his search for what Doc called "like-minded people." He was doing some manual work for one of my colleagues while finishing up this book, but knew he needed to get some background knowledge in child development to understand his experience with the trauma he and many of his fellow prisoners endured as children. My colleague recommended that he talk to me. Ken tucked my name into his memory and finished up his day of work.

Later that same month, he and Jenn were out to dinner at a local restaurant that I sing at every Sunday night. When I happened to walk by their table, Ken immediately knew I was someone he needed to meet. He didn't know my name, or who I was, he just had a very intense feeling. They moved closer to where I was singing but didn't introduce themselves.

A couple of weeks later, one of the bands I'm in was playing at the Central Pennsylvania Festival of the Arts, a big event that happens every summer in State College. He and Jenn were taking in the sights when they happened upon the stage where we were performing. They both immediately recognized me from the restaurant, and Ken decided to come up and introduce himself when we finished. I distinctly remember Ken approaching me and saying, "I'm supposed to meet you." I said, "Well then hello, I'm Molly Countermine." The look of surprise on Ken's face was obvious.

Ken shook his head and said, "Molly Countermine who teaches child development at Penn State?"

"That's me!" I said.

He chuckled and said, "Of course it is."

We arranged to meet for coffee a few days later, Ken asked if he could sit in on one of my classes, and a beautiful friendship was born. We began playing music together, and the rest is history.

Not only do I consider Ken Baxter one of my best friends, I consider him one of my best teachers. He constantly pushes himself and those around him to be authentic, reach for the stars, and never, ever, ever give up. I have watched him grow as a human being over these past few years, and I can't wait to see what's next.

Here's a little taste of the next book:

Doc, had warned that this day would come. "You will discover someday that doing the right thing will turn out to be the worst thing you've ever done." How could he have known? How could he have ever seen this coming? But there she stood, right in front of me, hands shaking, tears streaming down her face... and I was the cause.

Molly Countermine
Associate Teaching Professor
Penn State University

QUESTIONS FOR DISCUSSION:

1. Think about the father-son dynamics in this book. In what ways did Ken's experience as a son influence the type of father he was. What unresolved issues linger for Ken with both his relationship to his own father and to his sons? You might consider using their attachment relationship to inform your answer.

2. Reflect on Ken's decision-making process after his arrest but before he went to prison. What do you think was Ken's motivation to go to prison? In what ways did privilege play a role in this choice?

3. Think about Maslow's hierarchy of needs model. In what ways did prison life for Ken meet any (or all) of these needs? Which needs did Ken work on the most in prison? Do you think Ken became self-actualized? Why or why not?

4. According to Plato, the key to a meaningful life is simple: you have to earn your right to be a part of society. You must achieve an inner balance with your Reason, Desires, and Spirited Aggression. Once this is achieved, you have reached a state Plato called Justice, similar to Maslow's self-actualization. Plato went on to say that then, and only then, do you have something to offer to your community. The ultimate goal is to become a Philosopher King, or one who has attained perfect inner balance. These individuals are often the leaders of their societies, as they have only the best interest of the whole. Do you know someone like this? Do any of our leaders in government or the private sector have these qualities, and if so, who? If not, why? (Perhaps Plato is simple, but the world surely is not.)